Independence and the Death of Employment

Ken Phillips

Published by Connor Court Publishing Pty Ltd, 2008

First Published in 2005 as an e-book by Voltan

CONNOR COURT PUBLISHING, PO BOX 1, BALLAN, VIC, 3342
www.connorcourt.com

National Library of Australia Cataloguing-in-Publication data:

Phillips, Ken, 1954– .
  Independence and the death of employment.

  ISBN 9781921421082

  1. Industrial relations. 2. Industrial sociology. I. Title.

331

This book is dedicated to everyone
who cherishes independence

About the Author

Ken Phillips is an independent contractor operating as his own business, as a researcher, commentator, consultant and lobbyist on labour and workplace reform issues.

Among his many activities, Ken is a published authority on independent contractor issues, directs external research on industrial relations versus trade practices issues, and promotes the concept of 'markets in the firm'. Through his articles in Australian newspapers, think-tanks and academic journals, Ken is known for approaching labour issues from outside normal perspectives.

He is also co-founder and Executive Director of Independent Contractors of Australia.

Acknowledgements

Ideas are seldom the product of a single mind. We all draw upon the history, ideas and standards of the society which surrounds us, coupled with our personal experiences. I have my parents to thank for raising a family in which the key objective was defining one's individuality within a framework of strong interpersonal and family relationships. I have my partner and two sons to thank for never letting me forget the joy of working together.

The ideas for this book emerged over my lifetime to date. The crafting of the words has been an eight-year exercise heavily dependent on two terrific friends, Michael James and Chris Ulyatt. They have pushed me, prodded me, guided me and, most importantly, pulled me back on track when I was running in odd directions. My appreciation also to Connor Court for taking a punt and publishing a book that doesn't neatly fit into orthodox publishing lists. Of course, final responsibility for the contents of this book rests with me.

Ken Phillips
August 2008

Contents

Introduction   1

1: The Employment Demon   5
The nature of employment — the common law — the nature of contracts — the nineteen indicators of employment — illustrative court cases: Mayne Nickless, Crisis Couriers and others — the US experience — employment tests: how universal? — employment and control

2: Damning the Demon   39
Independent contracting versus employment — Queensland's notorious Section 275 — Queensland shearers speak out on independent contracting

3: Tax   55
Employment and income tax — Australia — United Kingdom — independent contracting and tax — more Australian history — PAYG: a step forward — a residual problem: personal services income

4: Employment and Regulation: Changing to What?   77
Employment and non-tax regulation — vicarious liability — illustrative court cases — discrimination, sexual harassment and unfair dismissal — examples and comment — the contract at will and its demise — the role of the ILO — a worrying development: corporate criminality

5: To Work We Go; To War We Go: The Firm   109
The nature of the firm — the centrality of employment — workers, bosses and managers— Ronald Coase and transaction costs — Elliott Jaques and employment bureaucracies — employee loyalty — the myth of the employer — accountability — the 'independent employee' — managers and motivation

6: Labour Regulation   139
The hallmarks of labour regulation — labour regulation versus commercial regulation — labour regulation and justice — the pivotal case of Electrolux — state theft of the employment contract — the view from the academy: 'wage slavery' — free markets and employment — challenges to the employment contract

7: Markets in the Firm   169
The problem of the firm — free markets and the firm — free markets in the firm: franchising and other arrangements — examples and comment — a startling example of markets in the firm: Koch Industries

8: Values   197
Democracy and equality — political and economic freedom — the power of the commercial contract — individuals and employment — the values revolution — the death of employment

Postscript: Political Developments Since 2005   209

Introduction

Bear in mind that I can treat anyone exactly as I please.

— Emperor Caligula (AD 41) (Suetonius, *The Twelve Caesars*)

What is power?

In 2001, a 60-second television commercial appeared on televisions in the homes of many nations worldwide. It was not directed at the ordinary consumer but at the comparatively small number of heads and senior executives of multinational corporations who were sitting at home with their families in 'relax mode' after yet another hectic but power-filled day.

The advertisement depicted throngs of cheering, arm-waving crowds; masses of people surging with outstretched arms reaching for one spot. The grand stone temples identified the scene as that of ancient Rome. Chariots mounted by armour-suited soldiers carrying the eagle-topped staff of Roman military authority stopped as one and wheeled in salute. From the right-hand corner of millions of television screens the back head of a male figure emerged, turned and surveyed the scene. Adorned as it was with a half-wreath of golden leaves, it was clearly that of the emperor. The face exuded the arrogant, self-satisfied, assured but benevolent look of one who knew he had a vast empire at his single control. At that point the text and voiceover of the advert delivered its message: 'How can you control all this without effective systems?'

It was an advert for one of the rising multinational computer software companies eager to attract the interest of top decision-makers in large corporations around the world.

It was an advert about power and about control. It was about employers and employees.

In 60 seconds, the advertisement depicted the single most important image of how twenty-first-century society conceives of the modern corporation. Business is a form of authoritarian but benevolent government in which an all-powerful head rules and controls a vast organization. The adoring

1

employees know their place in a strictly hierarchical, machine-like, command-and-control system. The people adore and obey the remote but god-like figure at the head, the employer. In this vision, corporate business is like the business of ancient Rome: warfare and the glory of victory!

No matter how erroneous or even distasteful this vision may seem to some in the 21st century, it remains the single most important idea that determines the attitude to business of individuals, society, government, and business itself. It influences the legislation and regulation under which business operates, and has a vast impact on the structure of society. This vision dominates how formal people-management dynamics operate inside firms, influences how our careers are structured, and affects our sense of self-worth and happiness. It has profound impact on the psychology of the stock market and how companies and individuals make money. It is a vision that came fully into focus midway through the twentieth century by the victory of the capitalist war machine that conquered tyranny in the Second World War. It is a vision of success made possible by discipline.

But if that vision has succeeded, it has also reached its limits—for it is also a flawed vision that leads people to underperform throughout their working lives.

This book is mostly about power—the exercise of it by one individual over another in the work environment. It is about the social, organizational, management and legal structures which create and prop up the powerful in our daily working lives. But it is also a book about a belief, namely, that concentrated power is on the wane because it holds back social, economic and personal performance.

In particular, this book is about employment or, rather, the very specific legal, institutional and relationship nature of the employment contract that dominates work. It is the employment contract that sustains the flawed vision and practice of command-and-control business in a power-driven world. The legal idea and behavioural application of employment distorts relationships inside firms. Every day that we go to work, employment causes us to underperform, to underachieve, and to remain unfulfilled. Employment as a legal and operational force is a glue that holds power-driven organizations together, yet it also causes them to underperform.

If, as individuals, businesses and societies we are to move forward, we must recognize the nature of the employment contract. Where we reject employment, we find new liberty, strength, equality and self-worth. Societies function better without employment. Businesses are more successful without employment. Individuals are happier without employment. Yet working without being employed is not easy. In fact, non-employment goes against the natural grain of some powerful human instincts. But the revolt against employment, against concentrated power, is a sign that we are becoming more civilized.

Slowly, employment is being rejected—although its rejection is unrecognized and little discussed. Its rejection is witnessed in the slow but inevitable insertion of market-based principles into the internal workings of firms. It is witnessed in the huge rise in the number of people who earn their living as independent contractors, franchisees and small- and micro-business people. It is witnessed by the millions of people who are 'employed' in firms but feel in their hearts that the relationships are sour. However, even as this transformation is happening, we hardly understand what it is we are changing from or into. But the change is guided by a significant legal factor. We use (and want to use) the liberty available through the commercial contract to guide our economic actions.

That is the topic of this book.

1: The Employment Demon

When human beings relinquish their individuality and identity of their own volition, they are also relinquishing their claim to being human.

— John Paul Getty 1892–1976[1]

Every day when we go to work to be employed, we enter a legal environment in which we voluntarily give up, in exchange for money, our basic human right to control ourselves. Yet, as societies and as individuals, we have trained ourselves to ignore this essential fact. We prefer to pretend that our human dignity, our individuality, our identity is intact, whereas in fact it is formally stripped from us. The great nineteenth-century American jurist Oliver Wendell Holmes explained it this way:

> There are few employments for hire in which the servant does not agree to suspend his constitutional rights of free speech, as well as idleness, by the implied terms of his contract. The servant cannot complain, as he takes the employment on the terms which are offered to him.[2]

Holmes's words, written in 1892, have not dated. No matter how much the convoluted processes of the law in the twentieth century may have pretended to alter this legal reality, Holmes's words still set out the core facts about the employment relationship and the expectations constituted within the law.

During the twentieth century, the managerial idea and practice of the firm was wedded to this legal idea of employment. It continues to be so today, certainly in theory and most predominantly in practice. The legal concept of employment and the dominant economic idea of the firm are mutually dependent. Most importantly, this legal idea of employment has a vast impact on how we relate to each other in our daily working lives. To understand employment is to begin to fathom our working relationships. And in the quest to understand economics, the behaviour of individuals, firms and economies cannot be understood without an appreciation of the centrality of this legal idea and practice of employment.

5

Employment is a specific type of legal contract. Its essence is that the employer has a legal 'right to control' the employee. This legality is reflected in observed behaviour.

As the twentieth century turned into the twenty-first, everyone thought they knew what employment was—namely, a simple work-for-pay relationship. The International Labor Organisation (ILO)[3] uses the word with this narrow meaning, as do statisticians and economists. But talking of employment as a work-for-pay relationship is imprecise and incorrect. It is a source of significant misunderstanding of human behaviour at work and badly distorts labour regulatory approaches.

In explaining the modern legalities of employment, it is imperative to be precise if clarity and accurate comprehension are to be achieved. The historical context of employment must be understood because it is integral to the modern meaning of employment. Further, it is necessary to study employment in two separate but related contexts. The first is to understand the employment contract as it stands on its own and unrelated to statute law that surrounds it. Then it is necessary to understand how statute law (that is, law created by parliaments) has changed, moulded and modified the ways in which the employment contract operates in our daily lives. The first few chapters of this book undertake that task.

This chapter looks at the employment contract as it would live if it were untouched by the statute laws of the second half of the 20th Century. The second chapter looks at the reverse of the employment contract, that is, the commercial contract and how people supply their labour through the commercial contract. Chapters 3 and 4 look at how statute laws have layered themselves upon the employment contract to create significant social policy distortions which affect all of us in very real ways. Importantly, however, these layers of statue law have not changed the essential features of the employment contract.

The starting point and the focus of this chapter is the common-law definition of employment, which applies in all nations that are governed by the common law. Unlike statute law, the common law evolves over time as a result of judicial decisions. Although the common law has its origins in the English legal tradition, the common-law definition of employment extends beyond the English tradition and the concepts underpin labour law in most countries, despite national variations. (This is dealt with in greater detail in the section 'How Global are these tests?' later in this chapter.) Under the common law, employment consists of a specific type of contract. Evidence that such a contract exists consists of certain kinds of human conduct and the commercial relationships that exist inside firms. A common-law judgment that an employment contract exists thus amounts to a finding that individuals are behaving in a particular way.

What is the common law?

Common law is broad and covers many areas other than employment. Common law is not legislation created by elected representatives, although legislation often uses common law as its starting point. Criminal law has centuries of common-law principles embedded in it, protecting such rights as trial before a jury and the presumption of innocence. Common law is thus one of the core protectors of often taken-for-granted human rights. It is a set of guiding legal principles governing human relationships that has slowly evolved over centuries of social development, and so reflects both past and present social practices. Under the common law, judges have the power seemingly to override the intention of a legislature as embodied in statute law, but only if the legislature has expressed its intent in an apparently illogical, contradictory or confused way. A legislature that seeks to subvert or change common-law principles will find itself opposed by centuries of accepted legal understandings. But inevitably it is the people who protect common law. The people will reject legislatures that undermine the common law, not because they have a formal understanding of the law but because they intuitively understand it as 'common sense'. Most legislation is consistent with the common law because legal terminology normally consists of specific common-law definitions. The common law is thus the chief protector of the people against the ever-present threat of the tyranny of the legislature and of the excessively powerful.

What is employment?

Under common law, the word 'person' can be used to refer to individuals, partnerships (two or more individuals), corporations and associated trusts. Contracts between persons can thus be contracts between individuals, between corporations and individuals, between trusts and corporations, and so on. But what is unique about employment is that one party to the employment contract must be an individual natural person. This restriction is based on common sense. An individual, a corporation or a trust can be an 'employer', but only an individual flesh-and-blood human being can be an 'employee'.

So employment is a specific type of contract between an individual, a partnership, a corporation or a trust on the one hand, and an individual on the other. Under common law, a contract between two corporations or between a corporation and a trust is always a commercial contract.

In its broadest terms, the specific contract that is employment is a modification of the historical master and servant relationship. It is a contract that gives the employer a 'right to control' the employee. But what does this 'right to control' mean? Put simply, it means that the individual who is the 'employee' does not have the right to control the terms of the contract. The right to control the terms of the contract rests at law with the person who is the 'employer'. The 'right to control' employment implies, suggests, or means that 'employees', that is, individuals who normally are thought to control their own actions, do not have the right to control their own actions. Their actions are potentially under the control of someone else. When stated as simply as this, employment can appear as an affront to the dignity of human beings.

Compare this with the commercial contract, under which each person in a contract relationship has an equal legal right to control the terms of the contract.

This basic difference between the two contract types—employment and commercial—has huge economic and social implications which explain key social dynamics.

When employment exists, the legal understanding and the behavioural fact is that the employee does not have the right to control his or her own physical and psychological self. The right to control is transferred from the individual to the employer. Even if actual control of the employee does not occur, or appear to occur, or is constrained, it is the legal right to control that defines the employment contract. It doesn't matter if the two persons consciously want this transfer of control; if they behave as if control has been transferred, they will in effect enter an employment contract. With employment, the employer makes decisions and the employee functions only within the parameters set by the employer. In its crudest understanding, an employee is a piece of machinery, no longer a self-controlling person but instead a modified version of a wage slave! The acceptance of money by an employee in the working relationship called employment is the selling of one's individual legal right to self-control. It is the selling of individuality.

What is a contract?

For employment to exist, however, a contract must first exist and contracts exist only if specific human conduct is evident. For example, two people standing in the street talking have a human relationship but not necessarily a contract. The same two people, however, can create a contract between themselves. No lawyer need be present and nothing need be on paper. But five key pieces of behaviour must occur. The persons must intend to create a legal relationship—say, one wants to sell a book and the other wants to buy a book. There must be clear terms—namely, that a particular book is for sale. There must be offer and acceptance—one offers to sell the book and the other person agrees to purchase it. There must be 'consideration', that is, the legal idea of payment, which may involve money or bartering or something else! There must be genuine consent—that is, both parties understand that there is a contract and want the sale to occur.

These key common-law contract principles ensure protection for all parties. For example, if the persons were in dispute after the book had been sold and went to court, a court would review the alleged contract between the parties, and if any of the key elements of a contract were missing, the court could declare that no contract existed.

The upshot is that people can, and most normally do, have relationships without creating contracts, but if people do create contracts, they inevitably have some type of relationship. The two people who were involved in the book transaction may not have liked each other, or one may have felt sorry for the other, or they may have been blood relatives. These are all human relationships that inevitably involve feelings and all the other psychological possibilities that exist within human relationships. But the mere fact of a human relationship does not of itself cause a contract to exist. Specific conduct must have occurred and be evident.

The first question, then, is this: if people have a contract, what type is it and how does that contract affect or reflect the relationship they may have? With employment, the relationship is quite clear. The employer has 'the right to control' the employee. The employee sells his or her right to self-control.

How do we know when an employment contract exists?

Every day of every year in every country, countless millions of people enter and exit contracts without the formal institutions of the law ever becoming involved. Many of the contracts are contracts of employment. In a tiny minority of cases, the persons find themselves in dispute and choose to go to the courts for settlement. By looking at the court settlement of these disputes, a clear understanding of employment can be gained because the task of the courts is to examine the details of behaviour before making a decision.

Before considering the specifics of any legal contract dispute in a work situation, the courts always first consider the contract form to ascertain whether it is employment or some other form of contract. They look for what they call a *'contract of service'*, which is the universal legal name for employment. Employment is sharply distinguished from the commercial contract, which is called a *'contract for services'*. A small and simple change of preposition and from singular to plural identifies the core of employment and its alternative, the commercial contract. But at the same time, it masks a vast difference between the behaviour and human relationships involved with each type of contract.

Ascertaining the correct contract type is crucial because of the different human relationships and obligations that exist within the different contract types. When a relationship is being investigated by the courts, the judges conduct a series of tests, effectively a series of 'swinging pendulums' designed to establish whether employment exists. If employment doesn't exist, but a contract is still present, they will find that the opposite of employment exists, namely, a commercial contract known as 'independent contracting'. By studying how the courts distinguish between employment and independent contracting, we can come to a practical understanding of employment. This is easily done by examining real-life court cases and the way in which judges arrive at their judgements.

In determining the existence of an employment contract, the courts undertake a detailed investigation of the specific circumstances they have been asked to consider. The parties come together in court and are questioned by legal counsel before a judge or judges. The process is usually expensive but has the objective of establishing whether the alleged employer had a 'right to control' the alleged employee. The judges apply clear tests which that are broadly consistent across nations (although variations in content and interpretation exist: for example, some tests are held to be more important in some countries than in others). In each case, the judges have the task of making a decision based on the balance of the evidence brought before them, given the particular circumstances and in the light of the full matrix of tests. Inevitably, the judges find a series of behaviours that indicate employment and other behaviours that indicate its opposite. Ultimately, they must make a decision based on the balance of evidence.

The courts use up to 22 possible major indicators which, in one way or another, dissect control at work into its ingredients, and apply tests against each ingredient. These indicators have been identified through the study of hundreds of court decisions. The major indicators are as follows:

- What is the degree of control?
- What is the style of remuneration?
- Who provides equipment?
- Is there an obligation to work?
- Can work be delegated to someone else?
- What is the intent of the parties?

- Who determines the hours of work?
- Is money deducted for holidays and leave arrangements?
- How is deduction of tax handled?
- How do government regulations apply?
- What are the contractual obligations?
- How is the work performed?
- Who takes the commercial risk on the end product?
- Who must rectify poor work?
- Who pays for the expenses of production?
- How is the job appointment handled?
- What are the powers of dismissal and termination?
- What do written documents say?
- To what extent is a person integrated into the business?

This broad set of indicators is not used in its entirety in every case or in every country. What occurs is that a selection of indicators from this list is used, but the intent of the investigation is always the same: to establish whether one person has a right to control an individual in the work situation. To understand these indicators and how they all lead to the one destination of 'control', it is necessary to look at them individually.

The tests of employment

One: What degree of control does the alleged employer exercise over the alleged employee? A court will inquire into how much discretion individuals may have over the performance of their work. Are they under supervision on a constant basis? Are they told how and when to do a task or are they pointed to the end result required and left to achieve it? Take, for example, a jewellery manufacturer who has two people working for the business. One person may assemble bits to make a standard design to the exact requirements of the manufacturer. He is told the hand movements required and what type of flux to use, and production is done on a conveyor-type 'line' according to a strict schedule as to when lunch and other breaks can occur. A supervisor oversees his performance at every stage. This person would profile as being in a 'controlled' relationship. If, by contrast, the other person was shown the end product needed and given the bits to be assembled, but could come and go as she saw fit, and supervision was limited to checking the end product for compliance with the required standards, this person would profile lower on the 'control' scale.

Two: What is the mode of remuneration? If the first person working as a jeweller was paid on an hourly rate, was paid overtime rates, had an allowance for using hot flux, had holiday pay deducted from his hourly rate and took holidays at a time that suited the company, this would indicate control and the person would profile toward being an employee. If the second person received a flat hourly rate that included an amount to cover holidays, took holidays solely at her discretion, and received a bonus for each and every product finished to specification, this person would tend not to profile as an employee because she tended to control herself.

The remuneration test considers whether your time is being purchased, thereby indicating that someone controls you during the time you are at work, or whether you are being paid for the job you perform, indicating that you are focused on the end product as an independent contractor.

When you are employed, you are paid only on hourly, weekly or monthly rates. Piece rates can sometimes be used. But it is you that is being purchased and the right to your time.

When you are independent, you are paid when a job is finished for the whole of the job. You are not being purchased; rather, the product or service that you create or help to create is being purchased. Progress payments can be based on hourly arrangements for convenience, but the overall job is the key. Sometimes the job may be priced by considering the hours involved. Sometimes the job may have an intangible outcome and therefore be difficult to price; but the difficulty does not alter the fact of your independence.

Three: Who provides and maintains equipment and/or resources? If the company provided the first jeweller all materials, a factory in which to work, a table and a chair to sit at, the person would profile as an employee. If the second person could work at the factory if she chose, but could also take items home to work on and/or could buy materials required for which she was reimbursed in the final remuneration, she would tend to profile as an independent person.

Providing your own equipment indicates that you control most aspects of your work (independent contracting). If someone else provides equipment, then this indicates that you exercise a lower level of your control over your work (employment).

When you are employed, you rarely provide your own equipment, which is always provided by someone else. You are paid less than if you provided equipment. The firm that provides your equipment is the party that claims business tax deductions for the equipment.

If you are independent, you are likely to provide your own equipment and maintain it, or you are liable to provide it or could provide it. The degree to which you need to provide equipment will vary from circumstance to circumstance. Sometimes the nature of the work may mean you provide very little, if any, equipment. For example, seasonal fruit pickers are frequently independent contractors. The nature of the work means it is not normally necessary for them to provide much equipment. Not providing equipment does not mean that you are an employee, it just lowers your independent profiling. Providing your own equipment means that you need to charge more and can claim the equipment as a business tax deduction against your own income.

Four: Is there an obligation to work? If the first jeweller is required to be at the place of work at set times, must work overtime at the discretion of the company and can take holidays only when the company determines, he would profile towards a controlled employee. If the second jeweller informed the company when she was available for work, took absences when she chose for holidays or to do other work as she pleased or chose to work long hours some days and shorter hours other days, she would tend to profile as an independent person.

You may be surprised to find that, when you are employed, there is a legal obligation to work, indicating that you do not control your own life. If you are an independent contractor, you do not have a specific legal obligation to work, and so you exercise considerable control over your own life.

If you are an employee, you are required or expected to be at work at specified times. Your working time is dictated to you by the demands of the business for which you work. Even if you don't think you have this legal requirement—for instance, because you work under an employment award or 'industrial instrument'—the employment document usually contains provisions such as 'an employee shall be ready, willing and available for work when required by the employer'.

If you are independent, you work because and when you want to work. You can decide not to work, and you do not have to justify that decision to anyone other than as a courtesy which makes good commercial sense. If you don't undertake work when you had previously indicated that you would, you will earn a reputation for being unreliable. But making and sticking to your undertakings is the important thing. You may work when your client needs you, but that is your choice, not a legal requirement.

Five: Is the worker able to delegate the work to someone else and free to work for other companies, including competitors? If the company insisted that their jewellers could not work for anyone else (a common requirement) and would not let anyone else do the work required, the jewellers would profile as employees. In this instance, the company is seeking to have a measure of ownership over the time of the persons and thus prevent them from working for competitors or becoming competitors themselves. If, however, the jewellers could organize for part of their tasks to be done by someone else, conditional on meeting the required standards, and the jewellers were free to work where, when and for whom else they chose, they would tend to profile as independent persons.

Delegation relates to exclusivity of performance. If you can arrange for someone else to do a job, this indicates that you are in control of the end result. If the demand is that you personally do the work, then this indicates that you have been bought, and during the period of purchase you have lost your control over yourself. Sometimes delegation may be difficult because of the specific skills involved, but this is an issue of practicality, not legality.

As an employee, you are expected to be the person who does the work and you are prohibited from arranging for someone else to do the work for you. You are being purchased as if you were a commodity. You would never 'employ' another person to do your work or even help you. You don't have that authority!

When you are independent, you can organize someone else to help you with part or all of the work. You may 'employ' someone and become an 'employer' or engage other independent contractors who work with you on projects. It is your responsibility, however, to ensure that the end result meets the required standards.

Six: Intent. This is perhaps the most important test of all. In one court case, the judge said 'In the final analysis I find the genuine intention of all parties, as expressed in contractual terms and in their conduct to be more persuasive than any of the other indicia which I have dealt with...'[4] The intent indicator looks at individual attitudes and the attitudes of the persons with whom they work. The question is: do you want to control yourself or do others want to control you?

The question is deeply personal. If you are employed, you are content to have others tell you what to do. You don't want to ask whether an instruction is appropriate or not, because it's not your responsibility. You go with the flow. You are expected to be loyal to someone else and think that if you are loyal, you will be looked after. You are happy to be a cog in a system. You are happy to have your contract dictated to you by other people—whether an employer or a union or a tribunal.

If you are an independent contractor, you want to be independent. You want to control your own life. You are not willing to have people dictate to you and you stand up for your position, beliefs and the professional approach you bring to your work. You insist on being treated as an equal. You are loyal to yourself and your professional integrity and capacity. You insist on having control of your contract. You may accept some contractual terms with which you are not completely happy, but overall you are satisfied with the contract. You see the people with whom you work as independent beings as well. The people who pay you are your clients, not your employers.

Seven: Hours of work. If you cannot determine when you work, you are controlled. If you decide the hours you work, then you control yourself!

As an employee you are required to be at 'work' at certain times and must not be 'absent'. If you are absent, you must explain why. You don't have control over your working hours, but must seek approval from others to vary them. Your employer dictates your work lifestyle.

As an independent contractor, you choose when you work and how many hours you work. You can work on weekends and not mid-week. You can vary your hours as you see fit without seeking approval from anyone (though you may inform your clients as a sensible commercial courtesy). You can modify your work to suit your lifestyle, which depends, of course, on how much work you wish to do. This is tempered by the practical needs of your client, or the physical environment: for example, if you work as an independent contractor in a building that is closed at certain hours, then your choice of working hours is constrained.

Eight: Provision of holidays and entitlement to leave. The withholding of 'entitlement' money is a method of control. It is a critical pointer to employment.

When you are employed, your employer withholds a portion of your salary as a method of determining when you can take holidays or other 'leave'. You are paid less each week than could be the case. You run the risk that, if your employer goes broke, the withheld 'entitlements' money may be lost. You are told by your employer when to take holidays and are paid when you are on holiday.

When you are independent, you receive the full payment for your work. No money is held back from you. When you work, you earn. When you don't work, you don't earn. You don't run the risk of losing 'entitlement' money if a client goes broke. You take holidays when you want. Generally, your payments are greater than the net salary of an employee in the same line of business, because no money is deducted for holidays and other 'entitlements'.

Nine: Deduction of income tax. This is a common test across the globe, but only because governments find the status of employment a convenient administrative tool for the collection of income tax. It was used in Australia, for example, up until July 2000 because the authority of the Australian Tax Office to require a payer to withhold income tax from a payee and send the money to the tax office was legislatively tied to the existence of common-law employment. In effect, for the tax office to receive revenue, it had to push people into common-law employment. The Australian tax system changed in July 2000. Now the Tax Act stipulates the different administrative systems that require payers to withhold income tax from both employees and independent contractors. In Australia, deduction of income tax is now a neutral issue in relation to the common-law assessment of employment/independent contracting. In other countries, such as the USA and UK, deduction of income tax is still administratively tied to common-law employment and remains a factor in the common-law test. This is discussed at length in Chapter Three.

Ten: Characterization of relationship for purposes of regulatory provisions. Many pieces of legislation seek to regulate how we work or they collect tax from our remuneration. The provisions of the legislation vary among countries and jurisdictions. Some legislation is dependent on common law (as with some income tax acts). Some legislation applies to both employment and independent contracting. The implication for the common-law test of employment or independent contracting is that some regulations sometimes attempt to force you to be an employee, even if that is not your wish.

Relevant legislation covers income tax, payroll tax, worker injury insurance, equal opportunities, anti-discrimination, and occupational health and safety. Generally, however, industrial relations legislation is the most important.

When you are employed, for the most part you do not control your contract. In the Australian example of extreme regulation, industrial relations law controls most of your contract (sometimes your entire contract). Even if you have an 'individual' employment contract, the content must generally be approved by a tribunal. Industrial relations tribunals dictate the terms of your contract, whether you agree or not. The system is complex and legalistic, and you have no control. The law takes your control of yourself away from you. But, strange as it seems, the law also takes much of the control of the contract away from the employer.

As an independent person, however, your contracts are regulated under commercial-type law. If you are in dispute over your contract, you have access to commercial courts and small claims tribunals. Your contract can never be unconscionable and must be freely entered into by you. But the courts will not seek to interfere in your contract unless you have a dispute. The courts will not try to determine the content of your contract before you enter it. The content of the contract is left for you to control with your clients.

Eleven: Contractual obligations. If you freely enter a contract in which you agree to be held to the requirements of the contract, you tend to control yourself. Where you have agreed to obligations, you must fulfil those obligations. Your client also agrees to obligations to you which the client must fulfil. You are not independent if the contract tends to be open-ended and not result-orientated, leaving you with little control over yourself. If the obligations can be changed without your prior approval by the other party, you don't control yourself. You are employed.

In a commercial contract, the contractor assumes an obligation to perform the contract, in other words, to carry out the tasks specified in the contract. When those tasks are performed, the contract is 'completed' or 'fulfilled'. The other party to the contract (the client) has a right to the performance of the contract. In that sense, the contractor is obliged to the client but only because the obligation is to fulfil the contract which has been freely entered.

In an employment contract, the employee assumes an obligation of fidelity to the employer. The contract need not specify any particular task or set of tasks to be performed, but within the terms of the contract, the employer may specify such tasks. The contract is not, however, 'completed' by the performance of such tasks, because the employee's obligation of fidelity to the employer continues as long as the employment contract is in force. An employment contract is thus indeterminate about any tasks that may be performed under the contract.

This legal difference may appear to be fine (even academic) but it is important. The consequence is that, when employed, you are merely part of a process and need neither understand nor care about the end result. Your contractual obligation is to be 'loyal' to the employer. The employer may specify tasks for you to perform but the contract is not ended when those tasks are completed, since the obligation of loyalty persists as long as your employment contract persists.

If independent, you work to achieve a specific task. For example, you are engaged to build a wall or a computer program, or to solve a particular problem. Your obligation under the contract is to carry out the task specified in the contract. Your client has a right to have those tasks performed and an obligation to pay you for the completion of those tasks. When all contractual obligations have been performed, the contract is completed.

Twelve: How the work is performed. If you decide how you do a job, you control yourself. If you are told how to do a job, someone else controls you.

When you are employed, someone else tells you how you must do a job and you just follow their instructions, generally without question. You comply with legal requirements, but only because you are told to. If the job process is wrong, you aren't 'required' to care (even if you do care) because you are paid to do as you are told. Your work procedures change only as and when someone else so decides and issues a new set of instructions.

If you are independent, you have a higher level of discretion about how you achieve an outcome. The end result is the important thing, not necessarily how you get there, which is really determined by the price you are being paid! You have a strong incentive to respect occupational health and safety requirements, to be honest and generally to know and comply with the law. There may be safety or production requirements that need to be met to ensure a satisfactory end result. You may need training to understand and acquire the skills necessary for your line of business. But that does not mean you are 'controlled'; rather, you are simply adjusting to practical realities.

Thirteen: Risk. Commercially winning (or losing) from a job indicates that you control yourself. If someone else wins or loses from your job, this indicates that someone else has exercised the control.

As an employee, you do not have to care about profits or losses. You are simply paid for the time you spend at the enterprise. If a product proves faulty, there is no comeback to you. You walk away at the end of the day without a care!

As an independent person, you gain a profit or suffer a loss from your work. If your work is faulty, you can commercially suffer as a result. But you can win big-time commercially if the product or service proves to be popular.

Fourteen: Rectification. Being responsible for your actions is a key indicator of control. If you are held responsible, you control yourself. If you are not responsible, it's because someone else controls you.

When employed, if you make a mistake you may be disciplined, but you won't be required to fix the error in your own time. In the worst-case scenario, you may even face the sack, but someone else might fix your errors. You do as you are told, but after that you don't have to worry.

When independent, if you make an error, you have to correct it at your own expense. You probably need your own indemnity and insurance policies. You are happy to back up your work by being prepared to fix problems in your own time.

Fifteen: Expenses. Being responsible for incurring your own expenses indicates a high level of self-control. If you have to obtain prior approval for expenses, you are controlled by someone else.

As an employee, you find that you receive less money than an independent contractor for the same kind of work, but your employer pays your work-related expenses, such as telecommunications, accommodation, or transport. You cannot claim any of these against your income, but your employer claims them as business tax-deductions at the end of each year.

As an independent contractor, payments made to you are higher than to an employee in the same line of business because you have expenses that an employee does not have. You may cover all your own phone bills, work-related travel expenses, and so on. You must record and track these and claim them as tax deductions from your business income at the end of each year. Sometimes you may incur expenses that are passed on to your client, but this will covered by your commercial contract.

Sixteen: Appointment. If there is an expectation that your appointment through your contract is ongoing, this indicates that you have handed control of yourself over to someone else. If your appointment is for the period of each agreed contract, this indicates that you maintain control of what happens to you in the future.

Seventeen: Termination. If there is a clear understanding that the arrangements finish when the job is done, no-one really controls anyone. If there are complex processes involved when either party wishes to cease working, then this indicates that people are trying to control each other.

In most developed economies, it's almost impossible for employers to sack employees without the initiation of 'unfair dismissal' processes that are promoted through the unfair dismissal conventions of the International Labor Organisation. Termination of an employee by an employer used to be straightforward. But now the process of ending employment at the employer's request can be complex and messy.

As an independent person, you work from job to job or contract to contract. You accept that when the job or contract finishes, the work ends. You don't consider that you have a job for life or even want a job for life. Clients come and clients go, and this is accepted as a normal part of life. You are likely to be confident that you can move on to another job.

Eighteen: Documentation and terms of the contract. No matter what written documents may say, the courts will take notice of the documents only to the extent that conduct matches the written statements. If a written document states that you are an independent contractor, but your actions are those of a typical employee, or the other party behaves like a controlling employer and you acquiesce, then you could be found in law to be an employee.

With employment, documents use language such as 'employ, employer, employment', etc. Because of the use of the word 'contract', it is easy to be confused into believing that it refers to a commercial contract when in fact it refers to an employment contract.

Most employee documents are found in industrial relations instruments, often controlled by unions and tribunals, but not by employees. Employees often have difficulty finding the written contract, as industrial legislation and regulations are actually part of your contract even though you don't know the detail. Your contract can be changed by tribunals without even consulting you. Or the tribunals can prevent you changing your employment contract as you would like.

For an independent contractor, documents will have a distinct commercial look and use commercial terms such as 'contract', 'engage', 'client', 'user', 'contractor', 'independent contractor'. Independent contractor documents should be in the possession of independent contractors. People own and control their documents. Changes to written documents occur only with the agreement of both parties. The documents can and should be easily understood.

Nineteen: Integration. This test is rarely used in Australia, but is frequently used in the USA, the UK and other countries. It inquires whether a person is 'part and parcel' of an organization.

When employed, you work 'in' an organization and need to promote yourself inside the organization in order to move up the promotional ladder. You don't need or want to advertise yourself outside the organization—unless, of course, you intend to leave and are looking for other employment. You are a corporate player. Someone else, or the system, organizes your career.

When independent, you actively market or sell yourself. You live from job to job and are always mindful of the need to advertise your services. Sometimes a job can last a long time, but that does not mean that you have given up your independence. You actively control your career.

The foregoing tests cover most that a court may choose to apply. No single test is more important than any other, and no test is conclusive on its own. The tests are like a swinging pendulum: one test may swing strongly towards employment, while another may swing towards independent contracting. The judges charged with making a decision have to come to a balanced conclusion from the facts before them.

None of this is theoretical. It is all highly practical. The judges are looking for the truth in the relationship that will indicate into which legal contract framework the relationship fits. One is a relationship of control and inequality. The other is a relationship of self-control and equality.

The practical nature of the investigations, and the real-life understanding of 'employment', is revealed in legal cases.

Stevens v. Brodribb Sawmilling Company[5]
Stevens v. *Brodribb* is the leading Australian case identifying common-law employment. The legal judgment drew heavily on the history of English common law. The judgment is a good example of common-law employment applying in most common law-based legal systems across the globe. The key statement from Stevens and Brodribb provides a good summary of the common-law test. 'A prominent factor in determining the nature of the relationship between a person who engages another to perform work and the person so engaged is the degree of control which the former can exercise over the latter. It has been held, however that the importance of control lies not so much in its actual exercise although clearly that is relevant, as in the right of the employer to exercise it.'[6]

The facts of the case were as follows. Brodribb Pty Ltd was a company operating a sawmill during the mid-1980s. Logging was carried out by Mr Stevens (and others), who drove a truck, and Mr Gray, who operated a bulldozer used to load the logs onto trucks. In an incident, Mr Gray was negligent in loading the logs onto Mr Stevens' truck and Stevens was injured. Stevens sued Brodribb Pty Ltd on the basis that it was vicariously liable for the acts of Gray. The essence of employment vicariousness is that, because an employee does not control himself, the employer is responsible for the employee's actions. In this case, Mr Stevens claimed that Gray was an employee of Brodribb Pty Ltd and therefore Brodribb Pty Ltd (the sawmill) should pay compensation for Stevens' injuries.

The court found, however, that both Stevens and Gray were independent contractors and so Brodribb was not liable for Stevens' injuries. The court considered the fact that both Stevens and Gray owned and maintained their own equipment, that although they were required to deliver two loads per day they could set their own hours, payment was calculated on volume, no guarantee of work was given, both men were left entirely free to exercise their own skill and judgement, and there was a right of delegation. As a consequence of a finding of no employment, the court held that Mr Gray was responsible for his own negligence and blame could not be transferred to Brodribb Pty Ltd.

In this leading case, the courts conducted a detailed assessment based on a full array of 'swinging pendulums'. In their decision, the judges made the point that no one indicator was dominant and that no hard-and-fast rules governed the way the tests should be interpreted. Importantly, the judgment depended on the full matrix of tests and the totality of the relationship. In addition, the case highlighted the need for the common law to keep pace with a changing society. 'The relationship is a dynamic one which needs to be accommodated to a variety of different and changing social economic circumstances.'[7]

Mayne Nickless[8]
Mayne Nickless Pty Ltd was a large, listed, Australia-wide transport company that engaged numerous transport drivers, some as employees, others as independent contractors. In 1998, one of its contract drivers, Mr Sammartino, was dismissed. Soon after, Mr Sammartino lodged an unfair dismissal application. Before the application could be considered, the courts had to determine whether Mr Sammartino was an employee or, as was claimed by Mayne Nickless, a contract driver. If he was an employee, the unfair dismissal application could proceed; if a contractor, the labour courts would not have jurisdiction and the application would fail.

On the employer versus contractor definition alone, the case was exhaustive. It was first heard by a single commissioner in the Australian Industrial Relations Commission. Mr Sammartino lost at this point because the commissioner found that he was not an employee. Mr Sammartino appealed to the Full Bench of the Industrial Relations Commission (IRC), where three commissioners heard his appeal. The Commission referred the case to a higher court, namely, the Full Bench of the Federal Court of Australia (with three judges sitting). After resolving some points of law unrelated to employment, the Federal Court ordered the Full Bench of the IRC to rule on the application. As always seems to be the case, the legal expenses were large.

In giving instructions to the IRC on the conduct of the case, the Federal Court stated an important principle of common-law process: '... the decision maker [the IRC] must make findings of fact and determine whether the facts as found establish whether the person is an employee or not. No exercise of discretion is involved.' In other words, a common-law investigation looks at the real-life behaviour of the parties involved. The accepted common-law tests are clear and known and must be applied in a consistent manner. This is not to deny that judges may differ in their reading of the circumstances brought before them, but the tests to be applied are clear. This statement by the courts refutes the claim by some commentators that the common-law test for employment is not clear.

At the end of this exhaustive examination, the IRC found that Mr Sammartino was in fact an employee and could seek unfair dismissal relief. In effect, the IRC found that, in spite of what Mayne Nickless thought it was doing, its attempt to engage people as independent contractors had failed. Mayne Nickless had not operated within the managerial and behavioural parameters necessary for any genuine independent contractor arrangement with Mr Sammartino.

The facts of Mr Sammartino's engagement as tendered in evidence were as follows. Mr Sammartino had started working for Mayne Nickless in 1986 as a casual employee driver, and went full-time in 1987. He was promoted to his own run in 1989, at which time Mayne Nickless considered Mr Sammartino became an independent contractor. From 1989, Mr Sammartino was engaged as a 'contract carrier' under the terms of an unregistered industrial agreement with the Transport Workers Union of Australia. A term of the agreement stated that Mr Sammartino was an independent contractor. Mr Sammartino had not signed the contract but had provided Mayne Nickless with invoices on which he was paid. Mr Sammartino provided his own vehicle but stated in evidence that he had always considered himself an employee. Mayne Nickless had provided the union with a list of independent drivers who had full-time contracts with the company.

Based on the evidence of Mr Sammartino, Mayne Nickless managers, and documents supplied, Mr Sammartino's engagement strongly reflected the terms and processes contained in the industrial instrument which Mayne Nickless had with the Transport Workers Union (TWU) and which also covered Mayne Nickless's employees. The agreement covered the timing of holidays, rostering issues, changes to and timing of changes to pay rates, and requirements to belong to the TWU superannuation fund. Warnings on work standards in Mr Sammartino's case were handled in exactly the same way as they were handled with employees. Mayne Nickless had entered an agreement with the union to cover conditions for 'contractors' after Mayne Nickless had conducted detailed negotiations with the TWU. Mr Sammartino's engagement was considered permanent by Mayne Nickless. Mr Sammartino was paid and taxed as an individual person. Mr Sammartino supplied his own vehicle, but so did employees of Mayne Nickless. Allocation of runs was at the sole discretion of Mayne Nickless. The contract that Mr Sammartino had not signed, but which was allegedly in place, was the industrial instrument that Mayne Nickless had created and signed with the union. The TWU–Mayne Nickless agreement was collectively agreed to by the TWU members and was not an individual contract arrangement. The agreement drew on terms from the industry-based labour award that applied to employees. Mr Sammartino stated that Mayne Nickless had told him he was entitled to all the terms under the employee-type award. Further, in 1990, the union had notified Mayne Nickless in writing that it considered that the contracts with contract couriers were of the employer–employee type. All of these facts created significant pointers towards employment.

For example, several pages of the judgment discussed the pay rates. 'On balance we conclude that … Mr Sammartino was not independent in relation to any significant aspect of the remuneration package applied to him. The package was collectively negotiated. The labour rate was derived from award equivalent or perhaps over-award arrangements….'[9]

In addition, the contractual obligation was personal to Mr Sammartino. 'He had restricted opportunities to substitute his own work performance…'[10] If Mr Sammartino lost his driver's licence, a replacement driver must be accompanied by Mr Sammartino at all times, further indicating that the obligation was attached to Mr Sammartino. In addition, the judgment found that Mr Sammartino's capacity to work for any other client was effectively restricted and prevented. This all indicated the removal of Mr Sammartino's capacity to control his own work; as such, he was an employee.

Other aspects, however, indicated independent contracting. Mr Sammartino had to supply his own vehicle and keep it in the livery of Mayne Nickless. He had to meet operating expenses and to upgrade to a new vehicle every five years. The provision of the vehicle constituted 38 per cent of the payments to him. In commenting, the Commission said, 'We consider the obligation to provide and maintain a vehicle … is an important indication that Mr Sammartino's contract was a contract for services [independent contracting]'.[11]

But Mr Sammartino operated as an individual and was not incorporated. The Commission stated that, in its experience, in industrial relations matters in the transport industry 'A requirement by principal contractors for owner-drivers to incorporate has become relatively common'.[12]

On balance, the Commission found that Mr Sammartino was in fact an employee. The behaviours that indicated independent contracting were outweighed by the fact that he was treated little differently from employees of Mayne Nickless. Mayne Nickless may have called Mr Sammartino a contractor, but its managerial behaviour indicated that Mayne Nickless really wanted an employee, and Mr Sammartino thought he was an employee and acted as an employee.

Vabu Pty Ltd trading as Crisis Couriers and Australian Taxation Office 1996[13]
The Crisis Couriers case provides a good comparison with the Mayne Nickless case because of the similarities in industries and operations. Both companies were in the transport business and competed with each other. They were structured along similar lines; they both required their drivers to provide their own vehicles and sought to have independent-contractor relationships with the drivers. Both cases were tested in the Australian common-law system. Mayne Nickless failed and Crisis Couriers succeeded. The difference between the two cases lay in the detail of the management of their independent contractor systems. Comparing the cases demonstrates how the common-law test of employment versus independent contracting hinges on a balanced assessment of the full set of behaviours to determine whether the workers own or do not own the 'right to control' themselves.

Crisis Couriers is a courier business in Sydney. Its bicycle couriers deliver parcels and documents in and around the Sydney CBD office blocks. The colourfully clad couriers can be seen every day weaving in and out of traffic and pedestrians, standing beside suit-clad business persons riding the elevators of skyscrapers, or standing in groups beside idle bicycles waiting for the next radioed assignment. Their courier colleagues can be sighted in the business districts of most major cities of the world. The company began in 1980 and, by 1993, Crisis Couriers was paying about $A2 million a year to about 80 couriers, including bicycle, motorbike, car and van couriers.

In Australia, employers are required to make compulsory superannuation/retirement payments for employees. The scheme is administered by the Australian Taxation Office (ATO) under the authority of tax legislation that ties the ATO's powers to enforce compulsory superannuation to employment relationships. Crisis Couriers believed that its couriers were independent contractors and hence not subject to the compulsory superannuation provisions of the Tax Act. It believed that it paid the couriers for results and that the individual couriers looked after their own superannuation.

In 1996, the ATO took Crisis Couriers to the Supreme Court of New South Wales to enforce superannuation payments. The task of the court was to decide the legal status of the couriers, which would determine whether or not the Act could be applied to the company. The case assumed importance in the transport industry in Australia because most private transport companies engage couriers and drivers under similar arrangements to Crisis Couriers. The first ruling under a single judge was appealed to the Full Bench of the court; two judges found the couriers to be independent contractors and one judge found them to be employees. Crisis Couriers won. As in all Australian cases, the 'right to control' tests as identified in *Stevens* v. *Brodribb*, were applied by the court.

Three couriers gave evidence before the court. Two drove vans and one a motor bike. When first engaged, the couriers were interviewed by the company and given three documents to sign covering conditions and rules of work. The contracts required that the couriers be neat and tidy at all times, wear the company uniform, replace vehicles as required, observe starting times and work prescribed hours, not use foul language, accept work as given by the company, accept re-routing, and take no more time than was permitted. These elements certainly could indicate employment because Crisis Couriers sought to ensure certain behaviours from the couriers. But the court stated that 'However, a man may supervise others without becoming their employer'.[14] In other words, supervision does not necessarily equal control.

The court ruled that independent contracting existed substantially on the basis that the couriers supplied their own vehicles (car, vans, motorbikes) and bore the costs of running them. The company supplied uniforms and radios but the couriers' business expenses were considerable. The couriers had to supply their own street directories, telephone books, trolleys, ropes and blankets. The couriers did not receive a set wage or salary but were paid for the successful deliveries they made. Crisis Couriers allowed the couriers to use a company or trust. The court stated 'each courier conducts his own operation, permitting himself for his own economic advantage to be supervised by the company'.[15]

There were many similarities to the Mayne Nickless case, but also important differences. The transport couriers association to which Crisis Couriers belonged had entered an industrial agreement with the Transport Workers Union but, unlike Mayne Nickless, the couriers with Crisis Couriers had individually signed contracts with the company. Further, the terms of the contracts were not drawn from any union agreement but were independently drafted. Were the union to argue that its agreement with the industry association covered contractors, the counter-argument was that the terms of the industrial agreement could not apply to Crisis Couriers because the power of the industrial agreement was dependent on the Australian Industrial Relations Act, which could cover only employees.

Hollis v. *Vabu (Crisis Couriers) Pty Ltd (2001)*[16]

Hollis v. *Vabu* of 2001 was an Australian High Court case that followed the earlier 1996 case of *Vabu* v. *Federal Commissioner of Taxation*. On the surface, the two cases involving the same company and same procedures produced 'opposite' results. The detail reveals more.

Hollis v Vabu (Crisis Couriers) is a most interesting and critical common-law test case. On the surface, it appears to overturn the previous and near-identical test case of *Vabu* v. *ATO*. It was a second case involving the same company. When the decision of this case became known, many commentators claimed that it proved that the common-law tests for employment did not work and were completely inconsistent. The commentators argued that if two test cases examining (apparently) the same company operations produced totally opposite results then the tests used were flawed. What was actually demonstrated, however, was that every case is individual and specific to the circumstances. Further, it showed that the criteria for assessment which the courts use are consistent. Finally, interpretation of the criteria can indeed vary significantly given specific circumstances, and considerable debate can occur between the judges on interpretation.

The original (1996) Crisis Couriers superannuation case involved an application from the Australian Taxation Office alleging that Crisis Couriers owed superannuation on the payments it made to its courier drivers. The key to the decision was the fact that the van driver couriers provided and maintained their own vehicles. This was considered a decisive factor shifting the balance of evidence to independent contracting.

The Crisis Couriers/Hollis case (2001) involved the same company but different circumstances. A bicycle courier wearing a 'Crisis Couriers' jacket had knocked over and injured a pedestrian and had ridden off without giving personal identification. The pedestrian was suing Crisis Couriers for damages on the basis that the unidentified bicycle rider was an employee of Crisis Couriers and consequently Crisis Couriers was 'vicariously' liable for the 'employee's' actions. The High Court conducted a similar investigation to the 1996 case and, on examining near-identical operational procedures, found that the unidentified bicycle rider was an employee of Crisis Couriers.

The High Court, however, was careful to be highly specific in this seemingly contradictory decision. The Court limited the finding of employment specifically to the unidentified bicycle courier who had knocked over the pedestrian. The court was careful not to comment on other Crisis Couriers bicycle, motorcycle, or van driver couriers. The court finding of employment was based on a view that there was a big difference between a courier providing and maintaining a motor vehicle and doing the same with a bicycle. On the balance of evidence, providing a bicycle was a much less significant pointer to independent contracting than providing a car.

The decision was controversial. Three of the five judges found that employment existed. One judge found that no employment existed, but that the bicycle courier was an 'agent' of Crisis Couriers and that Crisis Couriers was still liable. One judge totally disagreed and found that there was no substantial difference between the way the couriers operated—that is, whether they were car couriers or bicycle couriers—and found that the bicycle courier was an independent contractor.

The Crisis Couriers cases are particularly important because they highlight the fact that in order to ensure that independent contractor status is solid, it is essential that daily operational procedures and the behaviour of parties consistently conform to independent contractor criteria. What the case also proves is that a single body of tests used to investigate the existence of employment can lead to the different findings even in similar circumstances. In fact, the nuances of specific behaviours can lead judges to come to different conclusions. The two Crisis Couriers judgments differed because of differences of view on matters of small operational detail.

UK IR 35

In the United Kingdom, the right of the tax office to collect income and welfare taxes is legislatively tied to common-law employment: if control employment does not exist in a working relationship, the UK tax office does not have the legal authority to collect the tax. Because tax authorities prefer to collect tax at the point of payment, they seek to give themselves the authority to decide what is or is not employment. Even if people seek to avoid the employment relationship for purposes totally unrelated to tax, the tax authorities will seek to enforce employment to safeguard their taxing powers. This has created great confusion because when tax authorities have lost court cases on common-law grounds, they then go to great lengths to try to redefine 'employment' in a way that suits their tax collection purposes. In so doing they frequently breach common-law principles, create injustice and severely distort the economic behaviour of taxpayers. This has been strongly demonstrated in the United Kingdom in a case that highlights the common-law principles involved.

In 2001, the powers of the UK Internal Revenue Service (IR) to declare a person to be or not to be an employee were challenged. The case involved tax issues but also significant consideration of what it meant to be an employee. The problem and the court case had their origins in the information technology (IT) sector, where it has become commonplace world-wide for workers to prefer to be independent contractors rather than employees—a major factor driving the industry's spectacular productivity growth and high remuneration levels. The UK government had passed legislation, known as IR35, that enabled the IR to determine whether workers were in an 'employee like' working relationship, even if they were independent contractors at common law. In effect, the IR was empowered in this respect to bypass the common law and the courts. The affront to justice is enormous but it's a common tactic being used by taxing authorities and other regulators around the world. It was this bypassing of common-law judicial process that the Professional Contractors Group, a UK association of IT contractors, sought to challenge. The case was heard before a single judge in the UK High Court in 2000–1.[17]

The case went though the normal process in which the ways in which IT independent contractors conducted their businesses were considered. In the judgment, the evidence showed that IT industry contractors chose to work where and when they wanted. Further, clients had difficulty negotiating long-term contracts with IT contractors, and in any case the on-off nature of the work militated against long-term arrangements. In addition, skilled IT people actively marketed themselves to find the best work and financial rewards. The evidence showed that IT firms did not 'control' IT workers, and that IT workers avoided the ties and disadvantages associated with employment, preferring the flexibility of being free agents. Most contractors had established their own companies to ensure their contractor status; of this the judge said 'A company gives the service contractor control of his own destiny'.[18] Each of the behaviours evidenced in the case strongly indicated that the workers engaged were not employees. The choice of working this way was, in this instance, almost entirely that of the IT workers themselves, who resisted pressure on them from large IT companies to become employees.

The judgment powerfully demonstrated the advantages of working as a professional independent contractor rather than as an employee. The contractors argued that if they were forced to be employees they would 'receive less remuneration than if they were their own masters'.[19] The judge made the point that the difference between the IT people who considered themselves contractors and the way the tax authorities thought of them was more 'a question of a different approach and a different mindset'. The evidence indicated that the tax authorities were locked into the mindset of employment and could not comprehend independent contracting. This difference of mindset is perhaps the most important difference between employment and independent contracting. Contractors see themselves as business people making their own decisions. By contrast, employees see themselves as cogs in a machine with other people making decisions for them. The tax authorities could not conceive of individuals working for large companies yet making decisions for themselves. In truth, it's a cultural problem for tax authorities because they engage their own staff on strict controlling employment terms. Further, the tax authorities have a vested interest in finding employment, because it is over employment that their legislative authority holds sway.

The judge indicated that contractors clearly and consciously gave up the benefits of being employees. '[The contractor] does not have automatic entitlement as against the client to all the benefits of being an employee (such as maternity pay or sick pay or statutory holidays or unemployment benefit …)'[20] Against this, the contractor received much greater remuneration. In effect, the issue of holiday and other entitlements is not one of economic benefit but of who has control over the entitlements. Employees have 'entitlement' remuneration withheld from them so that employers can decide when employees take holidays and other leave. Contractors are fully remunerated and determine when they take holidays and other leave. This sometimes is probably inconvenient for the companies that engage IT contractors, but is one of the advantages of independent contracting to the contractors themselves.

The case also demonstrated the economic nature of independent contracting. The judge stated, 'the service contractor, through his service company, is in competition with large companies, or even with small companies'.[21] In other words, the IT contractors accepted and sought competition with each other. By contrast, employees were protected by their employers from competition both external to the firm and within the firm. The economic mark of a contractor is the desire to be competitive. In the tax dispute, the point at issue for the IT contractors and strongly argued by counsel for the Professional Contractors Group was that the treatment of independent IT contractors as employees by the IR unfairly reduced their capacity to be competitive, particularly against large firms. Thought of in another way, employment is an anti-competitive practice that favours large firms by shielding them from new but smaller competitors. By imposing employment on contractors, the UK IR has become a protector of big business from the entrepreneurial drive of individual UK citizens. This sort of action is inevitably harmful to the public interest, a point of no interest to the IR, which simply wants to maximize its powers and its revenues.

A further indicator of employment was the issue of loyalty. Employees are supposed to be loyal to their employers, whereas contractors are loyal to themselves. The judge commented that contracting involved 'an important contrast to the duty of fidelity ordinarily owed by an employee' [to an employer].[22] 'Fidelity' involves the idea of adherence to obligations: employees are expected to be willing to fulfil the obligations imposed by the employment contract. In effect, it is a psychological process whereby the employer's authority relies on employees willingly making themselves subservient to the controlling authority of the employer. Independent contractors do not have, nor do they want, a 'duty of fidelity'. As noted earlier, both employees and independent contractors incur obligations and it is true that contractors need to 'keep faith' with their clients. But the nature of the obligations is quite different. Once a commercial contract has been fulfilled, the independent contractor is relieved of any further obligation to his client; indeed, he may next offer his services to a rival client. But an employee has a duty to his employer which is ongoing and open-ended.

A key indicator of non-employment is that the person doing the work can substitute another person to do that work. In the case of IT contractors, the evidence showed that substitution did occur but usually only with the approval of the client. The judge did not, however, see the need for client approval as necessarily an indicator of employment. '...it would not be right to make an absolute statement ... that the need to obtain the client's permission necessarily negates the existence of a right to substitution, and/or points to employment'.[23]

The final issue of interest was the evidence that a person could move in and out of employment and contracting on a regular basis. In fact, this proved to be a regular occurrence in the IT area. It proved quite normal for people to be working on several different projects at the same time; in some cases they could be employees in some projects and independent contractors in others. Everything hinged on the nature of each individual contract, and no broad sweeping conclusions could be drawn.

The UK IR case demonstrated the consistency of approach across nations to the tests which the common-law courts use in investigating the existence of employment, that is, a specific type of contract in which the human relationships give one person control over another. In this case, the court upheld the common-law principles in the face of a tax authority that wanted to change those principles.

Williams[24]

Not everyone is either employed or an independent contractor. People can and are still engaged in paid work under arrangements that are a throwback to medieval times. The case of Mr Williams is an interesting example. Mr G. Williams was a member of the Royal Australian Air Force based in Darwin. In March 2000, he was dismissed from the RAAF on medical grounds and sought unfair dismissal compensation. Under Australian legislation, unfair dismissal action is available only to employees. Mr Williams could make application for unfair dismissal only if he was an employee.

The initial question in the case was whether the Australian unfair dismissal laws applied only to employees. In its finding the IRC said, 'It has never been suggested that the expression employee, either in the Act or in any of its precursors going back to 1904, means anything other than employee at common law'.[25] The outcome was that the tribunal found that the *Industrial Relations Act* that allowed relief for unfair dismissal applied only to common-law employees. Non-employees were not entitled to unfair dismissal relief—in Australia, at least. This same interpretation could be expected from the courts in other English-based legal systems and is reflected in International Labour Organisation conventions.

The engagement of Mr Williams was investigated and he was found not to be an employee. But nor was he an independent contractor. In fact, the Court found that he was in an engagement contract that involved even greater loss of the right to self-control than employment. Williams was found to be a 'servant of the Crown'. People who work in the armed services, police and other government institutions are often found not to be employees. These 'servants of the Crown' are instruments of the state itself. They are supposed to be subject to greater control than employees because they exercise the full and awesome power of the state that it can exercise over individuals. Therefore, the state exercises complete control over its servants and is able to dismiss them at will.

People who work as servants of the state and other legal arrangements are not the specific focus in this book. What the Williams and UK IR35 cases demonstrate is how necessary it is to be careful and precise in the use of the word 'employment', because the word has a highly specific meaning at law, involving a specific set of behaviours and control processes.

Common-law employment as defined in the USA

As in the UK and Australia, employment in the USA is defined by common law. The courts look for evidence that the alleged 'employee' is subject to a right of control exercised by an alleged 'employer'.

For example, US federal legislation governs employee health care, disability and other benefits under the *Employee Retirement Income Security Act* of 1974.[26] 'Employment' is the key definitional issue for the reach of the Act, and in several test cases the US courts have identified the common-law test as being consideration of 'the hiring party's right to control the manner and means by which the product is accomplished'.[27] No one factor is decisive and the outcome depends on a balanced assessment of the facts.

Microsoft USA

One of the most high-profile cases that caused a detailed investigation of the common-law employment test in the USA was that brought against the giant Microsoft Corporation in 1999.[28] The case involved a class action against Microsoft by some 15,000 temp agency workers who had worked for Microsoft over various periods since 1987. Microsoft had an 'employee' stock purchase plan that was not made available to the temp agency workers. The wording of the Microsoft stock purchase plan was clear in its intention to restrict stock option benefits to 'employees'. In a class action, the temp agency workers sought to prove that they were in fact employees of Microsoft and hence entitled to access the stock purchase plan. Given the high share price of Microsoft, the potential liability to Microsoft stood at $US20 million.

In May 1999, the US Court of Appeals held that the temps were 'presumptively' employees and entitled to retrospective benefits from the stock purchase plan. The Microsoft decision hinged, first, on the definition of employment and second, on whether or not the court determined that the nature of the contractual relationship between the temp workers and Microsoft fitted within the definitions of the stock purchase plan. On the common-law employment issue, the courts applied the tried-and-tested matrix of tests discussed above. The temps were found to be employees and Microsoft became liable for a large payout.

Barnhart USA

The Microsoft case can be compared with earlier US cases in which people were found not to be employees. In *Barnhart* v. *New York Life Insurance Company*,[29] the court found that the behaviour of Mr Barnhart and the insurance company was consistent with their written agreement that Barnhart was an independent contractor. In evidence, it was found that 'Barnhart was free to operate his business as he saw fit, was paid on a commission-only basis, claimed to be self-employed on his tax returns and was free to sell competitors' products'.[30]

What Microsoft, Barnhart and other key cases in the US demonstrate is the high level of consistency between countries and judges across jurisdictions in their application of the common-law meaning of employment as an issue of control. There may be differences in the mix of tests applied to individual cases and in the interpretation of behaviours evidenced in the tests, but the tests themselves are highly consistent. Further, it doesn't matter what the parties to a contract call their contract or what written contracts say: the key issue is the behaviour of the parties. The terminology used by parties is merely one of the behavioural factors under consideration.

USA taxing power and common-law employment
This becomes critical, for example, with US taxing issues. US Federal Income Tax law is tied to common-law employment for the 'at source' income tax deduction powers exercised by Internal Revenue Service (IRS) officers. The IRS may not deduct tax from a worker at the point of earning unless the worker is a common-law employee. IRS agents are instructed on the assessment processes they must undertake when seeking to enforce their powers. As in the UK, and in the past in Australia, tax officials are given powers to decide the common-law status of persons for the purposes of tax. In fact, this is an exercise that should be the exclusive preserve of the courts. Tax officials have a vested interest in the outcome of an investigation, and no matter how hard the IRS may proclaim the genuineness and integrity of its processes, they are neither qualified nor impartial. As occurs in other countries, US businesses are exposed to action by the IRS if they do not pay 'employment' taxes on individuals they consider to be independent contractors. If the IRS investigates and seeks to declare the contractors to be employees, the company is liable for substantial back taxes. The only defence is to seek to appeal the IRS decision in the courts, a process that often costs more than the back taxes owed. In these instances, the state-sanctioned, privileged and financially intimidatory position of the IRS effectively forces acquiescence by IRS-targeted companies, and potentially breaches the individual civil rights of people who wish to be independent contractors. More discussion of this occurs in the chapter on tax.

At least the IRS has compiled a set of common-law employment tests that its tax inspectors must use when seeking to apply the tax code. Although the IRS's role as determining agent is objectionable, the tests (fortunately) are accurate reflections of the common-law tests as evidenced in Microsoft,

Barnhart and other leading cases. The core issue continues to be whether the alleged employer has the right to control the alleged employee.

The IRS's constructed tests are set out below; positive responses to the questions indicate control and thus employment.[31]

- Is a worker required to comply with another person's instructions as to when, where and how work is to be done?
- Has the person who wants the services trained the worker?
- Is the worker personally required to give their services?
- Does the person who wants the services determine the method by which the work is accomplished?
- Does the person who wants the services hire, supervise and pay the worker?
- Is there a continuing relationship between the worker and requirer?
- Are the hours of work set by the person who requires the services?
- Is full-time work required such that the worker is restricted in his or her ability to work for other persons?
- Is the worker prevented from following his or her own pattern of work?
- Is the worker required to submit written or oral reports on his or her work?
- Is the worker paid by the hour, week or month?
- Does the business pay the worker's travelling expenses?
- Does the requirer of services provide the worker's tools and materials?
- Has the worker *not* made any financial investment in the place or process of work? Does the worker *not* have any share in the loss or profits of the worker's efforts?
- Is the worker prevented from working for other persons?
- Does the engager have the right to fire the worker?
- Can the worker terminate the relationship without suffering penalty?

This list is consistent with common-law tests applied in other English-based, common-law countries, and takes up 17 of the 22 possible tests examined earlier. As with all common-law tests, under the IRS, no one test is definitive, but the courts consider the balance of the total picture as applied to each case.

How global are these tests?
But how universal is the definition of employment? Are there big differences between countries, regions and legal systems?

Since 1996, the International Labour Organisation has being wrestling with a precise understanding of employment to identify the exact scope of labour regulation. The ILO has had three major conferences on the issue since 1996 and another conference is being held in 2006. In preparation for the

2006 conference, the ILO studied the laws which define employment in 60 countries with a diverse range of legal backgrounds and regional locations. In the report released in 2005, the ILO found that there is a common thread across the globe to understanding the definition of employment:

> What is surprising is the amount of convergence between the legal systems of different countries in the way they deal with this [distinguishing employment] and other aspects of the employment relationship, even between countries with different legal traditions or those in different parts of the world ... Irrespective of the definition used, the concept of a worker in an employment relationship has to be seen in contrast to that of a self-employed or non-dependent worker...[32]

The report described the term 'worker' as a generic term that can mean employee or self-employed.

The report looked at common-law countries and found similar terms and definitions being used. Countries it cited, for example, included Kenya, Nigeria, Lesotho, Indonesia, Ireland, New Zealand, Cambodia, China, Malaysia, Australia and Pakistan. These countries used terms such as 'to serve an employer', 'contract of service', 'contract of employment' and so on. These terms and understandings are consistent with the explanation provided in this chapter.

The report also looked at legal definitions used in a range of non-common law countries. These included Argentina, El Salvador, Chile, Colombia, Costa Rica, Nicaragua, Venezuela, France, Benin, Burkina Faso, Democratic Republic of Congo, Gabon, Niger, Rwanda, Portugal, Morocco, Bahrain, Qatar, Angola, Botswana, Slovenia, Mexico and Nicaragua. The defining terms from these countries included 'dependency', 'subordination', 'permanent dependency', 'delegated direction', 'conditions of subordination', 'direction', 'supervision', 'control', 'orders' and 'for the employer's account'. These terms used in non-common-law countries all point to an idea of employment being that as described in this chapter and which is the central thesis of this book.

Facing a hard fact

How then, should the idea of employment be understood and why this interest in discovering the true nature of the employment relationship?

Unfortunately, the word 'employment' is used in everyday language to denote every form of work-for-pay relationship. The word is used without reference to its precise and accurate meaning. As a result, it is often used incorrectly. The consequence is that this very broad usage creates misunderstanding of the vitally important issues about our own conduct when we work, the very nature and operations of business in society, and the functioning and regulation of economies. The misunderstanding causes serious distortions in each of these areas, distortions which will be examined throughout the remainder of this book.

We have to recognize and accept that 'employment' is a specific type of contract, which, like all contracts, is the legal expression of particular human behaviours and intentions. Under employment, two persons enter a contract whose very essence is that only one party—the employer—can control the terms of the contract. The employee has only limited power to control the contract terms and hence cannot exercise legal self-control. And this 'control' under contract is not some legal technicality removed from human actions.

Employment is an identifiable process in which we demonstrably choose either consciously or by default to give up our capacity to exercise full control over our own actions in return for money. It is fair to say that few people are consciously aware of this fact. Certainly, few people talk about it in these terms. Those few people who do talk about employment as a control process find themselves subject to severe criticism and rejection. So there is silence. And most people would find the idea of employment as control abhorrent and reject it. But the additional truth is that rather than clearly confront the fact of what employment is, we have as individuals and societies chosen instead to pretend that employment is not control but something else. However, that something else is never defined. The purpose of this book is not to ignore the truth of employment but rather to confront it and understand it.

In its crudest understanding, when we enter employment we sell our souls, maybe just a little bit, but we sell them nonetheless. Other people buy them. It is a process by which some parts of our psychological and physical being are delivered to other persons who exercise psychological and physical control over them. This is the human experience of employment and we need to confront it.

This first chapter has had one purpose: to look at the facts of what employment is by studying its clear legal contract form. The rest of this book looks at how we have, as societies, responded to employment, how we have chosen to regulate it and accommodate it and how this regulation has worked both for and against successful human interaction.

But to understand employment even more deeply, it will help if we understand the reverse of employment, namely, independent contracting. That is the task of the next chapter.

Endnotes

1. In Peter Krass (ed.), *The Book of Business Wisdom*, John Wiley & Sons Inc., USA 1997, 299.
2. Walter K Olson, *The Excuse Factory*, Martin Kessler Books, USA, 32.
3. International Labour Organisation Website: www.ilo.org
4. *Odco Pty Ltd and Building Workers' Industrial Union of Australia*. No VG 151 of 1988. Federal Court of Australia.
5. *Stevens v. Brodribb Sawmilling Company* (1986) 160 CLR 16.
6. *T Sammartino and Mayne Nickless Express t/a Wards Skyroad*. Australian Industrial Relations Commission. Dec 555/00 S Print s6212, at 57.
7. *Loc. cit.*
8. *Loc. cit.*
9. *Ibid.* at 93.
10. *Ibid.* at 96.
11. *Ibid.* at 95.
12. *Ibid.* at 102.
13. *Vabu Pty Limited* v. *Commissioner of Taxation*. New South Wales Court of Appeal. CA 40206/95.
14. *Ibid* at 14.
15. *Ibid* at 50.
16. *Hollis* v. *Vabu Pty Ltd* [2001] HCA 44 9 August 2001. High Court of Australia.
17. Queen, IR and PGA High Court Case No CO/2302/00, April 2001. [IR 35].
18. *Ibid.* at 3.
19. *Ibid.* at 19.
20. *Ibid.* at 50.
21. *Ibid.* at 30.
22. *Ibid.* at 48ii.
23. *Ibid.* at 49.
24. *Williams* v. *Australian Defence Force*. Australian Industrial Relations Commission. Print T2042 17/10/00.
25. *Ibid.* at 9.
26. *Employee Retirement Income Security Act* 1974. http://caselaw.1p.findlaw.com/scripts/title_search.pl?keyword=Employee+Retirement+Income+Security+Act+1974&title=uscodes.
27. *Ibid.* at (1a).
28. *Vizcaino* v. *Microsoft Corp.*, 173 F.3d 713 (9th Cir.1999) (Microsoft III). See: http://library.findlaw.com/1999/jun/i/127430.html
29. *Barnhart* v. *New York Life Ins Co*, 141 F.3d 1310,1312-13 (9th Cir 1998).
30. *Ibid.*
31. IRS website: http://www.irs.gov/business/small/article/0,,id=99921,00.html
32. International Labour Office, *The employment relationship, International Labour Conference, 95th Session, 2006. Report v(1) ILO, Geneva, printed 2005.*

2: Damning the Demon

As a contractor, I am my own boss and I make my own choices. As
an employee, I am always under someone's thumb … There is more
teamwork as a contractor

— Moera, 38-year-old woolclasser, Queensland, Australia, 2000

What is not employment? Independent Contracting!
To gain a deeper understanding of the legal reality of employment, it
is necessary to understand what is *not* employment. For although the
employment demon lurks deep within our societies, in truly free societies
the demon can be purged. People can and do reject employment and opt
instead for its opposite—working with commercial contracts and becoming
independent contractors.

Independent contracting is the contractual and relationship opposite of
controlled employment. Independent contracting often goes by other names,
such as free agent, freelancer, self-employed, and contractor. It is both a
method of and an attitude to working that is spreading fast and, at the start
of the 21st century, is recognized as having been adopted by up to one-third
of the private-sector workforce in many developed countries.

Independent contracting is the relationship obverse of employment. With
independent contracting, the contract deployed is the commercial contract.
The parties to the contract have equal rights under common law to control
its terms. In the eyes of the law, neither party has superior rights to the other,
even if one party is richer or apparently more powerful than the other.

Independent contracting utilizes the contract that protects the most basic
human rights of each and every person. The commercial contract delivers the
core legal structures designed to prevent or resolve the abuse of individuals
when they are involved in economic relationships. The commercial contract
provides fundamental protections to the weak, gullible or naive against the
powerful and manipulative. It is not perfect and cannot stop all abuse, but
it is one of the most important mechanisms available in civilized societies
to redress abuse. Its only similarity to employment is that it is not some

39

theoretical construct thrust upon people. The commercial contract is founded in the human relationships that actually exist in any given commercial transaction. It is the legal bedrock of economic activity.

Specifically, independent contracting involves the use of the commercial contract; a contract of equality existing between one person (whether an individual, company or trust) and another person. Independent contracting requires a contract in which parties agree that they exercise equal control over the terms of the contract and they therefore both control themselves. On the surface, the differences between the commercial contract and the employment contract may appear to be subtle, but they are, in fact, huge and their implications profound.

Both employment and independent contracting require (and are dependent on) very particular attitudes if they are to hold solid. Parties to an independent contract will have difficulty sustaining the integrity of the commercial contract if one party insists on wanting to exercise exclusive control. Likewise, if the employee in an employment contract objects to being 'controlled' and wants equality, the relationship and the employment contract itself will come under stress. Relationships are the key to contracts. Relationships do not cause a contract to come into existence but, when a contract exists, a relationship always exists. A contract is, above all, formed on the basis of mental attitudes that determine relationships and which underscore the integrity of a contract. The mental attitude of an employer or an employee is not appropriate to independent contracting; indeed, it would cause an independent contract to collapse.

Independent contractors are typically people who desire to be in a business relationship. Neither party is dominant and both accept and expect that the nature of the contract necessitates a business-type relationship focused on mutually beneficial outcomes. Professionalism is the key mental attitude required of an independent contractor, whether a high-powered surgeon or a cleaner. Subservience, lack of responsibility, avoidance of accountability and a lack of interest in the outcome are not the attitudes of the independent contractor. Instead, the attitudes of the independent contractor are self-assuredness, acceptance of responsibility, preparedness for accountability and a focus on outcomes.

The massive differences between the employment contract and commercial contract underscore significant differences in behaviour and outcomes in businesses and economies. To understand this extraordinary arrangement called the commercial contract, it is best to look again at specific legal decisions in which the finding of employment or independent contracting was the judicial task at hand.

The judicial decisions examined in Chapter One focused on the indicators of employment and independent contracting. All those cases involved dissecting the differences between the commercial and employment contracts. In the case about to be discussed, however, the workers subject to the testing were found to be independent contractors, not employees. The very evidence the workers gave in this case illuminates some key points about the attitudes and behaviour that are the hallmarks of independent contractors and the commercial contract. These independent contractors truly did control their own work, but that did not preclude their clients from exercising control as well. The control process was one undertaken by people exercising mutual control to achieve mutual benefit.

The Queensland fight for independence

The case involved an application under a highly unusual piece of legislation passed in the Australian State of Queensland which came into law on 1 July 1999. It is a piece of aggressive legislative activism that confronted and opposed the centuries of common-law development regarding commercial and employment contracts.

The legislative provision (called Section 275)[1] of the Queensland *Industrial Relations Act* sought to declare that common-law independent contractors could be turned into employees, even though their independent contractor status continued to exist and be accepted at common law. Section 275 was (and is) the equivalent of a parliament seeking to decree that an apple is an orange even though it accepts that the object is still an apple. One thing about common law is that, in lay terms, it is common sense. One odd thing about legislatures is that they are not legally constrained by common sense. Their only constraint is the alertness of the people to nonsense. So legislatures can (and do) declare things to be what they are not!

Section 275 falls into the nonsense category. So strange is the legislation that one court, when having to make a ruling on an application under section 275 that a company should be declared an employee, said

> We were initially concerned that the relief was so wide that a corporate subcontractor ... might be caught. There is some conceptual difficulty in treating a corporation as an employee. However in the context of a legislative provision which deems relationships to be that which they are not, there can be no objection to bringing such a relationship into existence.[2]

In effect, the Parliament of Queensland has discarded centuries of common-law principles and human rights protections, and sought to force people into relationships of inequality (employment) against their will. As with most oppression initiated by any state throughout history, the public justification usually claims the moral high ground. In taking such aggressive legislative action, the Queensland Government claimed that it was protecting the weak and the oppressed. But this mask of moral purity was only a diversion.

It was not surprising, then, that the first test case of this destructive anti-independent contractor legislation should contain substantial human drama and colour. It was a seminal test case within the context of Australian folklore, history and political ideology, and in its own way cut to the heart of the great political debate about labour and capital. The case was played out in the dusty, rural outback town of Charleville, Queensland, where sheep shearers confronted union officials in a battle of hearts and minds over the authority of the collective versus the rights of the individual. It was a battle between those who sought to organize and control workers through state-imposed collective systems and those who sought freedom of individual thought and action as independent contractors. Yet this grand battle of ideas was played out in a most civilized, refined and almost innocuous manner in the local Charleville court room.

The case involved an application by the Australian Workers Union (AWU), once the largest of Australia's trade unions, to force a group of independent contractor shearers led by Barry and Moera Hammonds to be declared employees under section 275 of the Queensland *Industrial Relations Act*. The background and history to the case, the town of Charleville, and the importance of shearing to the labour movement need to be understood if one is to appreciate the importance of the Hammonds case.

More than one hundred years ago, the Australian union movement and its political wing, the Australian Labor Party (ALP), were born from the beer-and-blood violence of the workers' war of the 1890s. When Australia rode on the sheep's back, the economic boom depended on fleece being shorn from millions of sheep in rural Australia. The dusty, hard life of the Australian shearer typified the working-class struggle against the landed gentry who were the woolgrowers. This rugged, matey and sexist environment gave birth to the Australian union movement in the form of the Australian Workers Union; and the resultant images have long been ingrained in the psyche of an Australian nation eager to establish its identity. The Australian union movement and the Australian Labor Party came into existence in the shade of a large but now gnarled old tree in a Queensland country town which, like Charleville, depended on the pastoral industry and sheep. Within the Australian labour movement, the symbolism of shearing in Charleville is strong. It's a symbolism of workers versus bosses that underpins unionism internationally and deeply pervades the cultural approaches to labour regulation worldwide.

The historical and ideological underpinnings of these two great and powerful Australian institutions — the union movement and the ALP — were threatened, so the union believed, by shearers who refused to be employees. The anti-contractor provisions of the Queensland *Industrial Relations Act* were created specifically by these two institutions, which controlled the Queensland Parliament at the time.

In the 1990s, almost a hundred years after the AWU and Australian Labor Party were formed, Charleville and the surrounding districts were infiltrated by immigrant New Zealanders. Many of these were darker-skinned Maori, who brought new efficiencies to shearing, first with the use of wide combs for shearing and, following that, with the revolutionary ideas and attitudes of independent contracting. Barry and Moera Hammonds were at the forefront in both reform endeavours. In both instances, they faced fierce and often violent opposition from the White-Australia-inclined, Anglo-Saxon shearers who controlled the powerful AWU. In both instances, the full force of statute law was thrown against the newcomers. The Government of the State of Queensland, being a political creature born from the AWU, utilized its full force against individuals who dared to flout the rules it chose to impose on workers.

Many laws were imposed on shearers. Chief among these was the ban on shearing work on a Sunday, in place for nearly 70 years. Never one to be told what to do, Barry Hammonds, supported by his wife, Moera, stood against the State, and in his first encounter with it, Barry dared to shear on a Sunday. He did this in 1992 and for his 'crime' he was tried and convicted and spent six days in the Charleville jail. As extraordinary as it seems, in an allegedly developed, democratic, civilized and free society, an individual could be jailed because he chose to work on a Sunday. The power of the union-controlled State had prevailed in that instance, but Barry had won a greater moral victory for the rights of individuals to work when they chose.

Barry's real crime, however, was to work in a shearing industry in crisis, because the price of wool had long since collapsed and the once-rich farmers of the district had become asset-rich but cash-destitute. No-one was making money and no-one could see a way out of the decades-long industry crisis.

For whatever reason, Barry and Moera were stubbornly determined to find better ways to work. They were at the forefront of the introduction of wide combs in the early 1990s and then introduced the first independent contractor systems into the Australian shearing industry. By the late 1990s, Barry and Moera had more than 300 individual contractor shearers working the rounds of the Queensland spreads, shearing sheep. By this stage 'employment' had dwindled to a fraction of the Queensland shearing industry. The AWU's influence amongst shearers had disappeared, principally because shearers found that the AWU's rough and arrogant approach hindered their ability to perform and make money.

Barry and Moera and their teams of shearers and shed hands were also at the forefront of improving work practices that were the key to the survival of the wool industry. It was not the big things that made a difference, but hundreds of small items. The 1920s' shearing 'award', still operating in the year 2000, stipulated the type of food that had to be served and the precise starting and finishing times of work. The required menu still reflected the 'meat and vegies' tastes and habits of the 1920s. What people ate was stipulated by law. Shearing work was ruled by laws that declared when start and finish bells were to be rung. Barry and Moera breached the union laws, modernized and improved the shearers' diets, and introduced flexible work hours that reflected the preferences of the shearers.

The Hammonds introduced better grading or classing techniques for the wool, since it is in wool classing that the revolution is most marked. In 2000, wool prices varied according to the quality of the wool. Most baled wool leaving the farm gate averaged 20 microns in thickness and fetched \$A3.50/kg for the woolgrower. By comparison, 19-micron baled wool could be worth \$A7.00/kg and 16-micron (relatively rare) \$100.00 plus /kg. Better 'people systems' in the shed made possible more exacting baling and treatment of wool and therefore better financial returns.

At that time, the future of wool-growing depended largely on the higher prices that better-quality wool could command. This was and is the free contractors' focus. Moera Hammonds is an ace wool classer. A wool classer grades the wool according to its thickness. She came fourth at the prestigious International Golden Shears wool handling championships in New Zealand in 2000, the highest placing ever achieved by an Australian entrant. Her professionalism with wool classing is reflected in the training she gives new contractors, the standards she and her teams expect of themselves, and the business mentality of the contractors towards doing a quality job. The ability to class fine wool as the sheep is shorn is not only critical to the wool price that the farmers receive but, just as important, to their ability to identify high-quality breeding sheep and thus to improve the quality of their flocks.

Part of Barry's strength was (and is) his easygoing, laconic personality. He tells the story of the union hiring a mob of town thugs to beat him up at the back of the Charleville Hotel. With his back to the wall, he faced the mob, sizing up who he would take out before he was overpowered. The mob sized Barry up and decided a drink with Barry would be more productive than a beating. Unbeknown to the union, the union paid for the drinks out of the money given to the thugs!

But the waning of the AWU's influence was not due to Barry and Moera, who, in reality, were simply examples of a much larger shift in the culture of the Australian workforce. In the days of the newly emerging 'e-economy', where the smart information technology experts operated as 'free agents', it transpired that the cutting edge of the change in worker attitudes was not only in major cities but in country Queensland towns and in mature, 'old' industries. The new, young breed of wool handlers, shearers and the like are educated, business-savvy, well-travelled and worldly wise. Business sophistication is not defined by where one works but by the attitudes of individuals. When it comes to these attitudes, the new shearer is the equal of the futures trader working at a desk in a high-rise glass tower. The AWU had become culturally time-warped, incapable of accommodating the new shearer. Worse still, from its point of view, it did not know it!

In the new shearing industry, most workers are staunchly independent contractors—or want to be! The shearing award is ignored because of its millstone-like effect on shearers' incomes. Sure, cold beer is still drunk in large quantities to cope with the extreme heat—frequently a harsh, bone-dry 40 degrees plus—but the workers themselves do not tolerate drunken colleagues who destroy the productivity of the whole team. And in Barry and Moera's shearing teams, for example, workers are in their early 20s and many are women. This was a big turnaround for an industry which, until recently, was dominated by ageing men and a looming workforce shortage. Although men may continue to do most of the shearing, the days of rough handling and abusing the sheep being shorn are diminishing. A shearer harming a sheep is likely to receive a reprimand from any of the female wool classers, who are sensitive to the sheeps' well-being.

According to farmers, the outcome is a better wool clip and higher wool prices. And, for this, the farmers pay more. The contractors' remuneration consistently outstrips that of the antiquated award, which tends to 'dumb down' both attitudes and pay.

The real point of interest, however, lies in the attitudes of both the shearing teams and the people for whom they work. Under the old system of employment, the farmers were seen as the bosses and the shearers as the workers. Relationships were of the 'them and us' kind which are typical of employment. But independent contracting is the legal identification of different mental approaches to work and to the relationships between the parties. In the Hammonds' Section 275 court case, these attitudes were demonstrated in the statements made by all the people who gave evidence.

It was in these new attitudes to work that the court found clear evidence of the existence of commercial contracts and thus independent contracting.

Comments from the wool growers, traditionally thought of as the bosses, provide a deep insight into the new attitudes. The statements are not statements of political ideology but rather of a practical approach to business needs. The statements are very much demonstrations of the nature of independent contracting and the commercial contract.[3]

Michael is in his mid-30s and owns and runs a family farm of some 240,000 acres with about 30,000 sheep. He also works as a shearer during the shearing season. He said:

> The esteem in which shearers around town had been held was terrible poor prior to them [Barry and Moera] coming along … They have taught people going into shearing that it is a career and a skill and given them self-esteem …Younger people coming into the industry … are now approaching it more as a career.

> … the flexibility to shear on weekends is very important … It is essential to be able to ensure that the sheep aren't kept in the holding pens over weekends.

> … working over weekends goes both ways. If the shearing is tough, caused, for example, by having a high proportion of big wethers in the flock and you try to shear through into the weekend, the productivity of the team drops.

> The TSA [Barry's and Moera's] teams tend to have a higher ratio of wool handlers to shearers. Since there is more time to spend on the fleece, the 'fleece to pieces ratio' can be greatly increased and this can make a big difference to the return for the wool clip.

David is 38 and the owner/manager of a local produce and hardware store in town. In addition, he owns and manages a 14,000-acre property with about 2,500 sheep.

> It used to be union controlled starting at 7am with a bell and when the bell rung to finish, the gear was dropped.

> I pay TSA a bit more than I do the employees, but it is worth it for the quality of work they do and their reliability.

> … when I had sheep with fly strike … I could have lost 100–200 sheep if they were not all finished off quickly … The TSA team will always do them more quickly to help save as many lives as possible.

Brad is the owner of a 14,000-acre family farm with 4,000 sheep.

> It is now much more a matter of mutual agreement between the shearers and the farmer about wet sheep. The farmer doesn't want to shear wet

sheep either because he has spent 12 months growing the wool and doesn't want to ruin it by shearing wet sheep. On the other hand, he doesn't want the sheep starving in the holding pen while the shearers keep voting them wet, which was the situation years ago.

Howard owns a 34,600-acre family farm with 17,000 sheep.

... the whole attitude of shearers we have seen over recent years with TSA which we believe has now permeated through the industry. The shearers are much younger, much more professional and out there to make a quid.

I believe a lot more goes into the training of wool classers and this shows through in the quality of the wool clip presented at the end of the shearing.

The TSA workers [contractors] are more attuned to what the market demands by way of wool presentation and this reflects in the price obtained for the wool.

The changes spoken of here by farmers were not possible under the old employee-dominated 'workers award' regulation regime. The law dictated behaviour that simply entrenched class warfare and stopped practices developing in the farm shed which would have enabled people to move forward with their working lives. The level of control exercised by law through the award was extreme in its detail and pervaded almost every work activity. The new breed of contractor-shearer developed a business attitude akin to that of the wool grower. The new attitude reflects an understanding that the shearing teams are in the same business as the wool grower, namely, to make money out of processing wool. Every person has a different role and all have individual expertise and needs that have to be accommodated and bought together for mutual benefit. The central recognition is that all that matters is the price for wool that the farmers are able to receive now and in the future. This dictates how much the shearers can receive.

This businesslike approach to work is reflected in the words of the independent contractor shearers in the wide variety of attitudes they display to their work. These are people who are effectively running their own businesses. They make decisions for themselves within the practical framework of the need to co-operate with others to achieve an end result. They meet their personal needs by voluntarily working to achieve identifiable, specific outcomes in harmony with other people of like-minded focus.

Amber is a 24-year-old wool classer with a degree in agribusiness. She wholesales woollen products as an additional business unrelated to shed work.

> I like being a contractor ... Barry does not mind if I take time off in the middle of a shed to go to lectures or to line up to enrol.

> If we are forced to work because of the wet weather, it's not anyone's fault. Also, getting behind in the shearing would affect the farmer.

Robert is a 32-year-old presser. He collects the graded wool, places it in large wool presses and, when full, activates the press to form the large wool bales that are delivered to market.

> ... when I first started working with TSA, I thought supplying my own equipment was a rip-off, but now I realize that I get the quality I want out of having my own gear. Nine out of ten of every grinding paper supplied by the farmer has been wet, damaged, run out or just failed to be provided.

> I like looking after my own equipment and I know where it is and what condition it is in.

> I have never been forced to work on a weekend and I have said no before. This was about two years ago because my girlfriend wanted us to stay in town because her father was very sick.

> Penalty rates are stupid ... I don't think any penalty rates would work. All the shops are open on Saturdays and Sundays anyway so why do the unions try to make us feel guilty when we do occasional work on a weekend?

> I have heard a little bit about this AWU application. I don't want to be deemed an employee and bound by the award. It should be my choice. Other employees work weekends, not because of TSA but because it is sensible.

Jacqueline is a 25-year-old cook, and some say has the most important job on the team.

> I get paid at a higher rate than working as an employee ... As a contractor, I am freer and I am governed by myself.

Justin is 23 years old, has a degree in Agribusiness and is a shearer.

> It seems as though the AWU never does anything in the shearers' real interests. The AWU application would affect me because then I would not be able to work weekends or more than 8 hours per day.... We would not be able to start shearing earlier in the day which we often do to either finish earlier on a Friday or to avoid working in the very hot afternoons.

Gavin is a 47-year-old wool handler and presser.

> I like working for TSA because I am my own boss and I make money by putting the bales out. It is up to me how much I earn.

Oscar is 21 and a penny-upper and shearer. A penny-upper organizes the sheep in the holding pens before and after they are shorn.

> Last week for example ... There were more rams in the group than they expected, so we worked on the Saturday and Sunday. Shearing rams usually breaks more combs and they are harder to hold.

> On my weekends, I usually catch up on sleep and work at one of the local pubs.

> If I have to work on the weekend, I don't mind missing this work because I get paid better for my work at the shearing shed [than at the pub].

Moera is 38 and a wool-classer.

> I started in the shearing industry when I was 15 years old ... I actually started bull handling when I was 12 years old.

> As a contractor ... I am my own boss and I can make my own choices. As an employee, I am always under someone's thumb.

> I like the idea of my money going into my own bank account and me not having to sit around the contractor's house for half a day on Saturday and not being able to have my money.

> There is more team work as a contractor.

Rhonda is a 32-year-old wool handler and classer.

> The problem with this is that it [the award] slows the whole team down. I have seen this at most places that are subject to the award.

> I remember last December [1999], a lot of sheep had fly-strike. If the sheep are not shorn relatively quickly, they could die from this.

Angela is a 25-year-old roustabout. Her tasks involve picking up the fleece once it is shorn, placing it on the classing table and sweeping up around the shearer.

> I started working through TSA ... The pay is better with them and that is important ... I take time off whenever I want. I have taken off today [Monday] so that I can go to the dentist. As an employee, they would have punished me for taking a day off...

Geoffrey is a 35-year-old shearer.

> I like being a contractor as it gives me peace of mind.

> I know that some farmers have specifically requested that I shear for them. I also get higher income as a contractor. I get $12–$13 extra per 100 sheep.

I prefer using my own equipment.

I take more holidays off as a contractor than when I was working as an employee and take off a couple of months each year. I usually go home to my farm ... and sleep. If I was working as an employee, my employer would want me to be more permanent.

I would like to see the workers have the choice of when to work and not be told by the unions what I can and can not do.

William is 24 years old and a shearer.

I've worked on shearing teams which are staunch in their observance of the award. They have the 3 minute bell which is a warning to all the shearers that the end of the run will happen in 3 minutes and they have to finish up their last sheep and can't start another one in that time. They also do not do any weekend work or extra hours during the week or any hours outside the exact allotted hours in the Award.

Those teams are okay and they get by doing their thing. However, that is too restricted for me. I would rather have the choice whether I wanted to work weekends. I believe it is up to the individual. I don't have any problems with the teams who don't want to work weekends and work strictly according to the award but it's just not for me. I believe that if I want to work weekends then that should be okay.

These are the attitudes that define independent contracting. Contractors look at the practical issues affecting their work and make decisions for themselves based on the needs to achieve results. This is not the mentality of wage-slave employment; contractors resist attempts to control them. In the Section 275 case, it was the union and the State of Queensland that were trying to force the workers into controlled employment relationships.

These attitudes, expressed both by the shearing workers and the people whose sheep they sheared, are the necessary, uncomplicated attitudes that underpin the legal status of independent contractors. Taken together, the attitudes show that no-one is controlling anyone. What controls the way of work is all parties' recognition and understanding of the practical things that have to be done to complete the job and achieve a commercial result. It was these attitudes that were the primary evidence in the Section 275 case.

Yet what does seem odd is that these independent contractors, working through the Hammonds, had their life's values challenged by the doyens of the old economy. The Australian Workers Union made application under Section 275 of the Queensland *Industrial Relations Act* to force the free contractors to be bonded employees, and attempted to require them to work under the shearing award on lower remuneration and under inferior conditions. And it was the State of Queensland that created the legislation that sought to deny these workers their right to achieve independence.

Ultimately, however, some commonsense did prevail. After an 18-month and highly expensive legal case which cost the independent contractors some hundreds of thousands of dollars, the Commission ruled against the AWU. The application to force these people into wage-slave employment was rejected. The courts perceived the established reality of independent contracting and did not rule against the contractors.

The case attracted widespread interest in Australia because of the fundamental challenges it posed to the functioning of commercial contracts and hence commercial activity. Many other industry associations sought to make representation to the Commission hearing to put on record the broad principles that were at stake. The Housing Industry Association (HIA) demonstrated how the case challenged fundamental principles that underpinned the very structure of the Australian economy. It said:

> The regulation of employment contracts contrasts sharply with society's regulation of commercial relationships, where legal equality is the basis of contracts...
>
> The Commission should be slow to interfere in normal commercial contracts—to apply industrial relations outcomes to commercial contracts is to intrude into an essentially foreign area, which will create great uncertainty for businesses and over time will damage the legal underpinning of commercial activity.
>
> HIA submits that it would be contrary to the spirit of the IRC Act to dragoon unwilling contractors into employment.
>
> The Commission should accept and uphold both contracting and employment as, in principle, two equally valid systems for organizing work.

These are the principles at stake in the way societies look at, consider and seek to control how people will work. They are principles that have their roots in the rich soil of every person's everyday working experiences.

Endnotes

1. *The Australian Workers Union of Employees AND Hammonds Pty Ltd and others.* Queensland Industrial Relations Commission No B885 of 1999.
2. *ALHMWU and Bark Australia Pty Ltd* No B1064 of 2000. Queensland IRC.
3. Hammonds case Affidavits and Witness Statements.

Regulating the Demon
Overview

So far, this book has focused on exposing the nature of a particular type of human experience. Employment is the relinquishing of individuality and identity at work. The task of the common law is to discover whether individuality and identity have been relinquished; if they have, then the work relationship is governed by a particular form of legal contract known as the employment contract or contract of service.

The contract of service reflects, identifies and governs the way the employer and the employee interact. Employment is mostly governed by the common-law processes of the courts. During the twentieth century, however, and particularly since the Second World War, common-law oversight has become overlaid by a complex mass of statute law that has its roots in the thoughts of Karl Marx and current generational devotees. Marx objected to the unequal power inherent in the relationship between employer and employee, calling it wage slavery. Regulation has as its heart one basic assumption: that the human inequality inherent in the employment contract is bad. The state assumes that it has a duty to regulate the employment relationship for the purpose of protecting the legally powerless employee.

The intention is noble, but the process of regulation is flawed. The power of the regulators has expanded to the point where the regulators themselves have become oppressors of both employees and employers. The forms of regulation developed have seriously distorted human behaviour. Inequality of power has not been diminished; on the contrary, it has been expanded and shifted.

How this has occurred, how it is occurring and how social regulation creates inequality can be understood only by looking at the detail. And there's lots of detail to look at. The first is tax!

3: Tax

The Tax Commissioner may (a) treat a particular event that actually happened as not having happened and (b) treat a particular event that did not actually happen as having happened.

— The Australian *Goods and Services Tax Act* (165–55), **2000**

In perhaps no area does the state choose to give itself greater power than in tax. The state is prepared to hand legal powers to taxing authorities that defy the laws of nature and common sense. In Australia, legislators have been prepared to give the chief tax officials authority to change reality. On a whim, tax officials can declare that a person travelling north is actually travelling south, that a war that occurred did not actually occur or, more likely, that an expense that an income earner incurred did not actually exist. Tax officials are granted powers that are granted to no other. Thus it has always been and thus, regretfully, it always will be.

And with this all-powerful authority, the attitude of tax officials to employment since the Second World War has been the most important regulatory influence on working relationships. It has been all-important for one simple reason: that the power of tax agencies to collect income tax at source, at the point of payment, has been legislatively tied to common-law employment. Where people have worked but not been employed, tax authorities have not had the authority to require the payer to withhold tax from the receiver of the payment and to send the withheld tax to the tax authority. This legislative model for the collection of income tax at source has been used in the USA, UK, Canada and Australia, to name just some countries. It is the 'at source' income-taxing model used by most developed and developing nations.

In effect, the common dependence of income-tax collection systems and labour regulation on determinations of master-and-servant employment has, over time, caused tax-collecting authorities to become allied with labour regulators. The two authorities with outwardly different agendas have found themselves in the same colluding bed. Tax-collection powers have been of key importance to the powers of labour regulators.

This outcome has corrupted the integrity of tax collection systems.

To understand how this occurred and how it exists, the historical background is important.

Historical background

With some regret, one of the giants of the post-Second World War economics profession, Milton Friedman,[1] describes his role as one of the architects of the income-tax system in the USA—a system replicated in most Western countries and now being transferred to developing nations. Friedman says that US federal income tax was meant as a temporary measure to overcome the problem of funding the Second World War. In the 1940s, the US Treasury was concerned that massive debt funding of the First World War had been a major contributor to the Great Depression, and feared that if the Second World War were also funded by government debt, then the seeds of a second great depression would have been sown. The solution was the income tax system. This now familiar tax system imposes tax on each individual income earner. A key part of the system is that it requires 'withholding'—a person making a payment to a worker must take out tax and send it to the tax office. This gives government a steady, reliable and continuous stream of money. Government can spend without resorting to debt, so long as it keeps its spending in line with tax receipts.

Milton Friedman bemoans how temporary measures become permanent and grow when government has its hands in the public's purse. Income tax has become huge and is a dominant source of government revenue. Here, then, is one of the sources of the 'employment' problem, because 'at source withholding' was and is legislatively dependent on the existence of common-law employment. No contract of service means no income-tax withholding!

In the 1920s, '30s and '40s, the legal master-and-servant employment model was perhaps at its height as the method for organizing business in capitalist societies. It was understandable that, in designing income tax systems, tax legislation should tie the power of tax officials to collect income tax at source to common-law employment. In the mid-twentieth century, common-law employment-dependent tax powers had caught nearly the entire working population in their net. However, things began to change.

Around the late 1970s, significant shifts in legal work engagement methods began to emerge and have since accelerated. People started to desert the master-and-servant, wage-slave model for reasons unrelated to tax. But as a consequence, tax officials feared that their legislative reach was diminishing.

The scale of the social movement away from wage slavery has only recently been authoritatively identified. In Australia, for example, the first survey on this issue was undertaken by the Australian Bureau of Statistics.[2] It found that, as of August 1998, 20 per cent of the workforce identified themselves as self-employed and only 59 per cent of the workforce identified themselves as working in full-time employment. Significantly, 28 per cent of the private-sector workforce were identified as working without being 'employed'. The best available surveys in 1989 put the Australian self-employed figure at somewhere around 3 per cent,[3] indicating the large and rapid scale of the growth of the independent contractor sector in little more than a decade.

In many other English-based legal systems, such as the USA and Britain, the trend away from employment has been even more marked. There are some indications that, in the USA, perhaps more than 40 per cent of the working population have deserted employment and work under independent contractor-type arrangements.

These trends have alarmed tax authorities in USA, the UK and Australia, to name just some. Many tax commentators and designers have not understood or accepted the social movement away from command employment, but have instead interpreted the movement as a tax-avoidance scam. From their perspective, it is perhaps tax avoidance; but, if it is not avoidance, the decline of employment certainly presents tax officials with an administrative problem, since their job is to ensure revenue for government. When that revenue is diminished, they come under pressure from their political masters.

The response of most tax authorities to the diminution of their collection powers has been a combination of accommodation and aggression. The aggression has come in the form of co-ordinated attacks against independent contractors by tax authorities, certainly in the UK, Australia and the USA. Ultimately, however, the movement away from employment cannot and should not be stopped. It is occurring for reasons unrelated to tax and is being pushed by new attitudes to the nature of work relationships: part of a redefining of the nature of control in social and economic structures. Aggression by tax authorities will only bring them into conflict with vast sectors of society and damage the effective working of economies. Tax authorities will not win by trying aggressively to enforce a tax collection regime that was designed in the mid-twentieth century. Yet tax officials can successfully accommodate the emerging social movement away from employment, and they have largely done so in Australia in the 2000s. It is a lesson that developing economies should heed.

First, however, it is necessary to understand the problem from the tax system and tax officials' perspective. Tax officials are charged with a legislative obligation to collect tax. From an administrative angle, the most effective tax systems are those in which voluntary compliance is maximized and in which tax is collected at the time a payment is made (at source). Tax auditing and compliance are expensive, not cost-effective, and something which tax designers seek to minimize. Voluntary compliance is a key objective.

In most nations, pay-as-you-earn (PAYE) arrangements have evolved as the primary 'at source' collection system. It is the system in part designed by Milton Friedman. It is around PAYE that the tax authorities' administrative systems are constructed. But, commonly, PAYE legislation gives the tax authorities power to collect an individual's income tax at source only if the individual is in a common-law master-and-servant employment relationship. The normal legislative wording requires 'employers' to deduct instalments of tax from payments of salaries or wages to 'employees' and to send the proceeds to the tax authority.

Industrial and post-industrial societies have largely been constructed around big businesses employing large numbers of people. The legislative process of requiring businesses (employers) to take tax from their employees and send it to the tax authorities has made for comparatively simple tax-collection systems. Income earners have been legally liable for income tax, but employers have been legally liable for collecting it. It has been much easier for tax authorities to administer the collection of income tax from tens or hundreds of thousands of employers than from many millions of individual income earners. The master-and-servant arrangement has well suited the administrative taxing systems of the nation-state, particularly before the onset of the IT revolution.

But when large percentages of people leave employment, this challenges the established taxing authority of the state. The shift from employment to contracting has seen large numbers of businesses continuing to employ many persons but 'engaging' many others through independent contracting. Consequently, and in relation to contractors, businesses no longer have a legislative obligation to withhold tax. In fact, to withhold any amounts from the contractor without the contractor's consent would breach businesses' common-law commercial contract obligations.

The response of the tax authorities to this community shift has largely been one of aggression, as reflected in the choice of language tax authorities use when referring to contractors. Independent contracting has been termed 'disguised employment', contractors are said to 'exploit the fiscal advantages offered by a corporate structure' and to engage in 'means to avoid paying a fair share of tax',[4] and tax authorities are said to need to establish 'rules to tackle tax avoidance' and to have a moral obligation to 'ensure that they [contractors] pay a fair share of [tax] compared with those directly employed.' These quotations come directly from press releases issued by the Internal Revenue Service in the UK.[5]

In short, the tax authorities have sought to demonize independent contractors in the court of public opinion in an effort to justify the tax authorities' aggressive push beyond their legal limits. It amounts to officers of the state using the power of the state to engage in crass bullying. It allows officers of the state to assume they have a moral responsibility to collect income for the state beyond the legal powers delivered to them.

In an important test case in the UK referred to in Chapter One,[6] the presiding judge referred to this sort of language from the tax authorities as 'wholly regrettable and unnecessary'. The judge offered the view that the language indicated a bias and predetermination of outcome on the part of the UK IR. The judge said, 'It seems to me to have been assumed without any or any adequate research, that all service companies [contractors] fell within that category [employment], simply by reference to the use in the initial publicity of words ...'

This evidence of the taxing authorities' determination to impose employment is a clear demonstration of the overstepping of the authority of the state and how the state, through the detail of regulatory administration, can become an oppressor of its citizens. Further, it demonstrates that regulators should not be the determiners of employment, since they have a vested interest in a particular outcome of any investigation.

Australia

As in the UK, the Australian tax authority (the Australian Taxation Office, ATO) has a long history of aggression against independent contractors. But the situation has rapidly improved thanks to a redesign of tax administration and collection.

In an effort to overcome independent contractor leakage from PAYE during the 1980s and 1990s, the ATO argued that the legislative powers under section 221A(1) of the Tax Act extended the Commissioner's powers beyond employment to include contractors.

The ATO sought to enforce this extension of its legislative powers. Australian courts, however, consistently disagreed with the Tax Commissioner. During the late 1980s and 1990s, the High Court of Australia (the court of final appeal) on 10 separate occasions rejected the Tax Commissioner's view that PAYE legislative powers extended beyond common-law employees. The Australian courts applied a strict common-law definition to the word 'employment' and consistently held that independent contracting was not employment. Yet even when a large number of legal decisions went against the ATO, it continued to take aggressive legal action against individual independent contractors. As of 2005, this remains the situation confronting independent contractors in the UK.

Naturally, the tax authorities can fund their side of these highly expensive legal cases from the public purse, while individual defendants have to pay for their defence from their own pockets. In some cases, determined to be test cases, the tax authorities will offer to pay the defendants' legal expenses, but not their accounting and personal expenses. In such cases, the individual taxpayer always suffers significant financial loss. Tax authorities, with the wealth of the state at their disposal, practise commercial intimidation against the citizenry. In this area, tax officials in many nations have a history of achieving their preferred outcomes simply because the individuals they target cannot afford the legal or personal expense of a defence.

But it is a situation that defiles the rule of law and reduces community respect for the instruments of the state. Ultimately, a community can come to see the state as akin to a robber baron who ignores justice and the law. This encourages a widespread belief that it is legitimate for the people to steal from the state because the state steals from them. If taxing authorities do not comply with the law, or seek to manipulate the clear meaning of the law, they inevitably encourage blatant tax avoidance.

It is of course a fine balancing act, because tax authorities have plenty of experience of individuals using legal loopholes and aggressive legal action to thwart legitimate taxing authority.

As well as aggression, another approach tried by the ATO in 1994 was to change income tax legislation so as to bring independent contractors into the income tax withholding net. The amendments, known as Taxation Law Amendment Bill No. 5, were, however, dropped in 1998 after significant turmoil and a change of government.

Amendment Bill No 5, like other attempts to apply income-tax deduction at source to all contractors, declared contractors to be master–servant employees. In effect, it sought to outlaw independent contracting. As one judge said, it amounted to legislatively calling a chicken a duck even though a chicken is still a chicken. It was an approach with parallels to the Queensland Section 275 legislation discussed in Chapter Two. Had these tax amendments succeeded, they would have turned the Australian Tax Office into an instrument of the labour regulators and would have put the ATO on a collision course with a broad social movement interested in freedom, equity and justice. Bad for tax collection and bad for society!

The problem with the ATO's approach is that it defies the common-sense, common-law reality that contracting is still contracting. Legislation does not change reality—even if governments give tax officials the power to pretend to do so.

Another approach taken by the Australian Tax Office was to create an administrative tax collection system at source for contractors. This was called the Prescribed Payments System (PPS). It was designed largely to create an 'at source' tax collection system for the Australian housing building industry, which is almost exclusively structured around independent contracting and is politically powerful enough to resists attempts by the ATO to impose employment on it. PPS existed between about 1983 to 1997 but was always seen by the Tax Commissioner as administratively messy and at best providing only a temporary plug for an expanding hole.

In Australia, the union movement conducted fierce scare campaigns against PPS, denouncing it as illegitimate and a source of tax evasion. But its real concern was that it provided a measure of tax legitimacy for independent contractors. A legitimate and safe legislative tool for collecting income tax from contractors does not suit the industrial objectives of the Australian union movement, which relies on the state enforcing command-style employment so as to sustain the 'class war' mentality upon which unions' claims to moral authority rest. Any taxing system that caters for contractors threatens union power.

The United Kingdom

The Internal Revenue Service (IR) of the United Kingdom has similar concerns with independent contractors. As noted earlier, the UK IR has acted aggressively against independent contractors. It has been involved in the at-source deduction issue, but has equally been concerned that independent contractors access lower levels of tax than employees.

The specifics of the issue are as follows. As in most income-taxing countries, tax is imposed on any entity that earns income. Employee income is usually taxed on sliding scales so that people who earn less pay a lower proportion of their income as tax than do high-income earners. This is considered an important tool for reducing income inequality in the community. Employees are allowed comparatively few income tax deductions because it is considered that employers pay for the non-labour costs of production, which are not costs employees must bear in the course of earning income.

Businesses, usually thought of as employers, are also taxed on their incomes, but the method of calculation is more complex than with employees. A business has large expenses and is taxed on profit (net income), not revenue. To calculate profit, business expenses must be deducted from sales revenue.

Most arguments over tax evasion relate to the business tax area rather than to employee tax, since tax authorities disallow deductions on costs they do not consider to be true business expenses. In addition, tax authorities spend considerable resources chasing accounting-type scams whereby businesses may attempt to transfer expenses from one business unit to another, hide income, claim personal living expenses as business expenses, and so on. Huge sums can be involved and the accounting and legal scams can be highly complex.

The issue of the taxation of the income of independent contractors, however, is not at its core one of illegitimate tax deductions or the hiding of income. The primary issue is that of a cross-over from employee to contractor. If a person is an employee, the administration of their tax is comparatively simple. If a person is an independent contractor, their tax is and should be treated within the more complex business-tax framework.

The issue is one of both practicality and law. An independent contractor, by virtue of the way she works, will tend to incur expenses that an employee does not. An independent contractor is the same as a business. Before an independent contractor's tax can be assessed, her business-related expenses must be deducted from the revenue to find the true (net) income. In law, an independent contractor works under the commercial contract for services, like any other business, and should be entitled to business-tax equity.

The conceptual problem that tax authorities in most countries cannot seem to cope with, as reflected in the UK IR approach, is that a single person can be a business. Tax designers seem to have collectively concluded that the idea is preposterous. They can conceive of a plumber, for example, being self-employed and running his own business and being entitled to business tax deductions. But they have particular difficulty conceiving of a person whose main business activity is the application of brain-power running his own business and being self-employed. They have even more difficulty thinking of independent contractors working in areas where employment has been traditional and dominant, for example, in factories. Tax authorities have additional and huge conceptual difficulties where individuals set up company structures and where such individuals work principally for a single client. They seem to be convinced that independent contracting must be a tax scam of some sort and go to extraordinary lengths to deny contractors their commercial status. Their suspicious attitudes are evident in their afore-mentioned aggressive language.

In the UK, this contractor-denying strategy has manifested itself in 'composite legislation', known as IR35 after a UK Internal Revenue press release. IR35 is an administrative tax measure that gives UK tax officials the power to investigate individual independent contractors and to make a determination as to whether they are employees or independent contractors. IR35 has caused uproar in the UK independent contractor community because of the *ad hoc* and selective denial of business-tax status to independent contractors. As a consequence, an independent contractor association was formed in the UK in 1997 (the Professional Contractors Association)[7] specifically to fight the measure, and within four years it had over 14,000 members. IR35 has strong similarities to anti-independent contractor legislation in other countries.

What is extraordinary about IR35 and other similar measures is the denial of natural justice in the tax attack. The determination of employee or contractor status has always been the preserve of common-law court processes. Independent judges hear evidence and make rulings based on the individual facts of each case and in the light of case law principles established over hundreds of years. Contractor status is not some glib, light foolishness. It is a reflection of conscious contractual relationships into which people choose to enter and around which they organize their work. Tax authorities have a financial vested interest in the outcome of a contractor or employee determination, and IR35 gives the applicant (the IR) the roles of prosecutor, judge and jury. More than that, they are the potential beneficiary of any decision they make.

But what is the core concern of the taxing authorities? And do independent contractors avoid tax? In the major test case of the legalities of IR35 introduced earlier, the ruling judge explained the general circumstances, which are common to contractor-tax issues in all countries where the 'concern' exists.

People who wish to cease being employees commonly set themselves up under a company structure (service companies) or even operate as a partnership. The company typically has one or perhaps two employees, who are often the directors of the company—it is a structure commonly used by self-employed independent contractors. The company invoices its client or clients, and is paid. The company takes on the risk of bad debt. The company has expenses that are a necessary part of operating the business. The company pays the owner or owners as employees and sends PAYE tax and, in the case of the UK, National Insurance Contributions to the IR. If, after deducting all their expenses, the company makes a profit, the profit is taxed at company tax rates.

If people using this structure run a shop, the tax authorities accept the business-tax status because a shop is a business structure that tax officials see in their daily lives. If the business employs a few other people or even tens of thousands of people, the tax authorities accept the business status. But if the company is the smallest of small-business structures, namely a one- or two-person self-employed entity, supplying services such as, for example, IT, tax authorities become suspicious. Why?

Tax authorities argue that, by purporting to be independent contractors, people who should be taxed as employees are able to reduce their tax liabilities through the service company. For example, in the UK, the IR promotes the view that people take advantage of the sliding scales of PAYE tax—that is, lower rates of tax for small companies—and do not have to pay National Insurance Contributions on dividends (which the IR sees as disguised employee income). By juggling the declaration of employee and dividend income, individuals can minimize their tax.

Does this occur? Probably yes. But is it illegal or illegitimate or immoral? No!

People have a right to decide how they wish to work and how they wish to manage their lives. In relation to tax, 'the problem' that the tax authorities think they are facing is not that people are rorting the tax system but rather that the world is changing. And that changing world does not fit the neat employment view of society around which tax authorities have structured their administrative processes and their personal working lives. The problem is not that of contractors rorting tax but rather of tax authorities failing to respond to new social trends or failing to redesign their tax systems to reflect emerging community practices.

The fact is that, in the UK, lower tax rates are available for small business. This is not of independent contractors' making but a decision of government. An independent contractor is the smallest of small businesses and has a right to access tax regimes created by government. If there is something wrong with the tax regime, the tax officials' appropriate response is to seek to redesign the regime, not to impose a selective view of the system's application. Tax authorities do not have the moral right or a right under common law to decide who is or is not allowed to be self-employed. The decision is always that of the common-law courts and the most that tax authorities have ever achieved is an administrative power under statute. Tax officials have a duty to collect tax. This does not confer on them the authority or right to decide the social and legal structures that people use in a society.

The great concern is that the law sets up the UK tax authority as a sole arbitrator of what is or is not a legitimate business structure. Yet the UK IR has a vested financial interest in the outcome of determinations. They are not qualified to undertake the consideration or make the decision. Only the courts can do that.

This was demonstrated in the IR35 test case[8] in which the judge cited the failure of the IR's tax inspector to apply contractor determinations accurately and consistently. The judge observed that '…two different inspectors wrote, quite independently to the accountants a month apart, without reference one to the other, giving entirely inconsistent answers: the one who gave the answer that IR35 would apply relied upon an entirely erroneous construction of the contract in question.'

The simple fact is that there is a clear legal distinction between the status of employment and the status of independent contracting. Independent contractors are self-employed business people subject to common law and legislative commercial regulation. They are not by nature, nor should they be, within the jurisdiction of labour laws. It is simply not possible within common law for a person to be a contractor and a 'little bit an employee'. Yet legislatures give the instruments of the state the power to perform acts of legal nonsense. When the state is both the lawmaker and the financial or other beneficiary of the law, the bounds of common sense and legal principles seem not to prevail, or at least are distorted.

This appears to be the case with the UK IR35. The tax authorities believe that independent contractors are tax rorters and legislatures have given the authorities total discretionary power on the basis that 'you can trust us'. But do independent contractors legally set themselves up just so they can minimize tax? The answer is that there is no general answer. It may be the case or it may not. Take the following simple but real-life example.

Independent contractors and tax deductions
A company needs an information technology specialist. The company can either employ the person or take him on as an independent contractor. Assume that the job will last 18 months.

If the company takes him on as an employee, it takes on a complex series of employer responsibilities. In most countries, by employing a person for 18 months the company enters a situation where labour laws assume that the person is full-time and effectively has ongoing ownership of the job. The company must factor its 'employer' responsibilities into its arrangements. When the company pays the person as an employee, employment regulation determines that the 'employer' must deduct certain items from the payments to the employee. This includes amounts to cover holiday pay, sick leave and other leave requirements. In Australia the amount that has to be deducted amounts to about 18 per cent of the employee's income. The employee does not see this money until he takes leave, for which he is paid although he is not working. The employer must keep detailed records of these deductions to ensure that the employee eventually receives back the money deducted. The withholding of money from the employee by the employer is, in effect, a forced loan from the employee to the employer. The system is disadvantageous to the employee and costly to the employer to administer, but it is all part of the complexity of the master employer–servant employee contract.

If the company takes the IT specialist on as an independent contractor, it does not take on any of the complex employer-type arrangements. The payment system is very simple. Nothing is withheld from the contractor for the purposes of holidays or leave, and the contractor receives total payment for the periods he works or the job he performs. When the contractor decides not to work, he does not get paid for not working. His holidays are his own choice which has nothing to do with the person paying him. Consequently, the payments made to the contractor are higher and the contractor takes on the responsibility of looking after himself. The contractor will often incur expenses that an employee will not. For example, a contractor is likely to take out personal income and public liability insurance, have self-training expenses and supply tools and equipment that are appropriate to the work he does. These additional costs incurred by an independent contractor will be reflected in the fee that he will charge, which is therefore greater than the wages that he would receive if he were an employee.

For example, an employee doing an IT job might receive $35 an hour. When on holiday he is still paid. An independent contractor doing exactly the same job but engaged in a completely different way might receive $50 an hour or more. This difference reflects the significant costs that a contractor incurs before a true comparison with the employee's remuneration can be made, such as the costs of taking a holiday.

Travel expenses are another example. With employment, employers normally provide their employees with work-related travel facilities. An employee arrives at work and takes a work car to go out and do her job. While the employee cannot claim the travel as a tax-deductible expense, the employer can claim it as legitimate business expense. A contractor, in contrast, has to charge her client a fee that is higher than the equivalent employee's wage in order to cover her travel expenses, for which she is solely responsible. The contractor can rightly claim the travel expenses as a legitimate tax-deductible business cost. The same arrangement holds with home office expenses: whereas employees are normally supplied a work station, the expenses of which are covered and claimed as a business expense by the employer, contractors, particularly in the IT industry for example, often work from an office at home, whose expenses they have to cover from their fees and which are legitimately tax-deductible.

On the surface, the contractor may appear to be earning more than an employee, but in truth may simply be receiving more in the hand because the contractor receives the 'employee benefits' in a cashed-out form. Whether this is true depends on the circumstances of each case. No one answer fits all cases and many other factors come into play that may complicate any calculation.

In traditional industries, it may be possible to calculate the difference between contractor and employee rates. But information technology—to take a relevant example—is a new industry that has grown up and is near wholly structured around independent contracting, making comparisons with employment virtually impossible.

The point, however, is that for tax purposes the payments an independent contractor receives are exactly like the payments any small business receives. Business expenses must be deducted before the business's 'profit' or true income can be calculated. The tax authorities' attack on independent contractors ignores these expenses and clearly seeks to disadvantage independent contractors. By insisting that independent contractors be treated like employees, tax officials impose higher rates of tax on independent contractors than those imposed on employees. A natural reaction of independent contractors would be to abandon independent contracting because of financial intimidation and to seek employment. By not being prepared to accept the business legitimacy of independent contracting, tax authorities become enforcers of employment.

When they adopt this stance, tax authorities are determining the nature of relationships in the work environment. Employment is about one person controlling another. The way people are paid is part of the control issue. Money is withheld from employees for holidays as a controlling mechanism. Employers want employees to work when and where the employer wants, at the employer's convenience. Holiday and leave pay is used by employers as a bargaining chip. With independent contracting the situation is completely different. No money is withheld and so no such control can be exercised. Negotiations over when a contractor takes unpaid holidays are done on an equal basis and are resolved in the normal businesslike way by finding commercial common ground between the parties. By insisting on employee taxation, tax authorities enforce inequality of employment bargaining.

Another complaint made by the UK contractors was that the IR ruling took away certainty of contract and was discriminatory. Before IR35, contractors knew that they enjoyed a business-tax status and could plan and operate accordingly. But when the IR sought to impose on them an employee status for tax purposes, the contractors considered they were being subject to state-imposed discrimination. Further, the actions of IR35 breached important principles of commercial activity in which 'A norm cannot be regarded as a "law" unless it is formulated with sufficient precision to enable the citizen to regulate his conduct; he must be able ... to foresee to a degree that is reasonable in the circumstances the consequences which a given action may entail.'[9] Through the mechanism of IR35 the IR has created contractual uncertainty. People engage in business only if they know that, when they strike a deal, it will hold. IR35 creates an environment where the contractor's individual commercial contract is subject to retrospective bureaucratic destruction based on arbitrary processes that contravene the very common-law principles upon which commercial contracts are based. Note, too, that the IR applies such judgements only to individuals, never to big business: a practice that is clearly discriminatory!

It's an issue of attitude and choice!

Sometimes the imposition of employment stems from disbelief that anyone would not want to work as an employee. Tax bureaucrats come from employment environments. They have been raised and educated to be 'employed'. They spend their careers as employees in generally secure government jobs, fight their way up the employment career ladder, mix and socialize with employees and most often do not have professional life experience outside the restrictive employment paradigm. Personally, they are taxed as employees. It is no wonder that they do not understand independent contractors, who do not fit into their experience of the world and may even seem strange or sinister to them.

But independent contractors do not see the situation in the same light. Employment 'benefits' are not seen as benefits at all but rather as restrictions. Independent contractors genuinely seek freedom, independence, flexibility, the capacity to control their own destiny and, above all, the ability to control their own money. They seek to manage their own financial affairs rather than have an employer manage their money for them. They don't want holiday pay withheld from them but rather want the money paid up front. They want to work at a time of their choosing, or even not work if that is their desire. Stories of people choosing to work for six months then not working for several months are common in the independent contractor community.

Sceptics say that this cannot be true and that the whole contractor thing is an employer-orchestrated scam. But it is true and the sceptics simply do not want to confront the reality that the near-total dominance of employment is being challenged by the people themselves. This is a 'people movement' to which tax authorities must respond in a positive manner.

Further evidence of the genuine nature of the independent contractor movement can be found in investigations undertaken by tax authorities themselves. Such investigations have been limited. Unfortunately, most tax measures relating to contractors have been enacted on the basis of assumptions rather than facts. In Australia, however, the ATO's obsessive belief that independent contractors structure themselves in order to avoid tax was put to the test by the ATO itself in the late 1990s, by investing considerable resources in significant tax audits.

During 1997 and 1998, the ATO conducted the so-called Alienation of Personal Services Project. A total of 65,000 Australian taxpayers were profiled for investigation as likely income-splitters.[10] This was a comparatively large selection of the 590,000 Australians who worked through self-employed company-structured entities in those years.[11] Notices were sent to 55,000 taxpayers initiating reviews of tax returns. A total of 5,403 taxpayers were specifically targeted for tax review, and 1,104 tax agents were visited by the ATO. The outcome was that only 714 taxpayers were issued adjustments notices, and the increases in tax paid varied from 1.9 per cent to 11.6 per cent per taxpayer. A significant but unreported number of taxpayers received rebates, indicating that they had overpaid their tax.

It is understood that the additional tax raised from the tax audit was below that expected from any random audit of general taxpayers' returns. It is known that the project was wound down because the additional revenue raised did not cover the cost of the audit. Most importantly, the independent conclusion of the audit was that the vast majority of people structure for legitimate business purposes and not for tax purposes. The audit proved that tax officials' allegations of tax rorting by independent contractors were false.

This audit should have been used as a major element in the independent contractor tax debate that raged in Australia between 1998 and 2001 when the government was redesigning the tax system. But the audit was for all intents and purposes suppressed — thereby raising questions about the genuineness of the Australian tax authorities' devotion to the truth. In 2000, the Australian government commissioned a major public review of business tax in which the issue of independent contractors featured strongly. But the 1997–98 ATO audit was not highlighted and did not feature in the government-commissioned review and report. The findings of the business tax report (the Ralph Review) read as if the 1997–98 audit had never happened. An aggressive anti-contractor stance was maintained in the report and simply reinforced the predetermined ATO position that independent contractors 'split' income.

Income-splitting is one of those issues that everyone seems to think everyone understands, but when it comes to precise definition there is mute silence. Those who make accusations of income-splitting have a responsibility to define precisely the point in a transaction at which a payment to an individual from an entity ceases to be an expense in earning an income and becomes a tax dodge. This is never specifically addressed.

In a typical example, if the spouse of a carpenter contractor is a partner in the contractor's business, at what point do payments to the spouse cease to be legitimate partnership payments and become income-splitting? Are partnerships to be disallowed? Are two-person companies to be abolished? This seems to be the desire of most tax authorities, yet tax authorities' personal views cannot be allowed to determine tax policy. Policy can and should operate only on clear principles that apply equally across the entire community.

Clear legal principles

In relation to contractors and employees, the facts are simple and clear. The status of employment and independent contracting are distinct and separate. There is no grey area at common law between the two.

As a consequence, independent contractors fall within the business-tax paradigm, which they access with all the advantages and disadvantages that apply in each country. Independent contractors are denied access to any alleged benefits available from employment regimes and avoid the disadvantages of employment. It is not for the instruments of the state to impose work status on people.

Resolving the dilemma: the Australian approach

The contractor-tax dilemma as it stood through most of the 1990s in Australia was similar to that in most other countries. PAYE was being eroded and the tax office had developed tests to limit people exiting the PAYE system, but in effect the tests had become quasi-common-law rulings, a task for which the tax office had no expertise or authority. Because the quasi-common-law tax tests largely sought proof of contractor status on the basis of the existence of company structures, individuals had strong incentives to structure into companies or trusts. In the view of the tax office, structuring had enabled individuals to split income and claim deductions so as to avoid tax. Lurking in the background were the labour regulators, ever ready in their many chameleon disguises to use the tax dilemma to aid their own cause — namely, to force people into PAYE wage-slavery employment.

In short, the linking of the Australian Tax Office's at-source income tax collection powers to common-law, master-and-servant employment relationships amounted to a serious mistake in times of vast social change. It corrupted the tax collection system, making it an instrument of the labour regulation system. It limited the right of people to free themselves from the inequality and injustice of the master-and-servant employment relationship.

With at least one in five of the Australian workforce not working in a traditional employment relationship, and with the trend showing rapid growth, the tax collection system was forced to modernize. The Federal Government's recognition of this was reflected in a Treasury document, produced in 1998, which established the principles and structures of the proposed reformed tax system and on the basis of which the incumbent Howard Government went to the 1998 election.

This key document said 'Australia's core withholding system — the Pay As You Earn (PAYE) system — relies heavily on outmoded ideas of master and servant to define obligations. It simply has not kept pace with labour market trends and is falling further behind. Australia needs a modern, comprehensive withholding system for payments to workers.'[12]

The backdrop to the modernization of this aspect of the tax system was the highly politicized introduction of a Goods and Services Tax (GST) in Australia. Australia was one of the few OECD countries not to have a GST, and its introduction came on the back of a narrow electoral victory by the Liberal coalition government in Australia. The media focus was principally on the GST, but in many respects the real game was the complete redesign of the Australian tax administration system. And perhaps nowhere in the OECD had such a large-scale reform been attempted in one hit and within such short time-lines. The final key pieces of legislation were passed in November 1999, the starting date for the complete package being 1 July 2000. Almost no part of federal tax administration was unaffected by the changes.

As one of its primary objectives, the reform had to detach the Tax Commissioner's collection powers from common-law dependency. Exit the 50-year-old (plus) PAYE system with dependency on common-law employment! Enter the pay-as-you-go (PAYG) system, with legislation written not in common-law employment language but in new tax-specific language, much to the confusion of the accountancy profession!

Imagine the hair-tearing that went on in the accountancy profession which, as of 1 July 2000, had to process tax returns for the 1999–2000 year based on old language and abolished legislation, and then cope with the immediate administration of a new system. Imagine the challenge for the Australian tax office. Imagine the confusion and frustration of Australian taxpayers. Yes, the political fallout was huge and first hit the government in the face in early 2001 with a collapse of public support for it.

But other than the obvious political costs to a political party for reforming a nation's tax system, what are the long-term implications? Has the Australian tax system moved to reshape itself in line with a changed society? To answer the question, it is necessary to consider the legislation itself and the psychology of the tax collectors as reflected through the legislation.

The new tax legislation delivers powers to the tax office through three key planks. The first is the Goods and Services Tax. The second is the Australian Business Number (ABN) legislation which requires every business entity (trading above a certain yearly turnover), including corporations, trusts, partnerships and individuals, to register for and quote its ABN when involved in most commercial transactions. The ABN gives the Tax Commissioner the capacity to trace each and every declared commercial transaction in the Australian community. It is the primary tool in a Big Brother tax cross-reference system that facilitates computer-generated tracing of Australians' commercial activity. (Save for undeclared 'black economy' transactions!)

The third plank is the PAYG legislation, which contains an instruction from the state to every business as to how and when it must remit tax. In all, the combined tax legislation stands 45cm high in five volumes, runs to thousands of pages and is printed on near 'see-through' tissue paper. The legislation hardly passes one test of good government, namely, to provide legislation that can easily be understood, but it is successful when it comes to severing the link between common-law employment and the Tax Commissioner's power to collect tax. To provide proof of this is difficult, because proof is found in what is *not* in the legislation rather than what is.

The administrative outcome of the legislation is that common-law employees are clearly caught within PAYG under one set of legislative wordings. Independent contractors who work through labour hire are caught within PAYG under a different set of legislative wordings. Individual contractors who work direct and have an ABN can choose to be caught within PAYG by signing a 'voluntary agreement', and this is described in a third set of legislative wordings. Contractors who do not wish to enter PAYG can remit their own income tax at source but will require an ABN if they don't want their clients to withhold 48.5 per cent of the value of their invoices. This multi-pronged process is designed to maximize pressure on all income earners to keep within the PAYG system. It successfully and broadly nets income earners no matter what their common-law work status and neutralizes the interest of the tax office in being a determiner of common-law status.

In many respects, this multi-pronged attack may upset some Australian income earners who do not want to be caught in an at-source income tax collection system. But the issue is not whether at-source collection is good or bad. The issue is whether or not the system responds to social developments and whether or not it treats all persons in an equitable manner. On this score, the Australian tax designers deserve praise.

Personal services income
The residual tax issue for Australian contractors is the 'alienation' issue. This is the view within the ATO that contractors divide their income with a spouse or other 'associate', thus lowering their tax liability and claiming tax deductions to which they should not be entitled. This issue has been largely addressed in Australia, although not in as complete and certain a way as with the withholding issue resolution under PAYG. It is, however, vastly better than the UK IR35 and the tax discrimination that independent contractors in the UK suffer.

The resolution did not come easily and was the source of considerable political pain to the Australian government during 2001. Initially, the independent contractor legislation had strong overtones of UK IR35—in particular, the high level of discretionary interpretive power given to the tax office. In addition, the rules would have denied many independent contractors legitimate business-tax status and would have been applied inconsistently. It took some time for the independent contractor community to realize the extent of the problems with the legislation, but when that realization sank in, a political storm erupted some six months away from an election. The government moved to quell the storm and amended the legislation to produce a much more reasonable statute.

The result is the Personal Services Income (PSI) legislation, finally passed in the Australian Parliament in late September 2001. The key to understanding the PSI legislation is that it applies a test for access to business-tax status that is essentially built around the common-law test for independent contractor status. With some qualifications, people who can clearly demonstrate independent contractor status have a higher level of certainty in receiving business-tax status than existed in the past. (There are, however, some unresolved issues which will not be discussed here.)

Principally, however, if an independent contractor passes the PSI legislation, she is entitled to be treated as a business for tax purposes and potentially can retain income in a company or trust and pay tax on the company or trust's income under company tax rules. Further, she can usually make payments to partners or associates who work with her and have those payments allowed as tax deductions from the business. In addition, she can claim certain business expenses as tax deductions. (This is predicated on the general tax avoidance provisions that declare that transactions entered into for the purposes of avoiding tax are disallowed.) In essence, these are normal tax rights and circumstances that every person in business has and reflect the commercial reality of how income is earned and expenses incurred when doing business.

For those with a technical interest, the final PSI legislation says that, to be allowed this business-tax status, four major tests are applied. First, a common-law employee cannot be treated as a business for tax purposes. Income will be treated as personal income and taxed accordingly. Second, the primary test is the 'results test'. A person who earns at least 75 per cent of his or her income as an independent contractor in a year will be treated as a business for tax purposes. If this test is passed, the person need not consider any of the other tests. However, a person who fails this test may still be entitled to business-tax status if he or she does not receive more than 80 per cent of income from one client in a year and has unrelated clients or employs people or has separate business premises.[13]

The clear intent of the legislation is to allow independent contractors to be treated as businesses for tax purposes. For practical purposes, the results test is the common-law test for independent contractors with two minor qualifications. In effect, the common-law test for independent contractor status is the key to accessing business-tax status. This is how the situation should be.

The point of discussing the contractor tax issues, with its sometimes endlessly circular arguments, is that the tax treatment of contractors is one of the strongest examples of how labour regulation is dominated by distorted understandings of labour contracts that have been locked in through historical circumstance, officials' personal experience and views of human relationships, and academically time-warped constructions of labour relations.

This is important to understand because it lays the basis for comprehending how these distorted understandings create problems in other areas of labour regulation—the subject of the next chapter.

Endnotes

1. Milton and Rose D Friedman, *Two Lucky People: Memoirs*, The University of Chicago Press, Chicago & London, 1998.
2. Australian Bureau of Statistics, Cat. No. 6359.0, August 1998, released February 2000.
3. Mark Wooden and Audrey Vanden Heuvel, *The Use of Contractors in the Australian Workplace: Evidence from a survey of Employers*, Monograph Series Number 3, National Institute of Labour Studies, Flinders University of South Australia.
4. *Queen, IR and PGA High Court* Case No CO/2302/00, April 2001. [IR 35]
5. UK 1999 Budget news release numbered IR35. See http://www.inlandrevenue.gov.uk/ir35/index.htm
6. IR 35.
7. See Professional Contractors Association Website: www.pcg.org.uk
8. IR 35
9. IR 35 Case at 44. Note: As of 2005, IR35 remained in place and continued to attract criticism from the independent contractor community. See www.inlandrevenue.gov.uk/ir35/index.htm and www.pcg.org.uk/aboutus/PCGAchievements2004.html
10. That is, the ATO wants to stop a person who earns income artificially splitting income with a spouse, thus lowering the overall tax liability by accessing lower tax rates.
11. Australian Bureau of Statistics, *op. cit.*
12. 'Tax Reform not a new tax, a new taxation system'. Circulated by the Treasurer of the Commonwealth of Australia, AGPS, 1998. (ISBN 0642 26153 9)
13. A basic explanation of the relative distinctions and their implications may be found at: http://www.contractworld.com.au/reloaded/ica-taxclarity2.php

4: Employment and Regulation
Changing to What?

To face tomorrow with the thought of using the methods of yesterday is to envision life as a standstill.

— James F. Bell

Describing the problem

If tax is the most dominant of the employment definition and regulation issues, what are the other regulatory issues? And how is regulation changing the way employment affects our lives?

Since the Second World War, not only has the employment contract been the focus of tax law, but it has also been covered with masses of regulation and government-induced control, to the point where the employment relationship is no longer a relationship between free human beings but is principally controlled and determined by the state. Although state control has been introduced for what might seem the most worthy of motives, the net outcome has been a souring and corruption of human interaction in the workplace. In essence, state control has overstepped the boundaries of reason and has, in many instances, itself become an instrument of negative social outcomes—perhaps most sadly by corrupting the creative potential of people when they work.

How this has occurred is both complex and simple. The task here is to see through the complexity to the underlying simplicity. First, some additional legal and managerial ideas about employment need to be understood. As already discussed, at its core, employment is about the right of one individual, the employer, to control another individual, the employee. Two additional ideas need to be comprehended. The first is the legal and managerial idea and practice of what is called 'vicarious liability': the process by which an employer is held to be responsible for the actions of the employee. The second is the legal and managerial loyalty that employees owe to their employers.

These ideas are critical to understanding employment and how the modern form of labour regulation has created negative social outcomes when combined with these two ideas. Odd as it may seem, both these legal and managerial aspects of employment exist for good commercial reason. The current ideas about the nature of business, firms and commercial activity in vibrant societies are wedded to these alleged legal necessities.

Vicarious liability: What is it?

In most areas of private life, people are held liable and responsible for their own actions. If we borrow money as private people, we are responsible for paying back the money. If we drive a car and cause a crash, we are held responsible to pay for the damage we caused. Generally, laws do not require the transfer of liability for actions from one adult to another. Yet this is what happens when people are employed.

Vicarious liability is a legal state in which an employer (a business) is held to be accountable and liable for the actions of its officers, agents and employees. Vicarious literally means 'acting in place of someone or something else'.[1] That is, an employee acts in the place of an employer and, therefore, an employer is legally responsible for the actions of its employees. Where the employer is an individual, that individual is responsible for the actions of others. Where the employer is a legal construct of a collective (that is, a firm), that legal construct is responsible.

For example, a corporation is a particular legal structure and at law is said to be a 'person'. A corporation can be very small and owned by one individual, or it can have hundreds of thousands of shareholders and huge numbers of employees. No matter what the size, a corporation is usually an 'employer' of employees, and vicarious liability is integral to the way in which human dynamics work within the corporation. As a 'person', a corporation is liable under commercial law but does not fall within the ambit of criminal law. Vicarious liability is critical to the existence of corporations and the way they are treated, because corporations assume collective commercial responsibility for the individual actions of the people who work in the firm—that is, the employees. The same applies to other legal 'persons' such as trusts.

Vicarious liability is a necessary and inevitable part of employment because, as we have already seen, employment is a legal status that gives the 'employer' the right to control the employee. Further, and by definition, this means that employees are taken not to have the capacity, desire or intent to control themselves physically, intellectually, creatively or emotionally. As a consequence, the employer is, and must be, vicariously liable for the actions of employees. It is the 'control' nature of employment that brings about vicarious liability.

Nor is this simply theory. Vicarious liability plays out every day in commercial activity and occasionally finds its way into court cases where its nature can be studied and understood. Take the following example of a damages action between a labour hire company and one of its clients.

Skilled Engineering case[2]

Skilled Engineering is one of Australia's largest labour hire companies and is listed on the Australian stock exchange. Among its activities, Skilled supplies blue-collar employees to industrial businesses in Australia. In 1997, an event occurred that culminated in a court case with a legal judgment handed down in 2001. The issue of Skilled Engineering's vicarious liability for the actions of its temporary on-hire employees was central to the court case and judgment.

Eric Sutton was a forklift driver employed by Skilled who worked at the warehouse site of a client of Skilled, Deutz Pty Ltd, for four days. Deutz stored diesel motors on racks of shelving in its warehouse. Eric Sutton's job was to unload diesel motors from trucks and place them on the shelving. The shelving was up to three metres high and the high-reach forklifts easily extended to that height. At one location in the warehouse a support beam extended between shelving lower than the three metre height. Eric Sutton was an experienced forklift driver and had all the necessary forklift driver licences. He had been instructed to ensure that when passing under the support beam he lowered the height of the forklift. On the fourth day of working, Eric was reversing his forklift with the lift at its full height extension and when passing the support beam he failed to lower the forklift. The inevitable occurred and the top of the forklift struck the supporting beam of the shelving. According to the court judgment, this resulted 'In a catastrophic chain reaction [in which] much shelving was caused to collapse and many valuable motors were damaged'. Losses to Deutz for damaged machinery amounted to $A369,000. Deutz Pty Ltd sued Skilled Engineering on the basis that Skilled was the employer of Sutton and hence vicariously liable for the damage.

The case was not a criminal case but a civil one. Skilled Engineering was found to have done nothing wrong in the selection and placement of Sutton, or in the fulfilment of any of its obligations. Eric Sutton's qualifications had been checked; he had all the correct licences and appropriate experience. The court found that the incident was 85 per cent attributable to Eric Sutton's driving—over which Skilled Engineering had no direct control, nor could have had control—and that Skilled could have done nothing practicable to prevent the incident. Nonetheless, damages of $A313,000 were awarded against Skilled because Sutton was an employee of Skilled and hence Skilled was vicariously liable.

This is not an unusual case, and such cases are not restricted to labour hire companies or to the Australian legal system. Vicarious liability plays out in many ways. Take this next case, discussed earlier, of the courier company Crisis Couriers, which was held liable for the actions of one of its bicycle couriers.

Hollis v. *Vabu* (Crisis Couriers)[3]

As discussed in Chapter One, Vabu is a privately owned courier and transport company operating principally in Sydney, Australia, trading under the name of Crisis Couriers. It has a fleet of vans, cars, motor bikes and bicycle couriers picking up and delivering parcels in and around Sydney. Significantly, it uses independent contractors who own their own vans, cars or bikes, and each driver or rider is paid per delivery. Crisis Couriers effectively acts as a booking, marketing, billing and organizing agency for the delivery services, and each driver runs his or her own micro-business. For marketing purposes, Crisis Couriers requires each driver or rider to wear a Crisis Couriers' identification vest.

The case of *Vabu* v. *Hollis* involved injury to a pedestrian knocked over by a bicycle courier wearing a Crisis Couriers' vest. According to the judgment:

> On 22 December 1994, Mr Hollis was leaving a building in Ultimo [a Sydney suburb] where he had attended to pick up a parcel. He had taken two steps on the footpath when he was struck by a cyclist and knocked to the ground. The cyclist went over the handlebars and landed in front of Mr Hollis. The cyclist stood up, said 'Sorry mate' and left the scene pushing his bicycle. He ignored Mr Hollis's calls. The cyclist remains unidentified. However, he was wearing a green jacket, on the front and back of which, in gold lettering, there appeared the words 'Crisis Couriers'. Mr Hollis suffered personal injury in the accident, principally to his knee. This required surgery, caused a period of unfitness for work and has resulted in a 25 per cent permanent deficit in the knee.

The pedestrian was suing Crisis Couriers for damages. Critical to the case was whether the unidentified bicycle rider was an employee of Crisis Couriers. If an employee, Crisis Couriers could be held vicariously liable. The case had reached the High Court, the court of final appeal in Australia.

The case was particularly significant because, in a judgment some two years earlier on a taxation matter (discussed in Chapter One), the courier drivers and riders of Crisis Couriers were found *not* to be employees but independent contractors. The High Court conducted a similar investigation to the earlier case and, on looking at near-identical operational procedures, found that the bicycle rider was an employee of Vabu.

In what was a controversial decision, the High Court limited the finding of employment specifically to the bicycle courier who knocked over the pedestrian, even though the bicycle rider was never identified. The court did not seek to make comment on other Crisis Couriers workers. In addition, only three of the five judges found that employment existed. One judge found that no employment existed, but that the bicycle courier was an 'agent' of Crisis Couriers and that Crisis Couriers was still liable. One judge totally disagreed and found that there was no substantial difference between the way the couriers operated—that is, whether they were car couriers or bicycle couriers—and found that the bicycle courier was an independent contractor.

As a result of the finding of employment by the majority of the Court, Crisis Couriers was held vicariously liable for the damage caused by their courier to Mr Hollis and was required to pay Mr Hollis $A176,000 compensation.

Comment

These two cases show how vicarious liability is tied to the nature of the employment relationship and how it causes the transfer of liability for individual actions away from the individual who performed the action. For example, in the Skilled Engineering case, if Eric Sutton had been an employee of Deutz, Deutz would have had to bear the cost of the shelving collapse. Further, if Eric Sutton had been a private person driving a car in the street, he would have been personally liable for the damages. In the case of Crisis Couriers, if the courier had not been working at the time but acting as a private person, the unidentified bicycle courier would have been liable for the damages. Eric Sutton and the bicycle courier were clearly in total and complete control of their respective vehicles and there was no suggestion that Skilled, Deutz or Crisis Couriers had any practical capacity to control any of the actions of these two persons. Yet because the persons were paid for their services in a way that was found to be 'right to control' employment, liability for actions was transferred from the individuals who committed the action to the persons who paid those individuals. This is the legal effect of vicarious liability under employment.

There is something disturbing and wrong about an institutional and legal arrangement that allows liability to be transferred. Why should people be able to escape the consequences of their actions simply because they are 'employed'? Why should the consequences be different when one is employed from when one is acting as a private individual? Personal liability for actions, which is necessary for social stability, is perverted because of a specific legal status created via a payment.

But there are other aspects of vicarious liability that show it is assumed to be necessary. It is bound up in the way we think about firms and human organization. Without vicarious liability, organizations would seek to deny legal liability for actions that were part of the organizations' operations. Ultimately, this could render the law powerless to prevent intimidation, corruption and thuggery. Take the following case of a trade union seeking to deny liability for breach of court orders.

Evenco[4]

This case involved a protracted and ugly dispute between a labour hire firm supplying building tradespeople to commercial building sites in Queensland, Australia, and one of Australia's most rugged building unions, the Construction, Forestry, Mining and Electrical Union (CFMEU). Australian construction unions consider that they own the commercial building sites in Australia and try to enforce total union membership on each and every site as well as dictating how work is to be done and on what terms it is to be paid for.

The CFMEU's motivation is to secure the power and revenue base of the union, but it also has other important and sometimes not-so-obvious motives. In complex processes of 'honour amongst thieves', union membership and site control are frequently used for determining who can win tenders for jobs and which companies are capable of constructing buildings. Unions act to prevent competition between building companies and to deliver commercial monopoly to favoured building companies. The financial stakes are high, frequently many millions of dollars. If an 'outside' player comes in and is prepared to supply non-union labour to building sites, the revenue of the building union is threatened. But, just as importantly, the interloper threatens the commercial colluding-type behaviour that operates to control the market for building construction. Through control of who can work on a building site, unions can ensure that only building companies with whom they have 'good' relationships can win building contracts. There is thus a coalition of interests between the building unions, which need members, and some construction companies, which aim to limit competition.

The process of ensuring union membership and control of the building market involves all the usual and known systems of thuggery, intimidation and harassment, often involving violence where unions think it necessary. Usually, however, all the players in the game, the builders and unions, know the 'rules' and abide by them without enforcement being required. But when someone breaks these unwritten rules, the cosy arrangement is threatened.

This is what occurred with the small labour hire company, Evenco Pty Ltd, in Queensland. It supplied trades-people to building sites, but did not insist that the 'tradies' abide by the union rules.

Evenco and the people it supplied were subject to prolonged harassment, but they were astute enough to record every incident. They eventually took the union to court and received a court order prohibiting the union from harassing them.

In March 1988, the CFMEU gave court undertakings that it would not harass Evenco or the people it supplied to building sites. The court order involved undertakings from the union and the union secretary, Mr Trohear. The union honoured its commitment and trained its organizers on the undertaking until 1995. From 1995 onwards, training of its organizers on the issue ceased and harassment of Evenco resumed, led by a paid union organizer, Mr Spinks. In court evidence, it was apparent that Mr Trohear was aware that the undertakings were being breached by Mr Spinks and other union representatives. Up to this point the issue had been a civil case, but became a criminal case as soon as the CFMEU flouted the court orders.

Evenco took the matter back to court. This involved making an application against the union for contempt of court. The court had to decide whether the union and Mr Trohear were responsible for the action of Mr Spinks and other union representatives. The case turned on whether Mr Spinks and others were employees of the union, and therefore, whether vicarious liability applied.

The judges took great care in applying common-law principles, because holding one party to be legally responsible for the actions of another is a grave matter. Further, this case had developed into a criminal case—albeit a low-level one—but jail was a possible penalty open to the judges.

On vicarious liability, one of the judges said:

> It is, I think, settled law that a master or principal is liable if his or her servant or agent breaches an undertaking given by the master or principal in circumstances where he or she is acting on behalf of and within the scope of the authority conferred by the master or principal.[5]

In this particular case, the court said:

> CFMEU and Mr Trohear were liable for the actions of the union organizer Spinks, an employee of the CFMEU as Spinks 'was acting in the course of his employment' when he offended the undertaking ... whilst there was no evidence that Spinks has specific authority to act as he did in offending the undertaking, his actions were committed

in the course of his employment ... the necessary authority may be tacit.[6]

The judges gave an insight into the historical precedents underpinning vicarious liability by drawing on decisions by the House of Lords in England as early as 1865:

the law in England has developed in the direction of holding the blameless employer liable for the unauthorized acts of an employee... The qualification of this is the employee must be shown to have acted 'in the course of employment' ... Under the law of tort [civil damages-type prosecution] an employer may be held liable for his servants' acts although clearly unauthorized.[7]

But the judges were not prepared to apply strict vicarious liability in the instance of criminal prosecution which this case involved:

the English doctrine of strict vicarious liability to which I refer [criminal] should not be followed in this country. The proper rule is that the employer must be shown to have authorized the act complained [of] or shown not to have taken proper steps to prevent it.

The judges stated that 'insofar as it can make an absolutely blameless person vicariously liable for the unauthorized act of an employee, vicarious liability for criminal acts is the exception not the rule.'[8]

The outcome was that, in this criminal case, vicarious liability applied, but only to the extent that the actions of the union employee representatives were done with the knowledge of the union and the Secretary who were parties to the court undertakings to cease harassing Evenco. 'As to Trohear, he was party to the undertaking and the same reasoning applies, but more simply, to him; he personally was obliged to obey the undertakings, and so had an obligation to do everything reasonably necessary to achieve that end.'[9]

In the end, the evidence showed that the union and Mr Trohear did know about the intimidation of Evenco by the union employees and could have stopped the actions, but chose not to do so. On the basis of direct knowledge of their failure to prevent the breaches of the court orders, the union and Mr Trohear were fined a total of $85,000. Any assertions by the union that they could not be held liable for the actions of their employee representatives were discounted. In this instance, a jail term was not imposed.

Comment

The Evenco case demonstrates the need for vicarious liability and why it is applied. Without vicarious liability, the risk is real that employers could avoid responsibility and liability for actions taken on their behalf. If employers could pick and choose which responsibilities to accept and which to ignore, elementary principles of justice would be breached and economic activity would be severely inhibited. It is imperative in the conduct of commercial trade that everyone has a reasonable assurance that they can act within known rules and undertakings that are supported by the courts. If firms were not liable for their employees' actions, the risk associated with dealing in commercial transactions would be that much higher—and could, in fact, undermine commercial activity. Take, for example, the following case of the collapse of the international trading house Barings.

Barings

In 1995, the giant international trading house, Barings, one of the world's oldest banks, collapsed because one of its employees undertook unauthorized multi-million dollar exchange and other trading gambles that failed. The employee, Nick Leeson, was jailed for fraud. If vicarious liability had not applied, Barings could have argued that Leeson's trading gambles and losses did not accrue to Barings but were the personal responsibility of the employee. If such an argument could be sustained, Nick Leeson could have been declared bankrupt. This would have effectively prevented the financial trading houses that had traded with Barings in good faith from recovering monies owed to them. Barings could have denied responsibility and accountability, secured its short-term financial future and continued to trade, leaving other trading houses to bear the losses. The result, however, would have been that no company would be prepared to take the risk of trading with Barings in the future. A precedent would have been set affecting the entire viability of the international money-dealing system, as traders could never be confident that the companies they dealt with would back the actions of employees or that the courts would back the system. Such an outcome would have had calamitous implications for worldwide economic activity.

The system of international money exchange (in fact, any financial transaction, no matter how small) is predicated on trust. International financial transactions occur with such speed that the legal niceties of documentation and signed security frequently lag way behind the transactions. Those who work in the international system operate on the assumption that the other players they deal with are as good as their word. Such transactions can occur only because of a belief that the courts will ultimately hold companies liable for the actions of their employees. This system of trust, supported by the courts, is a miracle of human behaviour made possible by the structure of open markets and, importantly, the existence of vicarious liability of an employer for an employee's actions.

But as important as vicarious liability is, its conceptual flip-side is employees' fiduciary and contractual duties of loyalty. Under employment, businesses can succeed only if the risks of vicarious liability are offset by the benefits that flow from employees' loyalty to their employers.

Loyalty

In no area of our private lives are we required by law to be loyal. Loyalty is something we freely give or withhold. Loyalty is a spontaneous outcome of a relationship. We can freely choose where we shop; no law requires us to keep shopping at any particular store. Even loyalty to a nation is something freely given. Yet, when we are employed, we are required by law to be loyal to our employer. When employed, we are not allowed to use our capacities, talents and energies in a way that may compete with our employer. This obligation is not generally stipulated in legislation but is found within the common law.

The legal principles of fiduciary and contractual duties of loyalty of an employee to an employer are meant to prevent and protect an employer from the potential competitive behaviour of employees. It is an idea that underpins the traditional concepts of the firm and economic activity. By virtue of having a right to control the employee, it is assumed that the employer imparts important commercial information to an employee which, if the employee were not loyal, the employee could use against the employer in a competitive manner, thereby causing commercial loss to the employer. Further, in paying employees for the right to control them, the employer is purchasing the right to the potential commercial benefit that employees may produce. These principles are frequently tested in the courts.

The case of *Digital Pulse v Harris*[10] demonstrates these points.

In the opening comments in the judgment on this case, the judge stated the commercial principle at stake. When:

> employees resolve to go into business for themselves in competition with their employer, they decide to give their new venture a head start by remaining in employment and diverting to themselves their employer's business opportunities until they are economically secure enough to declare their hands, throw up their employment and compete openly. No one doubts that the employees have breached their contractual and fiduciary duties of loyalty to their employer and that they are liable for damages, an account of profits or equitable compensation.[11]

Digital Pulse was a business that started in 1996, providing computer-based multimedia services including Web design and video production. By 1999, it had some ten employees. Mr Harris and Mr Eden were employees of

Digital who, while employees of Digital, set up their own business, 'Juice', in competition with Digital and unbeknown to Digital.

The judge explained the general duty of loyalty: 'An employee has a duty to act in the interests of the employer with good faith and fidelity. That duty is implied in every contract of employment if it is not imposed by an express term. In addition, the duty is imposed upon every employee by the law of fiduciaries.'[12] (Fiduciary means 'held in trust'.[13]) Further 'an employee may not take for himself or herself an opportunity within the sphere of the employee's business operations without the employer's fully informed consent....' and 'The remedy for breach of the contractual duty of loyalty is damages.'[14]

In delivering the judgment, the judge was clearly not impressed with Mr Harris, who, he said 'has demonstrated a capacity for extravagant falsehood'.[15] The judge found that Mr Harris had used Digital's advertising strategy document against Digital and awarded $A11,000 on that account. Other considerable amounts were awarded as compensation to Digital for loss of business or damage relating to a list of Digital clients whereby Mr Harris and Mr Eden had shifted Digital clients to themselves (Juice).

Further, the judge found that 'what Messrs Harris and Eden did was to defraud their employer of its valuable business opportunities and its confidential information'. The judge explained in clear terms the issues at stake. He said:

> the character of the Defendant's dishonest conduct strikes at the heart of commercial integrity, upon which the business community, and ultimately the community as a whole, depends. Employers should feel able to trust their business confidences to their employees with security. Employees should know that deliberate and dishonest breach of their fiduciary duties of loyalty, calculated to produce profit for themselves, will not go unpunished....[16]

As compensation, the judge ordered Messrs Harris and Eden each to pay $A10,000 to Digital.

In short, even if employees are not aware of it, they have a legal duty to their employer to be loyal and not to use their positions to their own advantage and/or in competition with their employer. Few employees are consciously aware of this legal requirement.

Volkswagen

This idea of duty and loyalty sometimes plays out for huge commercial stakes. In 1997, in a high-profile case, General Motors Corporation (GM) received a $US100 million pay-out in the first phase of the settlement of a $US3 billion dollar claim against Volkswagen (VW). The dispute began when an executive of GM left in 1993 to take up a senior position with VW. Seven other senior GM executives followed and GM alleged that, in the course of the desertions, valuable company documents and trade secrets were stolen. The legal action by GM alleged criminal racketeering, but at its heart involved the principle of an employee's duty of fidelity to the employer.[17] General Motors won significant compensation as a consequence.

Comment

In Chapter One, we examined the essence of the employment contract — that is, 'control'. So far, in this chapter, two additional elements of the employment contract — vicarious liability and loyalty — have been considered. These two elements should be seen as part of the employment contract as it stands on its own. The rest of this chapter looks at how statute law has been layered on top of and around the employment contract. Although ostensibly directed at creating social good, these legislative efforts have, in fact, resulted in significant social and economic distortions. When vicarious liability and loyalty have been joined with the development of unfair dismissal laws and anti-discrimination laws since the Second World War, strange, enormous and as yet unaddressed perversions have crept into the employment equation.

How it has changed !!!!

Since the Second World War, the common-law employment relationship has been burdened with reams of legislation that have fundamentally changed employment from a system of significant employer control to one of highly limited employer control. What has occurred, primarily, is the introduction of unfair dismissal and anti-discrimination legislation which, when combined with vicarious liability (in particular) and the duty of loyalty (to a lesser extent), has resulted in significant distortions of employment and of the idea and nature of the firm.

The change has occurred in several ways. Anti-discrimination laws come into play when someone denies a person a job on the grounds of the applicant's race, colour, religion or some other factor not associated with the needs of the job. Discrimination, as applied under the post-Second World War laws, is specifically defined prejudicial behaviour of one person against another. This is quite distinct from the discrimination we all practise every day, as when we choose one bottle of wine over another, or choose to keep the company of some people rather than others.

Liability for unlawful discrimination ought to rest with the individual who committed the act of discrimination. Yet, when conjoined with vicarious liability under employment, the liability for discriminatory action is transferred from the person who committed the act to the employer.

As a consequence, a strange notion has found legal form, namely, that a collective entity—a firm—can commit an act of discrimination. This happens only when the firm is either a corporation or trust and is an employer. If individual employees of a corporation commit unlawful discrimination, the liability for their actions is transferred from them to the corporation. In practice, this operates against the social and legislative objective of preventing unlawful discrimination. As will be argued, discrimination will effectively be stopped only when the individuals who commit acts of discrimination are held personally and directly accountable under law.

Further, the outcome of liability transfer in employment situations is that anti-discrimination law has become a litigious and, in many instances, arguably a money-making scam in which the law has become an active instrument of systemic abuse.

Likewise, unfair dismissal laws have frequently put employers in conflict with other statutory responsibilities in areas of health, safety and duty of care to customers and clients. Employers are expected to 'control' their employees and are held liable for the actions of employees, but employers have had removed from them some of their basic 'controlling' capacities—namely, the ability to decide who is in their employ.

Let us look at a few examples of such distorting behaviour.

Discrimination, sexual harassment and unfair dismissal
In the USA, pay-outs to people who have alleged discrimination or harassment in the workplace can now involve huge sums. And government in its role as employer has been one of the hardest hit. Often the very bodies involved in the rights protection business—both government and private organizations—have been the ones to suffer most severely from litigation.

During the 1990s, the New York City Department for the Ageing paid out $US1 million to its social workers as compensation on the finding of age discrimination by the Department against the social workers. The US Department of Labor paid $US5 million to settle a bias claim against it. A San Francisco legal firm which had a thriving business in the sexual harassment area was ordered to pay $US7.5 million, including the applicant's legal costs, in a successful sexual harassment case brought against it. The US Civil Rights Commission and the EEOC have repeatedly been hit with pay-outs. These high pay-outs are not unusual but rather the norm. In New York City, the average sexual harassment pay-out has been assessed as in the order of $US250,000.[18]

But these massive pay-outs are not necessarily the issue of concern. What is worrisome is how the application of these laws affects the way in which organizations are structured and operate, and how this, in turn, affects their capacity to perform. Sometimes the detrimental effects strike at core institutions that underpin a safe and secure society.

Police: In the 1980s and 1990s, the New York Police Force, Miami Police Force,[19] Washington DC Police Force and even the FBI became well known for endemic levels of corruption that were said to have had their roots in the way discrimination laws distorted those organizations' hiring procedures. Anti-discrimination laws had prohibited the Forces from considering minor criminal offences of applicants, with the inevitable outcome that ex-criminals became police officers, thereby creating an environment of endemic corruption. Other effects came from anti-discrimination laws that hindered the screening of applicant officers for literacy skills. In Washington DC, this resulted in murder cases not proceeding because police paperwork did not match the requirements necessary for successful prosecution. In one example,[20] the Boston Police Force was found guilty of discrimination because it sacked an officer who lied about his medical history on the application form. The issue for the Boston police was the integrity of the police officers employed and whether officers could be relied upon to act honestly and to give reliable testimony under oath. The offending officer was reinstated and awarded payment for discrimination.

Drugs: Caught between competing and conflicting laws, employers have sometimes found themselves in difficulty when they try to create safe workplaces without falling foul of anti-discrimination or unfair dismissal laws.

In Australia, the courts have found that a drug addict working in an ex-Servicemen and Women's Memorial Club could not be dismissed because it would constitute discrimination. This occurred because of interpretations under Australian law which declared drug or alcohol abuse a 'disability'.[21]

The Australian Industrial Relations Commission (AIRC) reinstated a worker who was sacked by his employer after being booked by the police for drink-driving. The Telstra worker (Telstra is a major Australian telephone company) had a blood alcohol reading of 0.110 (the Australian limit is 0.05) the morning after a heavy drinking session. The Magistrates Court fined the man $1,000 and suspended the man's driving licence for six months on the drink-driving charge. Nonetheless, the employment court determined that Telstra should continue to employ him.[22]

The AIRC awarded $15,000 unfair dismissal compensation to a train driver who was dismissed by his employer after a fatal train accident in which the driver tested positive to marijuana use after the accident. The driver was not found to have caused the accident but was in breach of the train company's drug and alcohol policy. The unfair dismissal award was made on the basis that the company had not adequately informed the driver of its policy.[23]

In a similar incident, an oil-rig worker was awarded 16 weeks' pay for unfair dismissal after testing positive for cannabis use. The award was made against the employer because it was alleged that the employer had not previously enforced its drug policy.[24]

Vicarious liability and harassment: Sometimes, no matter how diligent an employer might be in designing and implementing its systems, it is never enough to satisfy the courts. This seriously calls into question the ability of employers to control much at all.

In Australia, damages of $A55,000 were awarded to a teacher aide for sexual harassment from a principal of a State-run primary school. The sexual harassment did not involve physical contact but was on a smaller scale, involving standing or sitting very close. The State of Victoria, as the employer of both the aide and the principal, suffered the imposition of the fine on the basis that even though it had exemplary equal opportunity policies, it had nevertheless failed to train the principal adequately.[25]

In 1997, the Queensland Anti-Discrimination Tribunal awarded $A48,000 against a female apprentice fitter mechanic due to the harassment from mine workers at Mt Isa Mines. The award was made because Mt Isa Mines was held to have failed adequately to instruct its mine workers not to harass.[26]

In 2002, a 62-year-old driver, who had a 20-year unblemished work record at the Port of Brisbane Corporation, was reinstated following his dismissal for harassing a younger female worker. His sacking followed a complaint from the female worker to the effect that he had said to her, 'Gee you look lovely today, you give me half a woody'. (A 'woody' is an Australian slang word for an erection!) The man, who had been fully trained in the corporation's anti-harassment policies, admitted the comment but did not co-operate with attempts at further counselling, because counselling would allegedly have established his intention to cause harm by making the statement. The employment court reinstated the man on the grounds of procedural unfairness.[27]

Another case demonstrated the mismatch between employment law and anti-discrimination law. A Pakistani man alleged that discriminatory remarks had been made to him by a person at a boarding house in which he was staying. The action was being taken against the owner of the boarding house, but the person who had allegedly made the remarks could not be located. It could not be proved that the person was an employee of the boarding house owner and so no case could be established against the landlord. If, however, proof had been established that the comments were made by an employee of the landlord, the landlord would have been held vicariously liable.[28]

In short, the nature of the employment relationship has become critical to the ability to litigate under discrimination law, and a person who may commit an act of discrimination as an employee is able to avoid liability because it is transferred to another person, the employer. This makes it possible to make allegations of discrimination expressly for the purpose of soliciting money and has almost made possible state-sanctioned fraud.

But because discrimination laws do not take into account the distortions created by vicarious liability, they continue to lead to critical and damaging social outcomes. Often this puts vulnerable persons at great risk because the employer's capacity to exercise the duty of care owed to the public is dramatically curtailed.

In 1999, the Queensland Industrial Court ordered the Queensland Education Department to reinstate a man it had dismissed for inappropriately rubbing the thigh of an 11-year-old girl. The man had previously been sacked but reinstated after being acquitted of an aggravated sexual assault charge against a Year Five student in his class in 1993. Following this earlier incident, the man had been warned to modify his behaviour.[29]

Exxon: In an internationally high-profile case, the world's largest firm, Exxon, was found responsible for what had been, up until then, the world's largest oil-spill disaster when, in 1989, its supertanker Exxon Valdez ran aground in Alaska. The company lost billions of dollars in damages and clean-up costs, which reinforced its determination to improve procedures to prevent a recurrence. The Exxon Valdez's captain had a history of alcoholism of which the company was aware, and alcohol was a strong contributing factor in the ship's running aground. Yet when Exxon revised its policies after the disaster and began removing staff with drinking problems from safety-sensitive positions,[30] it was hit with 'at least a hundred challenges' on discrimination grounds. What *is* a company to do?

Sometimes it's even what a company doesn't do. Unfair dismissal laws provide for 'constructive' unfair dismissal. This involves situations where an employee leaves a firm but then argues that the circumstances in the firm were such that he or she had little option but to leave. In one case, an executive of a construction firm[31] was awarded $US8 million in a 'constructive' unfair dismissal case.

Cost: Sometimes it appears that the only outcome of anti-discrimination and unfair dismissal laws is the payment of monies to aggrieved parties, whereas the moral intent of the laws allegedly is to modify human behaviour so that discrimination and harassment do not occur and that only 'fair' dismissals take place.

In 1998, the Australian Industrial Relations Commission handled more than 8,000 unfair dismissal applications, of which only 20 resulted in reinstatement. Most cases never reached the court and were settled out of court or withdrawn.[32] Even though not documented, it is a common view that most unfair dismissal and discrimination claims are better settled by an early pay-out to the applicant because it is cheaper than mounting a defence.

In Australia, pay-outs awarded to successful unfair dismissal applicants usually amount to around $A6,500, with legal defence costs for the employer within the range $A5,000–$A20,000. The applicant's legal costs will rarely exceed $10,000 unless significant jurisdictional issues are involved. In 1995, it was estimated that the average cost of a relatively serious or complex harassment grievance claim was $A35,000, with legal costs of up to five times that amount. Pay-outs in less serious discrimination cases were usually about $A20,000.[33]

Sometimes the pay-outs can be huge, depending upon the legal jurisdiction in which applicants' lawyers choose to run cases. Often these high-pay-out cases involve actions against employers where the sacked employee was once the designated employer.

The sacked head of Coca Cola in Australia took a $A40 million action against Coca-Cola Amatil Ltd and Coca Cola USA through the unfair contracts provisions in New South Wales (NSW).[34] Using NSW unfair contracts provisions, a sacked Microsoft Human Resources director received an estimated $A10 million pay-out, a Westfield Holdings Ltd sacked executive was awarded $250,000, and a dismissed executive of Macquarie Bank won $775,000 plus costs.[35] A 58-year-old senior executive who had worked for the large, prestigious retailer David Jones for 35 years received $200,000 in a court-awarded pay-out under the same NSW unfair contracts provisions.[36]

A Rand Corporation survey found that Californian employees who won wrongful firing actions received on average $US500,000.[37] In the USA, lawyers' contingency fees in such cases are known to be as high as 40 per cent. Even if pay-outs are not made, the average cost of defending an unfair dismissal application in the USA exceeds $US100,000 and a sexual harassment charge $US200,000. With defence costs so high, many businesses facing an application give in and seek an out-of-court settlement, regardless of the facts of any situation. The mere making of a claim is likely to cause the employer to decline to mount a defence, on grounds of cost—hardly a situation contributing to justice!

Comment

The issue involved here is not the correctness or otherwise of anti-discrimination, anti-harassment or unfair dismissal laws, but rather whether employers actually have control of employees. In fact, the nature of employment law has been changed by legislation so dramatically since the Second World War that employer control is largely a social and economic myth. But it is a myth that forms the intellectual underpinnings of much new law, economic and managerial analysis and social analysis and policy.

This myth of actual control is, however, recognized by the judiciary in the subtle way in which it has modified the definition of employment to reflect the new reality. In the most important redefining statement of employment since the Second World War (discussed in Chapter One), the Australian High court said in 1986, 'It has been held, however, that the importance of control lies not so much in its actual exercise, although clearly that is relevant, as in the right of the employer to exercise it.'[38] This statement has become the principal starting point for all common-law test cases in Australia. It is strongly reflected in the approach used in North America and the UK at least. As one Australian judge said, it reflects the fact that 'the right to dismiss is in many cases strictly limited by law or by industrial matters'.[39]

It must be acknowledged, then, that if an employer does not have the right to dismiss an employee, he or she does not control the employee. At best, the control an employer exercises is strictly limited to the amount of control that the employee chooses to allow the employer to exercise. If employees wish to ignore an employer's control, they can easily do so. An employer's capacity to dismiss an employee without the employee's consent is limited to the uncertain situations in which employer tribunals will endorse the dismissal. Effectively, the ultimate tool of control — dismissal — has been removed from the employer and handed to employment tribunals. Employers have a theoretical 'right to control', but actually only have a mythical capacity to control. The state is now the controller.

The 'human resources' managerial function, now so prevalent among firms, has developed into an industry largely in response to the myth of control. Human resource professionals have a strange task in that they must persuade the employees voluntarily to acquiesce in the control requirements of the firm. Human resource managers seek to translate the 'employer control' myth into control reality. But these efforts by human resource managers do not stop the social distortions.

When the mythic capacity of the employer to control the employee is joined with statutorily imposed obligations under anti-discrimination and anti-harassment laws, it inevitably causes severe distortions to human behaviour in the workplace. The distortions take forms that do not occur within our personal and private lives.

First, the remedies to discrimination, harassment and other social ills are reduced to monetary compensation. As a consequence, laws which are supposed to modify human behaviour with a view to promoting greater social justice fail to do so.

Certainly, some people defend the awarding of damages against employers on the grounds that this induces employers to ensure that conduct within their organizations is appropriately modified. But because employers have only a formal capacity to control employees, such attempts to modify conduct are at best haphazard. And too often such arguments come from the legal profession, which has a vested financial interest in litigation rather than behaviour modification.

Second, the shifting of liability for discrimination and harassment from the employee to the employer involves an institutionalized injustice against the employer. The economic reality is that justice for the employer becomes a matter of luck in avoiding litigation.

Third, the shifting of liability away from employees for their personal actions must limit the behaviour modification objectives of anti-discrimination and anti-harassment law. When individuals know that someone else will be held liable for their actions, they are less inclined to change their actions or attitudes. Behaviour defined at law as unacceptable is likely to be pushed underground, displayed in less obvious ways, sometimes perhaps even displayed openly and in defiance of the law. To overcome these possibilities, the state-funded quasi-courts that have been set up to police anti-discrimination laws have difficulty operating on principles of true justice and can seem like kangaroo courts.

Fourth, the mismatch of unfair dismissal and anti-discrimination laws with the myth of employer control requires employers to become specialists in statute and case law in both areas in order to be sure that their operational practices conform with the law. This is a time-and-motion impossibility, as the law is so complex that even the legal profession must specialize to gain an understanding of it. The outcome is a huge increase in business transaction costs and an escalation in managerial uncertainty, both of which encourage the avoidance of responsibility within the firm. If employees are not held liable for their actions, internal systems within firms must ensure that liability is not attributable to anyone within the firm. This is bad for business, bad for people, bad for social justice.

How has this come about?
This situation has evolved because of the way the employment relationship changed during the twentieth century.

The contract at will
Before the Second World War, the employment relationship was structured around what was called the 'contract at will'. This operated as the principal employment contract until 1945 or so, and it was from the contract at will that the current employment contract developed.

The contract at will had simple principles. An employer could create an offer of work, and a prospective employee could consider the offer and, if acceptable, enter the employment contract. Once the employment contract was entered into, each party could choose at any time to exit the contract without having to give reason or cause. Both entering and exiting the contract were of interest and concern solely to the employer and employee; no external legal tribunals or processes were involved. Neither the employee nor the employer had a duty to the other beyond the actual daily work that was performed and the payment for such work.

This particular employment contract had long been in operation, received strong support from the courts, was a key pillar upon which the commercial might of the USA was constructed and was seen in the USA as vital to the securing of basic freedoms. In 1908, the US Supreme Court stated 'it is not within the functions of government—at least in the absence of contract between the parties—to compel any person in the course of his business and against his will to accept or retain the services of another.' How things have changed!

But this employment contract at will was still an employment contract in its truest form. It was a contract which, once entered, gave the employer control and authority over the employee. It is worth restating the quotation from the eminent American jurist Oliver Wendell Holmes, who explained it thus in 1892 in support of a decision to support the sacking of an employee. Holmes said, 'There are few employments for hire in which the servant does not agree to suspend his constitutional rights of free speech, as well as idleness, by the implied terms of his contract. The servant cannot complain, as he takes the employment on the terms which are offered to him.'[40]

So the employment contract at will was a contract which could be entered and exited at any time by either party but which, once entered, involved the employee being prepared to suspend his or her right to free speech and idleness. This was the idea of the master-and-servant relationship and is consistent with what we know about the employment contract as an instrument of control.

This contract at will was seen to be indispensable for economic activity and the operation of business. For the purposes of engaging in business and working inside a firm, employers needed employees to work, not to be idle, and to follow instructions in such a manner that they agreed not to express their opinions. In short, people agreed to suspend those basic freedoms and rights they had in their private lives while they were at work—in exchange for money. But they could also exit the contract at will when it suited them.

This was very different from slavery, under which people's rights were forcibly denied them and they could not exit the relationship at will. Slaves were owned and the slave owner had a right to hunt down fleeing slaves, punish them, and return them to unpaid work. Slavery, of course, is now outlawed across the globe and where it continues, it is illegal.

Many social and political commentators, however, saw the employment contract at will as a modified form of slavery, which they referred to as 'wage slavery' (Karl Marx was one such notable example). In exchange for money, people suspended their liberties and worked for others, who had control over them. It did not matter to Karl Marx and others that the employee could legally reject wage slavery, because, they argued, the entire capitalist system was built upon wage slavery. The only choice workers had was which wage-slave situation to enter. There was no real choice to reject wage slavery itself because the only alternative to it was unemployment, deprivation and starvation. In societies where employment was the only form of work engagement, the wage-slavery argument had great force.

From this view of the employment contract at will as wage slavery sprang the idea of the oppression and exploitation of the working classes by the capitalist (employer) class and the need for labour to organize itself in opposition to the employers. It was argued that the capitalist class organized economic activity exclusively around the employment contract at will and had a vested interest in keeping wages as low as possible. The only way employees could improve their incomes was to organize collectively and withdraw their labour *en masse*, stop other workers replacing them, and thus force the employer to pay more. Without collective action, employers would keep employees in permanent subjugation. When seen through this prism, economic and business activity is the site of a class struggle between employers and employees. But such a view is plausible only on the basis that the employment contract is the sole available contract of engagement.

At the turn of the twentieth century, the employment contract was at its peak. And in spite of its critics, it served society comparatively well in terms of enabling economic development. During the nineteenth century, economic activity and wealth exploded, dragging populations out of abject rural subsistence poverty into a level of comparative health and wealth not seen before. The Industrial Revolution was underpinned in large part by the employment contract at will.

Nevertheless, the idea of the inevitable class war between employees and employers took on international dimensions. Some commentators blamed both world wars, in part, on the conflict thought to be inherent in the employment contract at will. In fact, the International Labour Organisation (ILO, a division of the United Nations)[41] was established for the precise purpose of enabling the management of this 'inevitable' conflict between capital and labour. It was believed that if international labour and capital could meet in forums with governments to design appropriate labour regulations, then international tension would be eased.

Whether the ILO has contributed to lessening international conflict is hard to gauge. But the international and national labour regulation regimes that have been put in place since the ILO was set up have more or less killed off the employment contract at will in most advanced economies.

Death of the contract at will

The death of the contract at will did not happen quickly but occurred over time as common law evolved and labour legislation was introduced. The change began under US President Roosevelt's New Deal of the Great Depression years and achieved its greatest impetus through the strengthening of the ILO immediately after the Second World War. It reached its zenith (in the USA) with the *Americans with Disabilities Act* and the *US Civil Rights Restoration Act*, passed during the 1990s.[42] Both Acts, in part, dictate hiring and firing processes and rights under employment. The trend in the United States has been replicated internationally in most developed economies.

Up until the Great Depression, the US government had refrained from involving itself in labour relations. In July 1935, the United States Congress enacted the National Labour Relations Act designed to govern the labour relations of firms involved in interstate trade. Principally, the Act sought to give employees the right to organize collectively and to engage in collective activity to further their economic interests. The essence of this and all labour regulation is that it legalized a framework in which employees could engage in anti-competitive and collusive activity for the purpose of fixing labour prices. Employment regulation is anti-competitive in that it is designed to prevent employees from competing against employees: that is, if employees in a firm remove their labour (strike) to force higher wages, other employees from outside the firm cannot replace the strikers.

Employers, by contrast, are prohibited by law from engaging in anti-competitive collusion. Employers cannot act collectively to push up their prices or prevent other employers from competing for business. The prevention of anti-competitive activity is seen as critical to the successful functioning of a free market economy and the creation of wealth. In fact, the Combines laws of the USA act strongly to break up companies that have become too big within their markets. In 2002–03, the giant Microsoft Corporation was faced with potential break-up because it was alleged to have become so dominant in its market that it was preventing other businesses from competing with it. To avoid being broken up, Microsoft agreed to change a wide-ranging raft of its business practices that allegedly were at the core of its anti-competitive, monopoly-like power.

But labour laws do the reverse. Because employees are seen as a special case due to the allegedly exploitative nature of the employment contract, employees are given a legal capacity under labour laws to create price-fixing arrangements.

The USA development reflects law that had already come into force in other countries. For example, Australia created its unique form of labour regulation early in the twentieth century. This gave employees legal and state-funded institutional frameworks in which to collude collectively to fix labour prices.

ILO

The next major step was the internationalization of labour regulation efforts through the ILO. The International Labour Organization was created in 1919 at the conclusion of the First World War. The ILO was formed with two purposes in mind. The first was to improve the conditions of workers to prevent 'injustice, hardship and privation to large numbers of people'. The second was to prevent injustices in industrialized society that could lead to 'unrest so great that the peace and harmony of the world are imperilled'. In a period of endemic warfare, the ILO was formed to try to prevent the inherent conflict (even revolution) that was seen as an inevitable outcome of the employment relationship.

The big boost to the ILO came at the same time as the USA introduced its first national labour laws. In 1934, the USA under Roosevelt joined the ILO, even though it did not belong to the League of Nations. Even while the Second World War was still in progress, the ILO met in the USA, and in 1944 representatives from 41 countries signed the Declaration of Philadelphia, an annex to the constitution of the ILO which outlines the Charter of aims and objectives of the ILO.

Along with the United Nations, the World Trade Organization, the World Bank and other international institutions, the ILO is essentially a forum that seeks to persuade countries to pursue certain policies. The purpose of each of these organizations is to overcome specific problems that were perceived to have played a causal role in the outbreak of both world wars. The United Nations offers the opportunity for constant diplomatic dialogue and resolution of conflict between nations. The World Bank was established with the aim of preventing countries being crippled by debt. The World Trade Organization was designed to prevent the trade wars that preceded and contributed to both world wars. And the ILO has as its international objective the prevention of endemic conflict between capital and labour. Naturally, in the twenty-first century, these institutions' objectives have been revised in the light of new circumstances.

The ILO operates under a constitution providing the broad parameters for policy. It holds regular international forums in which participant countries pass 'conventions' laying out principles of labour arrangements that they agree are sound. It is then for each country to decide which conventions to ratify, upon which it has a moral obligation to embody such conventions in its domestic legislation. It is these ILO conventions which most frequently form the basis of the labour law that in most countries has killed the employment contract at will and turned employment into something different from what it was in the first half of the twentieth century.

In 1998, at its 86th Session, the ILO adopted its most recent Declaration on Fundamental Principles and Rights at Work, which included 'freedom of association, effective recognition of the right to collective bargaining, elimination of all forms of forced and compulsory labour, effective abolition of child labour, and elimination of discrimination in respect of employment and occupation'.

The two conventions that have had the most impact on the employment contract at will are those for the 'elimination of discrimination in respect of employment and occupation' and for the termination of employment under recommendations 119, 158 and 166 of the ILO. These conventions have been taken up with some enthusiasm in developed countries and replicated within legislation over an extended period of time. In effect, the outcome of the application of the two conventions has been the complete destruction of the contract at will within employment. As a result, the employment contract has effectively become a signifier of job ownership. That is, once employed, employees have quasi-ownership of their 'jobs' which they cannot ultimately lose unless the state agrees. Within post-Second World War labour laws, a job has taken on the features of a quirky property right.

It works likes this. On becoming employees, individuals sell their right and capacity to control their own lives. Employers purchase from those individuals the right to control them. Since the state takes the view that this right to control systemically puts employees in an unequal, unfair and exploitable position, it intervenes to prevent exploitation. Rather than addressing the core issue of whether employees should have their self-control removed, the state has allowed employers to retain theoretical control over employees but then legally limits that control.

Through anti-discrimination and unfair dismissal laws, the state prevents employers from dismissing employees on a wide variety of grounds. State tribunals oversee the process and give all employees an automatic right to appeal to the state if employers try to dismiss them. In effect, once an individual is employed, he or she acquires part-ownership of the job in conjunction with the employer. The employee loses ownership of the job only if he or she chooses to relinquish it or the state tribunal upholds a dismissal. The general concept of fairness in the dismissal process is only a mask for a deeper economic and behavioural process imposed on people by the state.

The idea of procedural fairness in job dismissal is supposed to be an attempt by the state to create or impose acceptable behavioural norms in society. The state attempts to dictate how people should relate to each other in the work environment. But it doesn't work very well. People still behave badly toward each other, and the state tribunals seem to be playing constant catch-up. The real outcome of the destruction of the employment contract at will—as we have seen earlier—is that an employer has to purchase a job back from employee if he or she wishes to dismiss the employee.

Unfair dismissal tribunals rarely require a job to be reinstated, because they recognize that it is not possible to force people to relate in constructive ways. For the most part, the tribunals award a financial remedy to the employee from the employer. Employers have learned that such pay-outs are the most likely outcomes of dismissal disputes. This knowledge, combined with the legal cost of defending an unfair dismissal action, results in employers taking rational economic decisions and, when a dismissal occurs, an up-front pay-out is frequently offered to avoid an unfair dismissal action. In effect, the employer purchases the job from the employee. The contract at will has been finally buried.

To summarize the explanation to this point: the employment contract is a contract of control where one party, the employer has the right to control the employee. The 'controlled' employee is required at law to be loyal to the employer. In return, the employer is legally required to take responsibility for the actions of the employee. Governments around the world have found this idea of employer control to be distasteful and have created laws to manage and control the actions of the employer. In effect, the state has forced itself into the employment contract and has taken over the control mechanisms within the employment contract. What has been the outcome?

Where are we at and where are we heading?

At the turn of the twenty-first century, the employment contract has become a strange beast because its clash with several regulatory regimes has distorted human behaviour. Regulation has not changed the core nature of the employment contract. It continues to have at its centre individuals selling their right to self-control. But now the employment contract involves legislated property rights to the job being shared by employer and employee, with control of the job largely in the hands of the state. The state has imposed itself on employer and employee, and now the state has the right to control the employer who, however, continues to pretend that he or she has control over the employee. The employment contract has become a quasi-contract between three parties: the employer, the employee and the state.

The outcome is an odd balancing act in which nothing is ever what it seems. Those who are said to have control do not have it. Control has become diffused and confused. And the question must be asked: where is this all heading?

As the state continues to entrench itself deeper in the detail and operation of the employment contract, the nature of the contract is likely to undergo further fundamental change by legislative design rather than through the comparatively slow, evolutionary and discovery processes of common law. This creates dangers which are largely unaddressed. Liability transfer is at the core of these concerns, which manifest themselves in two vital areas: discrimination; and work safety and accidents. The examples of distortions discussed above highlight some of the concerns.

In most areas of the law, individuals are held responsible and liable for their actions. In the criminal area, an individual who commits the offence is held liable and prosecuted accordingly. No transfer of liability occurs. Criminal legal processes devote great resources to trying to ensure that the perpetrator of a crime is correctly identified.

Under commercial contract law, when people have genuinely entered a commercial contract (contract for services), the parties to the contract are held financially liable and responsible for the consequences of events performed under the contract. If a product is sold and found to be faulty, those who made and sold the product are held financially responsible for the fault. This connection of accountability in the commercial area to the parties who undertook an action is fundamental in the commercial contract and is crucial to economic justice.

The problem with liability transfer in the areas of anti-discrimination and anti-harassment laws is that it encourages unacceptable behaviour on the part of employees, since employers are held liable for it. In this way the moral objectives fostered by legislation are defeated by the very legal and institutional approaches that are used to achieve those objectives. As well, individuals can use the accountability avoidance mechanisms to exploit others.

Corporate criminality: A nasty vision of the future!

These distortions became clear in Australia in 2001, when the Australian Federal government amended the national criminal code to create the new offence of corporate manslaughter. The first attempt to turn the Code into a legislative form occurred in Victoria in 2002 but, fortunately, was defeated. It was turned into law in the Australian Capital Territory in 2003—and is probably a world first.

The detail of the attempted Victorian legislation shows how the work safety regulators who designed and proposed the legislation misunderstood to a dangerous degree the nature of firms and the role of employment and employment liability transfer.

The Victorian Bill sought to amend the *Victorian Crimes Act* to create a new and additional offence of manslaughter by a corporation. Under the Bill, a corporation would have become criminally liable for the actions or omissions of its employees and agents. Specific individuals (senior officers) were targeted to become personally liable and to be jailed for up to seven years for the criminal actions of a corporation, even where those individuals were not personally involved in causing a death or injury.

The Bill sought to assign criminality to a corporate 'system.' Once the corporate system had been found to have committed a criminal act, individual 'senior officers' within the system could be sentenced on behalf of the system. This idea of a system being capable of a criminal act conceptually relies on the transfer of liability under employment from one party to another. The idea is that employees do not manage themselves but act according to the dictates of the system under which they work. When a work-related death occurs, the fault does not lie with the individuals who work in the system, but rather with the system itself, and the people who go to jail are the people who design or control the system (senior officers).

The close tie to employment could clearly be seen because the offence involved death or injury only to individuals *paid* by a corporation. It excluded individuals who were unpaid volunteers working for the corporation.

Government was to be exempt. The Bill held publicly-owned corporations to be criminally liable but it exempted the state and senior officers of the state from liability. The Bill applied a different measure of criminal liability to the managers and directors of a corporation from that applied to the managers and ministers of the state of Victoria or the Commonwealth. For example managers of the federal government owned corporation, Australia Post, would have been held liable, but managers of the public service-structured environment departments would not be liable.

Having untied criminality from individual actions, and made 'systems' capable of committing offences, the Bill proceeded to apply more contorted logic. It proceeded to apply criminal liability through a chain of commercial contracts. The Bill held a corporation criminally liable for the actions of an agent of an agent of an agent and so on. Under commercial law, firms regularly outsource functions and have other companies do work for them, purchasing the end product or service. The entering of a commercial contract with another party never involves the buyer of a service or good assuming the criminal (or financial) liability for something that may go wrong in the seller's internal operations. Yet the Corporate Manslaughter Bill sought to do just that. It made a corporation that purchased goods or services potentially criminally liable if a death occurred at a work site of the seller of the goods or services. And this process of criminal liability transfer could cascade all the way along a chain of contracts.

The idea of 'systems' being capable of criminality was tied to the idea of 'aggregate' behaviour. The Bill stipulated that the behaviour of a single employee was not to be attributed to a corporation, but the behaviour of all employees, even if in breach of written instructions, became the behaviour of the corporation, upon which it was capable of criminal action. 'Aggregating' reinforced the pivotal idea in the Bill that a corporate culture and its control systems were the cause of criminality.

By holding that a corporate culture could be capable of a criminal act, the Bill created a highly dangerous precedent whereby any culture could be seen to be criminally capable. Throughout history, individuals seeking power for themselves have sought to blame ethnic groups, specific cultures or religions on a collective basis for allegedly wicked acts. The alleged evils committed by collectives have been invoked to justify the wholesale slaughter of such collectives. The victims have been members of many races, religions, and classes. The defeat of the idea that collectives can be held culpable for wrongdoing has been a major step in humanity's march from barbarism to civilization.

The proposed Victorian Corporate Manslaughter Bill did no more than seek to translate into working legislation the principles of the Corporate Manslaughter Criminal Code which is contained within Australian Federal legislation but which, as a code, has no effect until translated into legislation. But the principle of collective criminality which has been recognized in Australia is able to take legislative form. The Victorian Bill was a world 'first'. The ground-breaking attempt happened in a country with a supposedly sophisticated understanding of the law and of economics and justice. It gives an indication of how the continuing trend within labour regulation has developed dangerously distorted concepts.

The trend reflects the distorted view of the world that results from an incapacity either to recognize, accept or cope with the liability transference aspect of employment.

At the beginning of the twenty-first century, the law and regulation of employment is drifting dangerously, with little thought as to the damage being done to the human quest for freedom, justice, and harmony. It is being driven by a blind obsession with enforcing certain social objectives, regardless of the damage being done to those same objectives by the very policy being pushed. It is driven by an obsessive conviction that the form of economic organization made possible by the commercial contract is and must always be exploitative. It is thereby based on a wilful devotion to a fiction.

EMPLOYMENT CONTRACT
At will

I...(write your name here)

of...(write your address here)

agree to become to become employed with
.... (write your employer's name here)
under the terms of the common-law employment contract at will.

I understand and agree that as a consequence of becoming employed I shall be paid certain monies to be established from time to time and that in return for those monies I understand and agree that during the period or hours of employment I:

- Shall refrain from expressing views or opinions that may not be in accord with the views of my employer.
- Shall not be idle and shall place my energy, thought and being at the disposal of my employer to be used by my employer at his/her discretion, direction and authority.
- Shall not make use of any information discovered when employed, for the purposes of competing with my employer for personal profit or the profit of another person.

I further understand that my employer or I can at any time and without any cause, reason or justification, terminate this employment contract without duress or redress other than the securing of monies owed for work completed under this employment contract.

.... (sign your name or place your mark here)

....(put the date here)

Endnotes

1. *The Living Webster Encyclopedic Dictionary of the English Language*, The English-Language Institute of America, Chicago, 1971.
2. *Deutz Australia Pty Ltd* v. *Skilled Engineering and Anor* [2001] VSC 194 (25 June 2001) Supreme Court of Victoria.
3. *Hollis* v. *Vabu Pty Ltd* [2001] High Court of Australia HCA 44. 9 August 2001 S149/2000.
4. *Evenco P/L* v. *Australian Building Construction Employees and Builders Labourers Federation and others.* Appeal Nos 3536 of 1999 and 3610 of 1999 SC No 1794 of 1988 and SC 4843 of 1986. Supreme Court of Queensland 4 April 2000. (Hereafter, Evenco.)
5. Evenco at 5.
6. Evenco at 6.
7. Evenco at 25.
8. Evenco at 27 and 30.
9. Evenco at 36.
10. *Digital Pulse Pty Limited* v. *Christopher Harris and Ors* [2002] New South Wales Supreme Court NSWSC 33. File number SC 50032/00. (Hereafter Digital.)
11. Digital at 1.
12. Digital at 20.
13. *Webster's Dictionary.*
14. Digital at 22 and 24.
15. Digital at 34.
16. Digital at 128 and 134.
17. *The Age*, 11 January 1997.
18. Walter K. Olson, *The Excuse Factory*, Martin Kessler Books, 1997, pages 235 and 282.
19. *Ibid.*, page 192.
20. *Ibid.*, pages 17 and 193.
21. *The Australian*, 29 January 2001.
22. *Burton* v. *Telstra.* Australian Industrial Relations Commission. Print R4998.
23. *Debono* v. *Trans Adelaide.* Australian Industrial Relations Commission 1999.
24. Print S0242 18 October 1999 AIRC.
25. *Gray* v. *The State of Victoria and Pettman.* Victorian Civil and Administrative Tribunal 9 June 1999.
26. Queensland Anti-Discrimination Tribunal. No H25/95 29 January 1997.
27. *Hopper* v. *Mt Isa Mines & Ors.* Queensland Industrial Relations Commission No 1221 of 2001, 11 April 2002.
28. *Shaikh* v. *Ian Campbell & Nivona Pty Ltd* Human Rights and Equal Opportunity Commission. No. 97/253.
29. Queensland Industrial Relations Commission. C42 of 1999. 20 September 1999.
30. Olson, *op. cit.*, page 268.

31. *Ibid.*, page 216.
32. *Australian Financial Review*, 22 October 1999.
33. *The Australian*, 21 March 1997.
34. *Australian Financial Review*, 22 December 1998.
35. *Australian Financial Review*, 6 July 2001; NSW IRC in Court Session 1829 of 1998.
36. *Australian Financial Review*, 5 December 1996.
37. Olson, *op. cit.*, page 240.
38. *Stevens* v. *Brodribb Sawmilling Co Pty Ltd* 1986 160 CLR16.
39. *Odco Pty Ltd* v. *BWIU* No VG 151 of 1988.
40. Olson, *op. cit.*, page 32.
41. See the ILO Website: www.ilo.org
42. Olson, *op. cit., pages 6–8.*

5: To Work We Go; To War We Go: The Firm

'A ruler will perish if he is good; he must be as cunning as a fox and as fierce as a lion.'

— Niccolo Machiavelli.[1]

Every day, people in advanced economic societies go to 'work' in firms. The dominant psychology inside firms is one of war; firms are conceived as empires at war with other empires in a winner-takes-all and loser-faces-disaster situation. This is the traditional view of how economies operate, how firms function in economies, and why it is thought that people who work inside firms must be subservient, controlled employees. It is thought that the firm will be vulnerable to attack from other, stronger firms unless internal control is maintained. This is the legacy of Rome.

We can all recognize a firm when we see one. But to define one is considerably more difficult. A firm can be a one-person operation or it can involve hundreds of thousands of people. It can have a corporate structure or be a partnership or a trust. It can be owned by shareholders, or a church, or a government, or a benevolent institution. It usually needs to make a profit to survive, but can often last for long periods of time even when it makes losses. It can hand its profit over to private owners or allow all profit to be ploughed back into its own growth; or it can exist for the purposes of donating to charity. A firm can be poverty-stricken or have more wealth than many individual nation-states. It can be a happy and rewarding place or soul-destroying or anything in between. But what is it?

When all else is stripped away, a firm is an organized set of human interactions directed towards the achievement of an economic or organizational outcome. The firm is most commonly thought of as the product of the owner or leader who directs it. The people who work in it are thought of as instruments of the leader.

In advanced societies, the law has come to play an essential part in the definition of a firm because firms are taxed, are subject to vast quantities of regulation, and have social expectations thrust upon them. They can often seem to operate in isolation from society, but are in fact among the most important elements in a society.

At one stage, firms were almost exclusively an extension of the family unit. Firms as corporations, as we now commonly think of them, are a comparatively new human experience dating back only 150 years. In Britain, 'until the Joint Stock Company Act of 1856 legalized limited liability, corporate enterprise was a rare form of organization. Incorporation required parliamentary sanction ... [and] it was rare for the entrepreneur to go to the trouble and expense of securing an Act of Parliament ... the characteristic unit of production was the family firm'.[2]

For most of the twentieth century (and now in the twenty-first century) firms have by and large been thought of as command-and-control structures. Although this concept is beginning to change, it still holds. The idea of the firm as a control structure has it roots in the paternal benevolence of the family unit and the idea of the nation-state headed by benevolent leaders.

The idea of the benevolent leader/ruler has additional resonance in the way firms usually begin, develop and grow. The idea of an entrepreneurial firm is of one created by a single person who identifies a need in a market, satisfies that need, becomes successful and expands the organization. The founding individual is thought to provide the driving force, but other people (employees) help manage the firm and so enable a system to develop and the firm to grow. Conceptually, the firm is taken to be the embodiment of the single entrepreneur's vision, creativity, drive and market success.

This understandable way of thinking holds that people working in the firm are (and need to be) subservient to the needs and wishes of the person at the top. After all, if the originator of the business was so adept at understanding the market and thus created the firm, surely the continuing success of the business is dependent on the same genius of the creator. This idea holds for government and charitable organizations too. The state perceives of a need, say, for welfare provision to the poor. A government-owned-and-funded organization is formed to create and deliver the service and is led by an appointed head. Or a church or charitable organization may fill the void. The driving vision is that of the state or the head of the church. The people who run the organization are seen to need to adhere to the dictates of the visionary at the top.

As a firm grows and takes on more and more employees, formal structures are developed to ensure that the originator's genius continues to drive the organization. The people working in the firm are seen (and see themselves) as dependent on the originator for their livelihood. Most people in the firm do not have the task of interacting with markets or replicating or competing with the genius of the originator, but must of necessity confine themselves to the organizational need to keep the firm's structure in place.

Firms typically go through several phases in this process.

The originator will operate on his or her own, with perhaps one or two other people, most often family members. Organizational issues and decisions relating to servicing the market are made by the originator—on the run, quickly and in reaction to changing market needs. And the firm may become no larger.

Or, as growth occurs and the number of people employed expands, the originator will gather around him or her a trusted coterie of people who become skilled in sharing the originator's vision and drive. Often, these will be family and/or close friends who work together in a bonded and trusting relationship. The trusted coterie works in a team; the human interactions are close and personal. Each member of the coterie gets to know and understand the others. All eyes are fixed on the originator, who exerts a pervasive guiding influence over the others. When successful, the coterie begins to think as one, in harmony with the spirit of the originator. To be successful, care is taken to ensure that the rewards attained by the developing organization are shared between the members of the coterie. Or, if the rewards are not immediate, a share of future rewards is structured into the employment arrangements. The proviso is that each person in the coterie can achieve a much larger income than if he or she were a salaried employee. This is the birth of inner management—people who exercise decisions over the company and share in its successes.

With the input of the managerial coterie a much larger business can be created and managed. More employees can be taken on. These employees continue to be thought of as operational instruments and not as essential to the capacity of the firm to succeed in the marketplace. The employees are paid considerably less than the members of the management coterie because their capacities are taken to be ancillary to the primary task of dealing with the market. In this familiar paradigm, workers are seen as controlled employees.

War between management and workers is thus born, because workers feel that they must fight to push up their remuneration. Management, ever mindful of the limitations and vagaries of the marketplace, wants to contain the operational costs. Personal communication between management and workers becomes more complex than when the firm was smaller and more intimate. When this stage has been reached, it's not that people have changed, but rather that the group dynamics have ceased to be personal and have become more crowd-like. Workplace relationships are no longer personal, intimate and family-like. The firm has become too big for this. Employees are simply cogs in a large organizational machine.

The small firm has now become a corporation. It needs organizational processes that manage, massage and formally control the organization itself. Additional people are employed whose entire task is to focus on the internal operation of the organization and hold it together. These people do not interact with the market but form a new level of the managerial class. They are decision-makers, but their remuneration is not tied to a share of the firm's success. They are wage-bonded managerial decision makers. They are like the white corpuscles that run through the bloodstream of the organization, repairing damage before it becomes too great, keeping organs in check and ensuring smooth running of the organization. They do not deal directly with the market, but ensure the smooth operation of the organization so that the market-oriented managers can do their job. The processes become highly formal and usually rigid.

If the originator of the firm is still alive and actively involved in the business, he or she can retain firm direction of the corporation. If the originator has died or moved on, the mantle of control and interaction with markets may have been handed to a blood heir, well trained and skilled in the vision and drive of the originator. Or the mantle may have been handed to a non-blood heir who is as skilled, trusted and capable as the originator—or so it is hoped. The originator or others in the upper coterie may have decided to cash in the latent financial value of the corporation and sell their shares, and may no longer be associated with the firm.

The listed corporation has been born. The corporation may now be owned by thousands of individuals, either directly or through superannuation funds, investment houses or a multiplicity of different entities. A pure form of communism has been created in which no-one owns the whole and in which ownership is available to anyone who wants to become involved and can afford the entry price. Still, a coterie of market-interacting and organizational control managers remains, whose importance is now vastly greater than when the founder was actively involved in the business. The non-operational owners are totally dependent on the specialist manager coterie for the delivery of trading profit. The only real sanction the owners have against poor corporate performance is to sell their shares. The shareholders may have the legal capacity to sack the board of directors but this is a logistically complex task only successfully undertaken when the corporation is in crisis.

The human dynamics within the listed corporation are now largely removed from any interaction with the market place. The employment bureaucracy has been born. Internal politics and individual situational need become the primary human dynamic that pervades the organization. People inside the organization know that the market is there, and know the total business is dependent on the market, but the bigger picture is so removed from their daily lives as to frequently disappear from view. People have a job description, mostly determined by a bureaucracy into which they may have a limited input. They do their job, fulfil their tasks, take pride in their achievements, are paid and have an income that enables them to lead a private life that may or may not involve others who work in the firm.

This employment bureaucracy also dominates public sector activity. Here the owners are even more removed from operations than in the share-owned corporation. It is the ultimate communist model. In a democracy, the public sector firm is owned by the total social collective. Control is exercised along lengthy procedural lines. Every now and then, voters elect persons who form a government. The government has control over the bureaucracy. The operation of the bureaucracy is the result of a complex interchange between the senior levels of the bureaucracy pushing agendas, public and private pressure for agendas, parameters imposed by legal principles and judicial interpretations, and formal policy dictates from the elected government. The market that the public sector bureaucracy is supposed to be serving often disappears from the field of vision in this complex mix of pressures. The people working in the public sector bureaucracy often become completely lost in a maelstrom of frustration. Their formal tasks seem to encompass the beginning and end of a process but without an identifiable higher purpose. They have little if any personal stake in the organization's fulfilment of its charter. Bureaucrats' success is measured by their capacity to advance up the career ladder structure to higher pay levels. It is why unionism levels in the public sector are usually much higher than in the private sector. Unions provide public sector employees with a countervailing force against the dominance of the government bureaucracy.

Ultimately, this idea of the firm as a bureaucracy is carried through to the police and armed services. Here, the focus on a market is totally lost. The owners of the corporation, the general public, are less important than the corporation itself. The system of government takes priority. The objective of the police is to ensure that the system is maintained. Police will protect individuals from other individuals, but will protect the state in preference to the individual. The objective of the armed forces is to protect the system—the nation state—from external assault. People working in the police or armed services find that the 'market' they serve is difficult to identify and isolate. These people are required primarily to understand the bureaucratic system, what it allows, not to question it, and to respond without question within a command-and-control framework. It is a system that necessitates the subordination of individual creativity and freedom of action to the constraints and dictates of the system.

There is nothing new in this picture and nothing sinister. It is simply the way societies have developed. It is also very successful. Any person who has worked at any of the levels described will recognize the core elements. The primary thread running through all of these descriptions of various levels of the firm during the twentieth century is that of command and control. In short, human organization requires the creation of reliable chains of command in which all people in the chain respond appropriately and reliably to the commands they are given.

This command-and-control process is a natural human inclination. It is the current development of the burning vision of Rome, but is not limited to societies historically steeped in the Roman tradition. Most people have ultimate faith in their own capacities, and if they make a decision they want to see that decision carried out in the way that delivers the best results from their point of view. Alternatively, where people lack faith in their own capacities, they may feel inclined to rely on the evident self-assuredness of someone else.

Further, this idea of the firm being dependent on command-and-control structures has been developed in highly formal expressions that have influenced the thinking of legislatures, regulators and business strategists.

Take two important and influential writers on the subject during the twentieth century — Ronald Coase and Elliot Jaques. Neither is a household name, but both exercised considerable influence over the formal concepts and approaches to the firm, particularly in the second half of the twentieth century.

Coase

Ronald Coase is an economist who is primarily interested in how markets operate. He wrote some of his most influential works around the middle of the twentieth century. The study of markets is principally the study of how people behave in their purchasing choices. One of Coase's significant contributions was his explanation of transaction costs. That is, that for every buying and selling decision that people make, there is a cost for undertaking the transaction that must be factored into the price.

In a simple example, buying an apple from a shop involves more than the cost of the apple. In the process of paying for the apple, we must pay for the time of the shopkeeper to undertake the transaction. In a more involved example, the process of buying shares on the stock market involves not only paying for the time of the stockbroker who arranges the transaction, but also covering the costs of the legislative and legal and regulatory environments that enable the transaction to take place.

Coase drew attention to the fact that, if transaction costs were too high, then transactions would not take place. And transaction costs are something we tend not to put a value on when we should. If, for example, every time shares were sold on the stock exchange the buyer and seller of the shares had to personally meet, sign documents, and lodge the documents with a registrar who took 30 days to record the transaction, few shares would be sold. If you were the buyer, the cost in your own time of meeting the seller and the delay in registration would probably dampen your desire to buy shares. You would trade in fewer shares than otherwise. The high cost of share-trading to you would not be recorded anywhere because you would not choose to trade. The opportunity for share-trading would be lost and never known.

Coase's contribution to understanding how humans behave was to establish that we all put value on our time and effort in a way that affects our decisions in life. Further, Coase observed and commented on how we organize ourselves to minimize these transaction costs. This is the significance of firms, according to Coase. Firms are a form of human organization that enables us to undertake complex transactions in a way that keeps transaction costs within affordable levels. He argued that the key ingredient in the organization of firms is command and control. More precisely, he identified in the legal form of employment, the right of one person to control another, the key ingredient that facilitated command and control.

Coase said:

> We can best approach the question of what constitutes a firm in practice
> ... by considering the legal relationship normally called that of master
> and servant or employer and employee ... The master must have the
> right to control the servant's work. We can thus see that it is the fact
> of direction which is the essence of the legal concept of employer and
> employee just as it was in the economic concept (of the firm) which
> was developed above.[3]

In short, the firm could not exist without the controlling elements of employment.

Coase made this observation in 1937. He had spent several years touring the industrial heartland of the USA researching the transaction cost idea by talking to business people and asking how they organized their firms and what affected their decisions.

Coase's observations may have been accurate in the 1930s and perhaps continue to reflect how most firms operate. Command and control is a natural product of human inclination. But Coase's observations were more than simply observations of reality. Coase's explanation has reinforced practice and has had a profound influence on what economists, managers and most people conceive to be firms. Further, Coase influenced how markets are conceived, that is, as competing and interacting firms seeking to appeal to the whims of consumers.

Late into the twentieth century and into the beginning of the twenty-first, the dominant conception of a firm continues to be that of an organization structured around command and control of employees by employers. This understanding of firms dominates the way we think about markets, in which command-and-control firms contain transaction costs, firms both interact and compete, and consumers make purchases from competing firms.

This idea of firms as solid command-and-control structures is developed in a more complete way by the author and management consultant Elliot Jaques.

Jaques

Jaques was a USA-based management consultant and a psychoanalyst by training and background. Jaques has an impressive history as a researcher in organizational forms and published several important works during the late 1970s and early 1980s. His real impact has been effected through his consultancies to large, multi-national companies, many of which significantly re-evaluated their internal controlling structures as a result.

In Australia, Jaques consulted to the mining giant CRA during the 1980s. CRA took Jaques's views and philosophies on board and adapted them to CRA's circumstances. The process resulted in a watershed change in approaches to workplace relations and the organizational structure of CRA which, on implementation, helped turn CRA into one of the most successful and largest mining companies in Australia. In the 1990s, CRA merged with the London-based mining company Rio Tinto in what proved to be an Australian management takeover. Rio Tinto is now one of the world's three largest mining conglomerates. Jaques's management philosophies had a pervasive influence on how Rio operates. Further, hundreds of students of Jaques's principles who worked in management in the Australian arm of Rio have left Rio over the last two decades to take up senior positions in mining and other companies and in the public sector across Australia. The management principles promoted by Jaques have had significant influence not only in Australia but also internationally in certain corporations.

Jaques's core proposition is the superiority of the employment bureaucracy as the model for the internal structures of firms in industrialized societies. That is, the legal form of the employment contract is a most effective tool for the management of industrial activity, and the bureaucracy built around the employment contract is the most significant ingredient in a successful firm. In essence, Jaques is interested in the employment model of 'control' as the basis around which to structure a firm. He studies the control system of employment and recommends a highly rigid process through which control can be effectively organized, thereby delivering success to the firm and a sense of purpose, place and reward to the individuals working in the firm. He points out, however, that his model does not apply to the small business sector and he remarks that he has found it difficult to apply the principles in the academic sector.

Jaques is critical of bureaucracy that is mindless and inefficient. His interest is in the process of designing and implementing a successful employment bureaucracy. His theorem is that every job has a 'time span' in which the person doing the task thinks, plans and executes the job. A factory process worker will have a time span of, say, one week, the works foreman, say, one month, and the executive director, say, five years. Jaques reasons that this time span for each job is scientifically measurable and its measurement will determine the exact number of bureaucratic levels required in any given enterprise. When the firm is structured around the required bureaucratic levels, it will have achieved its perfect form. It will not function properly if it has more or fewer levels than those prescribed by the time-span analysis.

Jaques proposes that achieving the perfect bureaucratic form makes possible a fair distribution of wages and salaries and of socioeconomic status for all employees. Fair enterprises[4] can be designed and implemented, he says. He rejects any idea that employee remuneration can be set according to the principles of supply and demand, and he claims that studies have proved that a free market for labour inside the employment bureaucracy is disruptive of the perfect form of the firm.

Further, Jaques argues that the employment bureaucracy can give workers a sense of purpose and place in society. He reasons that, at each level in the employment bureaucracy, fair and equitable levels of pay can be achieved and can be proven to be so. He calls this 'fair felt pay'. It is the level of pay that a person can achieve in the employment bureaucracy that is commensurate with any other person who is performing similar work at the same level in the bureaucracy. As long as these differentials are maintained, every person in the organization will feel that he or she is being treated fairly, thus achieving harmony within the bureaucracy. It is only when people in the bureaucracy seek to upset the 'felt fair pay' differentials that problems arise.

It was perhaps not surprising that Jaques had significant influence in Australia because his perfect form of the employment bureaucracy matched closely that of the peculiarly Australian system of controlling wages and work conditions throughout the entire Australian economy. In 1904, Australia imposed on itself a complex system of wage regulation that can best be described as a nationalized version of the Jaques 'felt fair pay' principles. It exists to the present day in 2005. Australia has quasi-courts that seek to establish measures of wage relativity across an entire spectrum of job and task descriptions. Presumably, the imposition of these 'fair' wage differentials and structures achieves harmony within the working population of Australia and strengthens social cohesion. Through their industrial relations institutions, Australians have, like Jaques, rejected the idea that wages and incomes can be set according to the principles of demand and supply.

These ideas of the firm as a rigidly structured command system have become institutionalized, not just within firms but within nations as well. In Australia, for example, the micro form of the alleged perfect firm has been replicated in the macro form of the nation's labour-regulating institutions. In effect, these national structures impose on firms their managerial form.

Loyalty

The dominant idea of the firm not only has these legal and managerial control elements but also psychological elements that are just as important and command-and-control orientated.

Nations have always expected and demanded loyalty—it is both morally esteemed and deemed worthy of reward. Disloyalty has resulted in social exile and sometimes in execution. But far from being a good, loyalty is most often a tool used by the cunning to entice the unwitting to surrender power. The psychology of loyalty is the psychology of subservience to command and control. It is the process by which people are seduced into accepting their place within a class-based social structure, where they willingly give up control of their own destiny to someone else.

As in nations, in the modern business environment loyalty has been a dominant operational imperative thought necessary for success. Loyalty is so psychologically ingrained that it is considered to be a key element of the glue that holds a firm together.

The idea of loyalty has its roots in the blood, mud, death and comradeship of the battlefields of every war since the birth of modern civilization in ancient Greece. Wherever a nation has existed, loyalty has been demanded. It has been accepted that, without loyalty, a nation could not survive external assault. It is not surprising, then, that loyalty should be a modern business catch-cry, because for the first 70 years of the twentieth century the business of conducting business was dominated by men whose approaches had been moulded by the experiences and demands of war.

Business in market economies has largely been seen as a war involving winners and losers. Loyalty has offered a prime conceptual framework for managing the firm for competitive war. The principal structure adopted has been that of class. Firms would invite people in and people would apply to become part of the firm. Individuals would be assessed for skills and abilities and slotted into formal, rigid class structures inside the firm. Incomes, status and decision-making prerogatives were all determined by the class structure.

This idea of micro class structures in firms, based on qualifications and acquired formal skills, replaced ideas of macro class structures operating across a society built on inherited position. The twentieth-century firm has been a scientific, sophisticated version of the traditional class system through which the lord of the manor managed his estate in medieval England. But in business, your position in life is not determined by birth, but by which part of the firm's hierarchy you are assigned to. The better-known class structures of old have became hidden within the class structures of the firm.

Within this class structure a simple set of unwritten rules applied that were meant to operate for the mutual benefit of the firm's members. The demands on the individual were simple: do the tasks allotted to you and above all conform to the hierarchical structures of the firm. In short, be loyal to the firm above all other considerations.

An individual's willing conformity or loyalty has often been more highly prized than success at allotted tasks. After all, mistakes at work can usually be corrected by other employees. And the firm's selection processes were surely so good that hiring inappropriate individuals could hardly ever happen! If an individual failed consistently over time, he or she could be reallocated to more suitable tasks. The system would protect the individual from occasional lapses, but was not itself threatened by individual task failure.

By contrast, lack of loyalty was cancerous and threatened to bring down the edifice. Exposing weaknesses inside the firm or questioning its hierarchical structures threatened the entire system. So, in return for loyalty, the firm would provide the employee with protection from the harsh realities of the war that was conducted daily between firms. The loyalty pay-off included financial security, longevity of engagement, security in retirement and a sense of place and purpose in the firm's class structure.

This dominant management model has been highly successful. Great industrial monoliths, larger than many nations, have been created. The principles of command and control, dependent as they are on loyalty-driven mindsets, have enabled spectacular and complex organizations to emerge, contributing to a twentieth-century explosion of material well-being.

But loyalty has never been solid. The trashing of corporations that began in the 1980s, with mergers, acquisitions, and downsizing, has sent the clear and unforgiving message that firms can and will be loyal to individuals only while it suits their purposes. In reality this has always been the case. Firms can be loyal to employees only while economic circumstances enable them to afford it: a lesson learnt by the Great Depression generation. When a business goes broke, that's the end of the loyalty pact!

Loyalty has always been sold to employees as a positive. But it has always had sizeable, never-to-be-mentioned personal downsides. Loyalty has always required the willing sacrifice of the employee's sense of, and desire for, freedom to the higher demands of the organization. Nothing is more completely lost than that which is willingly discarded. Liberty thrown away creates a gaping, unresolved emptiness in the individual's heart. In this environment, loyalty generates a culture of silence, fear, transference of blame and gouging of personal integrity. For example, most people feel uneasy when the system requires them to ignore corruption. Most people chafe at the limitations on their ambitions that the corporate hierarchy imposes on them. Ultimately, the loyalty system creates a culture of subservience to the whims, egos and personal ambitions of the corporate elite. Such a culture makes it impossible for an organization to realize the greatest combined potential of its personnel.

Above all, the loyalty thought necessary to a firm's performance has acted to dull performance by suppressing accountability. When loyalty is demanded, accountability becomes diffused and lost. All the signals in the loyalty-driven organization say 'the buck stops somewhere else'. Accountability that has been diminished by loyalty causes errors, corruption, and general underperformance that has to be absorbed and accepted. Loyalty causes the firm's systems to be corrupted and incapable of solving internal problems.

Systems cannot fix problems. Only the people in systems can do that. Demands for loyalty suppress people who would otherwise keep the organization operationally active, intact, alert and reactive to problems. A huge amount of informal conversation revolves around problems at work caused by people higher up on the firm's status ladder but which can't be brought to their attention.

The negatives of loyalty produce a major psychological dysfunction. As loyalty limits ambition and demands conformity to class structures inside firms, frustration emerges as a dominant but suppressed human emotion. As long as people are prepared to accommodate frustration, loyalty can survive. But generations moulded by peace have low tolerance levels of frustration. People want more. They want to explore the inner self, to find the thing that drives them, to risk and to create. They are less accepting of failure and negative behaviours in those around them. In short, the peace generations have become entrepreneurial and, as entrepreneurs, people find pathways to greater financial success and personal satisfaction.

In management thinking, loyalty has achieved a quasi-divine status. To challenge loyalty is to risk bringing down the wrath of the high priests of social and business engineering. Yet loyalty has an undeservedly good reputation. Its negatives have become apparent and are increasingly being rejected. The outcome can be maturity in the personal relationships operating inside firms, a maturity that promises greater dignity for people and improved performance for organizations themselves.

And this idea of the individual worker being controlled by the system of employment within the firm, of the firm creating and determining an individual's place in society, and of the firm needing loyalty and the individual giving it has had much of its justification in the belief that this is what the worker wants. One commentator said 'The organisation transports us ... We do not have to think for ourselves if we do not wish, and most of the time this is a comfort ... most of the time we love it'.[5] But others recognize the damage that this idea and structure of the firm inflicts. 'We have pictured two broad problems; the first arising from an individual's consuming desire to "belong" and his surrender of individuality to the organisation... The second arising from the way the organisation manages to defeat both the individual who runs it and the individual who works within it.'[6]

The myth of the employer

We have seen that the concept of a firm is taken to hinge around the legal right of the employer to control the employee. The employer is the embodiment of the firm. However, the idea of the employer, except in small businesses, is a figment of our collective and legal imaginations.

In most business situations, 'the employer' is most often a complex process of control of employees by other employees: employees who have been given the delegated authority of the legal construct of the employer.

This is a twist on the normal thinking about an employer but it is a fact that is seldom, if ever, addressed and will be explained further below. As with the king who had no clothes, as a society we fool ourselves into believing that the firm is a dynamic of employer–employee control. Employer–employee control is, in fact, most frequently a psychological and legal smokescreen that masks from our perception the true nature of the human work dynamic. In reality, employment control within a firm is control by one class of employees—the delegated employees called managers—over other classes of employees who do not exercise control, not even over themselves.

Losing control: A case scenario

The smokescreen happens like this. A person starts a business by identifying a market need, organizing finance, production, the workers and so on. She works hard. She makes a profit from the enterprise, but then realizes something. The business is financed entirely from borrowings. Machinery has been obtained on lease. Raw materials have been obtained on credit. Products are sold but credit must be provided to buyers, and bad debt exposure is now a possibility. If a worker is injured, the businesswoman will be up for costs and held accountable and financially liable. If product does not meet standards or, worse still, goes rotten and a customer is poisoned, the entrepreneur can be sued and even held criminally liable. Sure, there is profit, but it is not that great after all the negative possibilities are taken into account. The entrepreneur is not some industrial giant but an ordinary person with the full complement of human frailties. She has a family to care for and a mortgage on her house. So she has a chat with her friendly legal adviser.

The legal advice is, of course, to create a legal structure that protects the businesswoman's private assets from the commercial risk involved in the firm. A proprietary limited company is formed that takes control and ownership of the business. The entrepreneur is now a director of the company and may even be paid to work as an employee of the company. The proprietary limited company is at law a legal person. It has now become the employer. The employer is now not a physical person but a legal entity. The human relations charade has begun!

Now, employees of the firm are legally subject to the control of an employer that does not have a human form. Rather, it is a legal construct that is controlled by the entrepreneur. By this time the company has grown. One hundred and fifty people now work in the organization. The family that owns the business feels that the closeness of the personal relationships that the entrepreneur once had with the workers is beginning to diminish. It has become difficult to know and relate to large numbers of people. The entrepreneur now needs a management team. It is formed. One person looks after marketing and sales. Another is in charge of production. Another looks after relations with workers. The entrepreneur finds that the direct control she once had over the firm is rapidly disappearing. Now the firm has a life of its own. In the human sense, the firm is no longer an instrument of the founding entrepreneur but a product of a management class that creates and responds to a vast array of influences. The legal control of the employer (now the proprietary limited company) is exercised through the employees who are on the management team. The management employees exercise employer prerogatives over other employees. A general manager might be in place who acts entrepreneurially.

The original entrepreneur senses that it is time to move on, to spend more time on the golf course and with the grandchildren. A return trip to the solicitor occurs, but this time with the accountant as well.

The accountant and solicitor both advise their client to reap the latent un-cashed profit in the business and go public. The company is floated on the stock exchange and shares sold to the public. The entrepreneur retains 40 per cent of the shareholding but has made a windfall profit and could easily retire. Free shares were distributed to the accountant, solicitor and general manager—who have also done very nicely. The entrepreneur, however, is now largely removed from the day-to-day operations. One of her adult children works in the company as the marketing manager and is being groomed for the top job. Another adult child has disappeared overseas backpacking who knows where. The third child has started an Internet company using his or her share of the proceeds from the company float.

The funeral of the founder is a celebration of a productive life. The workers are advised in a memo that the 'boss' of the firm has passed away and will be missed by all. Further down the memo, workers are advised of the latest progress of the hourly pay-rate negotiations. The human relations legacy is an interesting one. The original employer in human form no longer exists. The employer is a legal entity owned by large numbers of disparate shareholders whose only concern is the share price and the dividend payments. If the company goes broke, the shareholders lose the value of their shares but are not held liable for the accumulated debts of the company. Banks, creditors and others who have loaned money to the company are the main financial losers. It is the company that has a duty of care to its workers, not any individual person. The company is no longer human but has become a system. The 'employer' does not exist as a human but is instead a management process involving many people. The relationship between employer and employee has become a conceptual phantom and a legal concept around which a vast amount of social and economic regulation has been written. But it is mostly a sham, because the employer–employee relationship is a complex process of formalized class structures inside the firm where the relationships are exclusively those of employee–employee. But if you work in a firm, don't dare say this in a management meeting, because you will immediately become targeted as a threat to the class structure. It is a truth that is not allowed to be spoken.

Accountability
But the implications of this control structure based around employment and class are not all positive. Sure, the employment-control firm has long been a successful model for the organizational conduct of a firm. But the class structures and the isolation and 'protection' of the individual in the firm from the dictates of the external market systemically destroy accountability. And with the loss of accountability the firm becomes vulnerable to systemic and institutionalized incompetence and corruption. This is constrained only by the morals, integrity and competence of each individual person working in the firm. Employment control, as a model for the firm, is a systemic breeding ground for low forms of human behaviour, particularly corruption and theft.

The loss and eventual destruction of accountability works like this. Employees in a firm are paid at an hourly, weekly or monthly rate. The firm assumes entrepreneurial risk and reaps the rewards or suffers the losses. The employee is protected by the firm from the harsh realities of the marketplace because the employee earns money but does not face the risk of losses. Employees act in good faith to the best of their ability, but if they make an error of judgement the firm will assume responsibility for the error. The most an employee could normally suffer as a result of error is lack of promotion, transfer to another job, or, if serious, dismissal from the firm. The employee is protected from the full consequences of his error. The control systems in a firm are supposed to ensure that, if the employee commits an error but stays within the instructions of the control system, then it is the system that is at fault and not the employee. The employers (the managerial class of employees) are responsible for designing the control systems in a firm. The firm acts as a collective to protect the individual—including the managers—from individual error. It's a parallel concept to the idea of the nation.

Nations primarily exist, so it is thought, to protect the individuals inside the nation from external threat. Markets are assumed to threaten the individual and so the firm exists to protect the individual from markets. But nations and firms can protect the people only if individuals accept that they will be controlled. And protection of the individual from accountability is one of the 'benefits' said to be delivered to an employee for his or her willingness to be controlled by the employer. In this sense, loss of accountability is a conscious, structured element of the employment-dependent firm. But it is a topic that management, managerial academics and labour regulators do not want to discuss. The pretence is that accountability is achieved or achievable within the employment control systems in the firm. And although this may often be true, the reality is that the control is fickle. Further, it is argued that, if individuals in the firm were held accountable in the same way that markets make individuals accountable, different human dynamics would come into play that would escalate the cost of operating a firm and threaten its very existence. This is another perspective on Coase's transaction cost theory discussed earlier in this chapter.

The destruction of accountability is at its worst when it aids and abets the people who work at the top of the firm, enabling them to rort the firm to satisfy their own greed. This occurs quite simply, for example, when the top managers of firms rewrite the policies of the firm to give themselves large financial or lifestyle perks paid for by the firm. Common things, such as lavish boardrooms and offices adorned with expensive artwork, are symbols of power and wealth which appeal to the egos of the top corporate players. Private jets and expensive cars do much more than enable the practical transport of time-poor managers from place to place. These are also usually symbols of importance giving the corporate player the sense of being Caesar-like in their own mini-empire. This type of cancer at the top of the firm can spread systematically right through the firm. When this happens, it further protects and enhances the largesse distributed at the top of the firm. This can be fatal and cause firms to collapse.

Around the turn of the twenty-first century, the giant US energy trading company Enron and telecommunications company Worldcom crashed. In Italy, the iconic milk and food giant Parmalat crashed. In Australia, the massive insurance conglomerate HIA crashed, as the Bond and Quintex (run by Christopher Skase) corporations had done earlier. In each of these cases, the ensuing investigations led to allegations that these giant businesses, led by high-profile corporate leaders, splashed their money around their subordinates inside the firm and around charitable and community organizations. The largesse given to others was, however, never as big as their own. The giving of money to others silenced the potential criticism of the giving of money to themselves. These allegations—many of which are subject to ongoing testing in the courts—also include claims of massive internal corporate fraud, in which money was routinely and illegally shipped from business to private accounts. The financial records of the companies, it has also been suggested, were doctored to hide transactions, and dubious accounting practices were used to make massive trading losses look like profits. And while this was happening, the banks who loaned money, the government regulators who allegedly oversaw the activity, the professional stock market analysts, and the thousands of professional business commentators who watched these firms failed to spot the impending crashes. Everyone external to the firms was blinded. But in each case the investigators from financial authorities found people inside the firms who knew, or had an inkling, that things were going terribly wrong. Those who knew and were involved were, like their bosses, criminally charged (many went to jail), others are still to face the courts, still others fled, hunted by the authorities. Some inside the firm who sensed that things were wrong could not or did not do anything before the collapses. Others were oblivious. But in all cases accountability and transparency inside the firms had collapsed. The command-and-control systems, dependent as they were on employment, were easily and routinely manipulated to avoid accountability and transparency. And this is not a rare occurrence. Every firm, every organization that utilizes command-and-control employment brings into its structure the psychological and institutional DNA for the destruction of accountability. Most firms contain and suppress the cancer, but they cannot eliminate it. Loss of accountability is the flip-side of the containment of transaction costs said to be necessary for the existence of the firm. But all too often the accountability destruction cancer destroys the organism it has colonized.

There is nothing surprising about this. It's the natural behavioural response when command-and-control employment systems are adopted in any human collective. It is changing, but not because governments, corporate regulators, corporate organizations themselves or shareholders are concerned about the systematic destruction of accountability within firms. These groups don't even recognize, let alone discuss, the problem for fear that to do so would threaten the very existence of the firm itself. These groups suffer from conceptual blindness to the problem. Where the change is coming from is the people.

The 'independent employee'
In truly democratic and educated societies, people are generally alert to the psychological processes of command and control. Even employees are not comfortable with command and control. People have become (and firms are now confronted with the 'problem' of) 'independent employees'.

'Independent employees' are people who work in firms, are captured under the command-and-control contract and structures of employment, but in their actions, desires, thoughts and ambitions are people of independence. They are people who, in their work, live the lie of employment but have all the personal attributes of independence. They are potentially firms' greatest assets because they enable firms to be creative. They are people who thrive on accountability. They have integrity and adhere to their principles. They are large in number.

The independent employee has emerged because command-and-control employment depends upon ignorance and willing compliance for its survival. But people in educated societies have become less ignorant and don't want to be controlled. And it's difficult to control people who don't want to be controlled.

Why has the independent employee emerged?

In democracies, people have become used to thinking that, in theory at least, governments are servants of the people. Government is not of a higher order than the people. People express their individual supremacy over government at the ballot box. Obviously, once elected, governments can and do behave badly and systems of government can and do disempower individuals. But in the latter part of the twentieth century, government became more 'light touch' than certainly was the case for earlier generations. The nation state exists to protect its people from external violence, to provide systems of law, order and justice within and to fund and often provide services. Frequently, in performing these tasks, the state assumes a higher importance than the individual. But in the modern state there exists an idea, at least, that the processes of governance should attempt to strike a delicate balance between the organizational needs of the collective and allowing the individual the right to be an individual—to find his or her own place, harmony and happiness. The idea of the state has moved from one in which it sought to determine the individual's place in society to one in which it is thought of as an organizational framework for individual freedom. This idea is clearly current, even if the practice is frequently haphazard and always far from perfect.

This idea of the individual being free from state control has firmly taken hold in the psyche of democratic societies. It is clashing with the concept and practice of employment by the command-and-control firm. In their private lives, employees are free voters and consumers. They decide what to buy and when. They travel freely. They demand that their needs and wants are satisfied by the service providers whom they pay to do so. The law protects and enforces their right to choose and normally prevents them being required to buy or use services they may not want. They borrow large sums of money to purchase cars or homes or to set up businesses. As private individuals, people are not controlled. Yet when they go to work, they know they are controlled. They know that their incomes are dependent upon their willingness to be controlled. But they are not comfortable with it. In their working lives they live a lie. Most pretend to be comfortable with being systemically controlled, but employer control runs against the grain of their private lives of self-control. Some people accept this willingly. Some are happy to be told what to do at work. Other people revel in the control structure of firms, seeking to climb the internal career ladders in order to achieve greater rewards, but also in order to control those lower down the ladder. But others—the newer, emergent and progressively dominant group—privately resent the control.

We have reached a moment in history when the problem of the independent employee has become real and pressing. Independent employees are vast in number. They are people who, to earn an income, live in a society that insists on employment and find that they must accept the control of the employment contract if they wish to work. These people are in every respect independent beings. They want to and do think for themselves. They are decision-makers. They are self-managers. They seek to control their own destinies and careers and not to have the firm decide either their current or future place in the world. And the more educated they are, the more they want to exercise self-control. These people, working in firms, are the greatest challenge so far to the idea, structures and operations of firms.

The firm as a command-and-control employment system is under challenge. And it is not coping with the challenge. Occasionally the challenge turns into farce.

In April 2004, a French economist, Corinne Maier, who worked part-time as a researcher for the French firm Electricité de France, wrote a satirical book on life within the firm. The book, *Bonjour Paresse* (Hello Laziness), subtitled *The Art and Importance of Doing as Little as Possible in the Workplace*, includes chapters with titles such as 'The Morons who are Sitting Next to You' and 'Corporate Culture—Stupid People'.[7] The book had a slow start when first published, with an initial print run of only 4,000. But it sprang into prominence and on to the best-seller list when it became widely known that Corinne's employer had called her in for disciplinary action over the book. Apparently her employer didn't like Corinne's depiction of large organizations as driven by internal politics, beset with boredom and inefficiency, and plagued with bad management. Her advocacy of 'active disengagement' and ensuring that one did as little as possible to climb the corporate ladder was perceived by her employer as 'aimed at spreading gangrene in the system from within'. But Corinne did no more than spell out what frustrated independent employees have learnt is the true nature of their positions. They are told that the system is more important than themselves and that to survive they must suppress the self for the good of the system. Corinne's book represents no less than the psychological response of the independent employee to being trapped within the command-and-control employment organization.

Within employment control, the system demands that the identity of people be subjugated to the greater good of the system. The reaction of the independent employee in such circumstances is to leave; otherwise they become disgruntled, de-motivated and disillusioned. Only those who seek to be controllers enjoy the system and rise through its hierarchy.

Sometimes the independent employee breaks out. This occurs most dramatically with whistleblowers, people who work in a firm or organization, see or experience fraud or great wrongs and errors in the organization, and go public with the problem. Whistleblowers are people, like Corinne Maier, who find bad within the system and whose conscience tells them they cannot sit by and observe or experience the bad and do nothing. They expose the bad. They are people who display all the attributes of independent employees. They are people who cannot submit themselves to the control of the employment organization, particularly when the organization is wrong. And their reward for exposing wrong is most frequently not credit for ridding the organization of wrong, but rather extreme pressure to shut up. They face disciplinary action, they are often sacked, and in extreme cases they put their own safety at risk.

In one typical example,[8] a police officer in the police force in the State of Victoria in Australia disclosed what become known as the 'window shutter' scam. What was occurring was that retails shops in Melbourne, Victoria, were having their shop front windows smashed at night. The incidents were reported to police who would ring window shutter security firms to have the windows boarded up the same night. The cost would be covered by the retailers' insurers. It transpired that sections of the Victorian police were receiving financial kick-backs from the security companies. Suggestions also emerged that some of the police involved paid criminals to organize the window smashing. One police officer objected to the practice and tried to have it stopped by exposing it internally. However, the corruption was so endemic that he found that the senior officers to whom he complained were also on the take. He went to the press; the accusations made front-page news. An official police enquiry followed and the officers involved were disciplined internally. After the scandal and the subsequent investigative process, the only officer dismissed from the force was the one who complained. He brought an unfair dismissal action against the Victorian Police, which he won, but the police appealed through several superior courts until the officer lost on the grounds that he was a 'servant of the Crown' rather than an employee, and so could not bring an unfair dismissal action for want of jurisdiction. Years later, corruption in the Victorian police force reached scandalous proportions. The top levels of the Force publicly accepted that they had deep problems at senior levels. Reports suggested that many of the corrupt senior officers were in fact the same officers accused of corruption in the shutter scandal, but since then they had been promoted to senior levels. The whistleblower was sacked; the corrupt officers were promoted.

This Victorian police case is not rare. And it seems that the problem for whistleblowers is that they find themselves subject to sustained attack by the organizations for whom they work. So common is the problem that, in many places, governments have enacted special whistleblower legislation to protect them. In so doing, governments have acted in the belief that people must be encouraged to be honest. Whistleblowers expose corruption and crime and must be protected and encouraged.

But enquiries into the whistleblower problem have not focused on what it is within organizations that allows cultures of corruption to become entrenched. Perhaps it is the systems of control established under employment that enable corruption to become more than simply the actions of isolated individuals. In fact, systems of control based on master–servant employment legalities have within them the seeds of systemic corruption. Systems of employment control face this constant problem. It's simply one of the many problems facing the human resources industry.

Human Resources: managers juggling the impossible to juggle

It is human resource managers who seem to have been handed the near-impossible task of reconciling the aspirational and individualized motivations of the 'independent employee' with the collective, bonding needs of the firm. Entire forests of trees have been converted into paper to produce the millions of books that have been churned out on the subject. None of these books seems to express the issue in terms of the mismatch between the independent employee and the concept and practice of control within the firm. Instead, the issue they all address is how to 'motivate' workers, how to get them to act with imagination, creativity and responsibility while remaining with the firm and not leaving to work for other, competing firms or to start up their own. The firm needs employees to create value that is retained by the firm. This is the objective of the employment-based firm.

In the 1950s, the human resource manager began to come to prominence. Academic schools of human resource theory and training began to emerge, seeking to solve the central problem of the firm: how to exercise control without destroying creativity and performance. During the latter part of the twentieth century, human resource management theory started to accept that command-and-control processes did not result in the most productive of workforces, particularly in large firms. Command and control de-motivated. It created an 'us and them' mentality, a psychology of war within the firm in which there were winners and losers. But the dilemma is that the firm is thought to be unable to exist without command and control.

The idea of command and control itself as the core structure of the firm has not been challenged. Why? Because even to think of challenging command and control assaults key psychologies of the senior management ranks of the firm. This includes their individual and collective egos, career ambitions, their perceived entrepreneurial flair and their ability to capture and retain the benefits of the firm for themselves and shareholders. Any manager who challenges the idea of command and control in a firm will rarely have promising career prospects. In fact, even suggesting that command and control has flaws is taboo. Above all, it is taboo to challenge the employment contract because employment is culturally accepted, if not always consciously recognized, as the key legal bedrock of control.

Instead, human resource managers and systems are supposed to reconcile the irreconcilable. The HR industry has been built around creating human, motivational, profiling and training propaganda and career systems that would entice legally bonded employees to perform at their peak, to give of their all, to want to stay with the firm and to willingly allow the firm to retain large shares of the value they create.

In this exercise, the HR industry has displayed genius. It has achieved considerable success, largely by focusing on the positives of the firm. It has downplayed issues of control employment and always looked on the bright side of life. Motivation comes from excitement, not negativity!

The most famous and perhaps most influential of management writers in this area is the late Peter Drucker, often billed as the world's greatest management thinker.[9] Drucker created the terms 'knowledge worker' and 'knowledge society'.

In the 1930s, early in his career, Drucker noted that, whereas economists were interested in the behaviour of commodities, he was interested in the behaviour of people. Again, whereas economists reflected on the interaction between firms and between firms and consumers, management was focused exclusively on the internal human dynamics within firms. And the two were not, and still are not, conceived as being one and the same. Drucker was deeply wedded to the free enterprise system. His focus was on making it work well. He was concerned that the industrial corporation had assumed the market's central place in society and that the new social structures were failing in the areas of freedom and equality.

Drucker's concerns about the alienation of the worker paralleled those of Karl Marx. Drucker said:

> Work appears as something unnatural, a disagreeable, meaningless and stultifying condition ... devoid of dignity as well as importance. [The worker] is not a human being in a society, but a freely replaceable cog in an inhumanly efficient machine.[10]

Drucker derided the authority and power of the executives in large corporations. Executives were no longer the owners of the firm but exercised illegitimate control over the corporation and its workers:

> In the modern corporation the decisive power, that of the managers, is derived from no one but from the managers themselves controlled by no-body and nothing and responsible to no one. It is in the most literal sense unfounded, unjustified, uncontrolled and irresponsible power.[11]

But Drucker was not a destroyer. The solution to the problem of corporate control by management was not to do away with the corporation or management or free markets. Rather, he proposed to bring the assembly-line worker into the picture of the whole of the firm and so remove his alienation.

Shortly after the Second World War, Drucker was commissioned by General Motors Corporation (GM) to undertake a study of its management. Drucker found in GM something different from what might have been expected. Under the leadership of its president of more than 20 years, Alfred P. Sloan, GM was a heavily decentralized corporation. But, at GM, decentralizing was much more than the norm. Drucker described the situation he found as follows. 'Alfred P Sloan has developed the concept of decentralization into a philosophy of industrial management and into a system of local self-government. It is not a mere technique of management but an outline of social order'.[12] Drucker recommended that the workplace should be democratized, not by law but by management itself, because it would make the corporation more effective. Drucker talked of treating workers as a resource, not as a cost, and of looking to develop the 'responsible worker'. But when, in 1947, Drucker made his recommendations for change within

GM, both management and unions turned against him. He had supporters, but the idea that management should manage and workers work held sway within GM, as it did in most corporations in the USA. And it wasn't until the 1970s, when Japanese car imports began rapidly to erode the dominance of the US car industry, that corporate America started to revise its thinking. Only then did Drucker's ideas of 'the quality of working life' and 'quality circles' and so on begin to find favour in the USA. More managers began to see that 'For the proper functioning in the industrial enterprise ... its members, down to the last sweeper and wheelbarrow-pusher, must have a managerial attitude toward their work'.[13]

How to achieve this? For Drucker, the first step was to eliminate power and fear from the management–worker relationship. Drucker thought that the power imbalance could be rectified. If the worker felt secure in his job, and had the right to withhold his labour without fear of being fired, then workers would cease abusing their power. There was thus an important role for unions. Management needed to be balanced by countervailing power. Job security was part of the answer but, for Drucker, management training was more important.

Drucker's most famous dictum was 'management by objectives'.[14] In 1954, he set out a conception of the manager as no longer the traditional delegate of the owner but as someone who sets objectives, organizes, motivates and communicates, develops yardsticks and measures, and develops people. And there is no doubt that this concept of management has taken hold and been dominant since the 1950s. Drucker characterized it as a situation where managers had control over themselves rather than control from above. Further, he believed that management's most urgent task was to find ways of motivating workers by banishing fear, especially fear of losing one's job.

But even more was needed, reasoned Drucker. In 1966, he wrote that the new knowledge worker 'needs opportunity, he needs achievement, he needs fulfillment, he needs values'.[15] Drucker heavily criticized the human resource management schools that promoted human relations simply as a device to get workers to do what management wanted. Instead, he was in favour of extending downward the management of individuals so that workers managed themselves. As early as 1969, Drucker saw the evolution of the worker as entrepreneur as a dominant development, in US business at least.

Drucker was not alone in holding these views. Others also identified the development of the independent-minded worker as a key social, psychological and even economic force. Tom Peters was another of the major thinkers on management after the Second World War who recognized the emergence of the independent worker.[16] He said in the late 1990s: 'We are

CEO's of our own companies: Me Inc. To be in business today, our most important job is to be head marketer for the brand called You'.[17] This was reflected in the reality of business of the late 1990s, when the vice-president of AT&T, James Meadons, said 'People need to look at themselves as self-employed, as vendors who come to this company to sell their skills'.[18]

Two further management thinkers are Mike Hammer and James Champy, who together came up with the idea of re-engineering the organization. In 1993, they argued that responsibilities and authority were so widely distributed throughout the organization that virtually everyone needed to become a manager, even if that management was only of his or her own work. And to accommodate this, they reasoned, organizations had no choice but to flatten the traditional command-and-control pyramid. By 1995, however, Champy claimed that re-engineering of firms was not occurring or was happening only half-heartedly, and that the obstacle to change was management itself. According to Champy, management had not changed but it would have to change its approach to control. He likened the problem to 'a communist regime introducing free enterprise into a controlled economy while trying to hold on to power'.[19]

Champy attributed the failure to change to the natural inclination of managers to conceive of workers only as machines. Managers 'rely on humans only at the most elementary level of their being ... The machines (firms) are basically organisation charts bought to life ... all held together by chains of command and lines of authority'. Managers' reasoning is that 'With careful command and control, sound navigation and maintenance, the ship should operate with perfect reliability and rationality (no subjectivity)'.[20] Champy went on to predict the 'collapse of the old corporate machine ... as customers make tougher and tougher demands on a company's services and products ... and it's specifically the chains of command and the lines of authority ... that are groaning and popping the loudest'.[21]

Champy claimed that 'what must be abandoned by the new management of our corporate ships — that is both officers and crew — is a whole ideology, a whole way of thinking about power'.[22] But what stopped companies re-engineering themselves in this new direction, according to Champy, was managers' fear of losing control: a fear that was greater than the fear of loss of status. He went on, 'we must wake up to the fact that authority is no longer vested in a place on the organizational chart, but in an ability to do a job'.[23] Champy was urging managers to revolutionize their thinking and their attitudes. The key to the new corporation was culture, not structure, and managers must start the new culture with themselves. The new culture could best be described as one of entrepreneurship. 'Reengineering demands that managers empower people to do the new operational work and to do whatever it takes to serve the customer's needs'.[24]

This same theme—the elimination of top-down, command-and-control management—was a consistent one among most profile management thinkers at the tail end of the twentieth century.

Rosebeth Moss Kanter is a Professor of Business Administration at Harvard Business School, author of numerous management books and consultant to many corporations and governments around the world on organizational change and renewal. Kanter sees the process of management reform as 'providing the tools and conditions that liberate people to use their brainpower to make a difference in the world of constant challenge and change'.[25] Kanter sees the management task as 'mobilizing and motivating individual human talent in pursuit of collective ends'.[26] 'Leaders must create cultures in which experiments, questions and challenges are not just for the courageous'.[27]

Along with other management thinkers, Kanter sees continuity of staff as critical to the success of the firm. 'Momentum is lost because of staff turnover';[28] 'in bureaucratic cultures, powerlessness, not power, can corrupt, turning the powerless into controlling, petty tyrants who guard their own patch of turf rather than strive to deliver value for customers'.[29] Kanter says that 'a debate has raged among business leaders in North America and Britain over whose interests should come first—those of shareholders, customers or employees'.[30] The new business strategies require managers to find new ways to guide action and motivate people, she reasons.[31] 'Most businesses today say they serve customers. In reality, they serve themselves'.[32] She puts the emphasis on finding new ways of motivating staff without using command and control. 'The new security is not employment security (a guaranteed job no matter what) but employability security—increased value to the internal and external labour markets'.[33] She promotes a 'kind of voluntary control through relationships among equals'.[34] She looks at Bell Atlantic, which transformed itself and in which 'Corporate staff were put on in a market-like situation, in which their budgets depended on selling their services, thus provoking an internal-customer orientation'.[35] Kanter says that 'creative managers are not empowered simply by a boss or their job; (but) on their own they seek and find the additional strength it takes to carry out major new initiatives. They are indeed corporate entrepreneurs'.[36] 'The idea that corporate staffs have internal customers became real at Bell Atlantic through Client Service group structure in which corporate staffs had to sell their services to line managers who were free to purchase them internally or externally'.[37] What Kanter is describing here is the new development of 'markets in the firm', a topic that is covered in Chapter Seven.

But what needs to be emphasized at this point is that, in all the management rethinking about control and power within the firm, the idea and practice of the employment contract has never been challenged. Management thinkers have not realized that the new desire to empower workers is at cross-purposes with, and defeated by, the legal underpinnings of employment: that the social, institutional and legal regulatory approaches to labour—embedded as they are in the employment contract—prevent the empowering of employees. Corporations may seek to operate with management by objectives, to empower workers, to have knowledge workers, and so on, but this is attempted within the legal framework of employment, which is entirely about control.

This creates irreconcilable tensions. Management cannot systemically achieve its performance objectives while it is trapped in the contract of employment. The tension can be resolved only by aligning management and philosophical ideas with the legal reality. If management wants command and control, the employment contract fits perfectly. But if management finds that command and control limits performance, and desires to move beyond command and control, this cannot be fully achieved while the employment contract is retained.

But the legal, social, institutional, and attitudinal paradigms within which labour regulation operates makes the move away from the command-and-control employment contract very difficult. This is the next topic for consideration.

Endnotes

1. Niccolo Machiavelli, *The Prince*, Penguin Books, 1981.
2. Phyllis Deane, *The First Industrial Revolution*, Cambridge University Press, 1979, page 180.
3. R.H. Coase, *The Firm, The Market, and The Law*, University of Chicago Press, 1988, page 53.
4. Elliott Jaques, *Free Enterprise, Fair Employment*, Heinemann, London, 1982, page xi.
5. J. Irwin Miller, 'The Dilemma of the Corporation Man' in *The Book of Business Wisdom*, Peter Krass (ed.), John Wiley & Sons Inc, New York, 1997, page 283.
6. *Ibid.*, page 289
7. 'Is slacking the only way to survive the office', *The Scotsman*, 16 August 2004; 'What's that stench in your office? Inertia', TimesOnline 16 August 2004 at www.timesonline.co.uk
8. *Konrad v. Victoria Police (State of Victoria) and Murray Neil Comrie, Chief of Commissioner of Police for the State of Victoria*. No VG 58 of 1998. Federal Court of Australian [1999] FCA 988.
9. Jack Beatty, *The World According to Drucker*, Orion Business Books, 1998.

10. *Ibid.*, page 45.
11. *Ibid.*, page 46.
12. *Ibid.*, page 56.
13. *Ibid.*, page 76.
14. *Ibid.*, page 111.
15. *Ibid.*, page 115.
16. Tom Peters, *Liberation Management,*. Pan Books, London, 1993.
17. Beatty, *op cit.*, page 171.
18. *Ibid.*, page 171.
19. James Champy, *Reengineering Management*, Harper Collins Publishers, 1995, page 5.
20. *Ibid.*, page 13.
21. *Ibid.*, page 20.
22. *Ibid.*, page 21.
23. *Ibid.*, page 27.
24. *Ibid.*, page 115.
25. Rosebeth Moss Kanter, *On The Frontiers of Management*, Harvard Business Review Book, 1997, page xiii.
26. *Ibid.*, page 6.
27. *Ibid.*, page 9.
28. *Ibid.*, page 11.
29. *Ibid.*, page 15.
30. *Ibid.*, page 21.
31. *Ibid.*, page 27.
32. *Ibid.*, page 54.
33. *Ibid.*, page 55.
34. *Ibid.*, page 62.
35. *Ibid.*, page 66.
36. *Ibid.*, page 99.
37. *Ibid., page 125.*

6: Labour Regulation

The system of wage labour is a system of slavery

— Karl Marx

Overview

Labour regulation is stuck in a conceptual time warp several hundred years old. It is distorting human relationships inside firms and hindering social progress.

Societies are changing quite rapidly, but the labour regulation that governments impose on societies is failing to keep pace. There is a singular failure to realize what the change is and why it is occurring, and so to design appropriate responses.

In essence, labour regulation is based on the view that relationships inside firms are relationships of inequality between the powerful and the powerless. Labour regulations are supposed to eliminate this power imbalance and so impose equality inside the firm. This in turn is supposed to make for more equitable societies.

Whether or not this view of power inequality is (or ever was) a true reflection of the reality of relationships inside firms, it is the central concept that drove the design of all labour regulation throughout the twentieth century, and particularly since the Second World War. But that concept is now under direct challenge. The idea that relationships inside firms are always and systematically relationships of inequality between the powerful and powerless no longer holds true. It may sometimes be true, but it is usually wrong. New ways of looking at labour regulation must be framed.

To understand labour regulation, some key sub-concepts need to be understood.

Bargaining power inside firms has always been discussed on the assumption that all firms engage workers under the employment contract. Legislation creating labour regulation has always been drafted to apply to where the employment contract exists, on the understanding that the employment contract is a contract of inequality and hence needs to be regulated with a view to removing the inequality. Where people work without employment contracts, labour regulation does not apply. The alternative work contract to employment is the commercial contract. At law, the commercial contract is a contract of equality and so should not be (and is not) regulated in the same way as employment contracts. Yet these legal facts are largely ignored when labour regulation is discussed. The academic discussion of labour regulation is conducted as if all contracts, whether commercial or employment, were contracts of inequality which therefore required 'power countervailing' regulation. Such discussion is therefore of little value.

Nonetheless, social change is posing a challenge to the 'power inequality' concepts of labour regulation and upsetting the comfortable and established paradigms of the existing academic debate. People increasingly are rejecting relationships of power inequality—within families, between the sexes, in politics, and in every social arena. It is affecting the firm, where the rejection of power inequality has two main manifestations. People who work under the employment contract behave independently as 'independent employees' and reject inequality in their behaviour. And further, people are rejecting the employment contract as a mode of work and choosing to work under the commercial contract as independent contractors. Labour regulation and discussion about it are both becoming rapidly outdated.

What is labour regulation?
Critical to understanding labour regulation is the recognition that labour regulation should not be confused with regulation covering taxes, social welfare, anti-discrimination objectives, equal opportunity, and work safety. Each of these areas of regulation interfaces and interacts with labour regulation, but each is separate and distinct, and has its own unique objectives. They cover issues of government taxation, income security for the less well-off, relationships across society, and safety. These regulations are connected with labour regulation because they are applied to and within the firm. Taxation law uses the firm as an administrative vehicle for collecting revenue for government. Social security laws use the firm as an administrative vehicle for facilitating income security when a person is out of work. Anti-discrimination and equal opportunity laws have application across all of society (and hence are applied to the firm), but their objectives are in fact distorted by the employment contract. Work safety laws are designed to ensure that people are not harmed as a consequence of firms' activities. These laws largely use the firm as an administrative tool to target broader social and other objectives.

Labour regulation, however, is different from these other kinds of regulation because it seeks to interfere with and control the interaction between the people who work in the firm. It does this by seeking to control the employment contract and by taking away employer control of the employment contract. But labour regulation disempowers not only employers but employees as well. Labour regulation is an instrument whereby the state assumes high-level managerial control of the firm while at the same time pretending not to do so. This is the traditional role of labour regulation as formalized and consolidated after the Second World War, and internationally institutionalized under the structure of the United Nations affiliate organization, the International Labour Organization (ILO). It is a body of law that distorts the ability of firms and the people working inside firms to reach for and discover their highest levels of performance and satisfaction.

The extent to which labour regulation performs this controlling role varies between countries and within countries, but the primary thrust of labour regulation is common across developed economies and is being incorporated into the emerging regulation regimes of developing economies. It is a primary factor that affects the success of economies and the competitive differences between economies.

Labour regulation vs commercial regulation
Labour regulation is different from the commercial regulation that applies to contracts between businesses and consumers and between businesses and businesses. It is essential at this point to understand this difference.

Labour regulation operates on one core understanding: that the employment contract is a contract between parties who have unequal bargaining power. And this inequality of bargaining power is built into the law of the employment contract. As demonstrated at length in earlier chapters in this book, the employment contract (under common law called the contract *of* service) at law and in practice is a contract of control. That is, the employer has 'the right' at law to control the employee. The legal and managerial idea is simple: once an employment contract is in force, employees agree to give employers the exclusive right to use and control their services. In practice, this means that the employer can control the terms of the employment contract and change those terms without the agreement of the employee. The only 'control' an employee can exercise is to terminate the contract.

This is quite different from the other principal contract in societies involving the provision of services, namely, the commercial contract, also known at common law as the contract *for* services. When a business buys a product or service from another business or sells to a consumer or another business, the type of contract in operation is the commercial contract. The essence of this contract is that both parties have equal rights, enforceable at law, to control the terms of the contract. This contrasts starkly with the employment contract. Under the commercial contract, for example, the terms of the contract cannot be changed by one party without the consent of the other. But under the employment contract the employer has the right to change contract terms without the employee's consent.

These two basic contracts could not be more starkly different and have hugely different implications for the application of justice in societies, how people in societies interact in their economic relationships, and the way the two contract types are or should be regulated.

The commercial contract provides one of the most important protections for economic justice and social stability. A consumer may be small and poor and the supplier of a good or service may be big, rich and seemingly powerful. But in the eyes of the law, and for the purposes of the commercial contract, both parties are equal. If the 'little' person has purchased a service, the big company must ensure that the service supplied is as advertised and is safe. The company cannot decide after taking the customer's money that it will supply a different service. If it does this, the law of commercial contract will require it to honour its original stated intent. In this respect the commercial contract is a contract of equality. It is a great social and economic leveller. It ignores might and power. It is the core legal basis upon which free markets operate. It is the contract that ensures that trust in society is reflected in and is enforced by the law. The commercial contract is hugely important for the achievement of social stability and economic success.

The commercial contract is heavily regulated, but in a particular way. The law of commercial contract allows people to enter the contract of their own free will. In free-market societies, the law does not say which contracts you can or cannot enter. The state does not force you into contracts you do not want or dictate the terms of commercial contracts before you enter them. The law will interfere in the contract only when there is a dispute which the parties cannot resolve. The law will then check that the contract was a genuine contract and resolve the dispute according to the terms laid out in the contract. This is done by the courts. The law will not seek to tell people what the terms or price of the contract should be, either before or after the contract is agreed. But the law will declare null and void contracts that do not conform to these key protective features of the commercial contract structure. This structure of the commercial contract and the comparable light regulation that goes with it not only enable economies to operate, but are also fundamental protections of human rights and a leveller of social status. Under the commercial contract, everyone is equal before the law. The commercial contract is a destroyer of class consciousness and class warfare. It is a noble contract, but is rarely if ever recognized for its fundamental importance to a just, fair and equitable society.

With the employment contract, the structures and implications are different. Under the employment contract, equality before the law does not exist. But few want to recognize or accept this legal truth and the simplicity of the difference from the commercial contract. Chapter One of this book detailed all the elements that go to make the contract of employment a contract of control. Effectively, the nature of the employment contract is that the employer has the right to control the terms of the contract without the agreement of the employee. This is not equality before the law. This is the entrenchment of class structure and class consciousness within the area of work and of the firm and it is recognized and enforced by law.

The reaction against this class-based employment contract—particularly after the Second World War—has seen the development of labour law that seeks to redress the power and class imbalance. Law-makers have taken the view that the inequality of the employment contract is wrong and must be addressed. But rather than giving legal power to the employee in equal measure to that of the employer, the law has instead taken power from the employer and assumed that power itself. This is the essence of labour regulation. It is odd. If the power imbalance inherent in the employment contract were so unacceptable, it would surely have been more logical and more equitable for labour regulation to empower the employee. But this has not occurred. The rhetoric of labour regulation claims to have empowered the employee, but in fact this is not the case. Both by design and in its operation, labour regulation seeks to empower the state under the banner of empowering the employee. It is a great social subterfuge conducted by the state against employees. In this respect, labour regulation is not a process of addressing power imbalance but rather a process of creating an additional power imbalance—with all additional power going to institutions of the state.

This is the modern form of labour law. And it is global. Rather than creating and protecting human rights and economic justice globally, labour law has distorted rights and justice and, in fact, created injustice. Because the state has stolen power from the employer, it assumes that it is has done the right thing. But, under the banner and illusion of justice and rights, the state chooses to be blind to the injustice it now represents and imposes.

Labour law: a system of injustice

When it is unencumbered by labour regulation, the employment contract delivers to the employer control over the employee, even if most employees are not aware of this.

The most obvious control is the expectation and requirement under contract that the employee will attend work each day as required by the employer. Since this contractual obligation is not written down when a person becomes employed, most employees are not aware of this legal fact. But it can be found stated in the judgments of courts adjudicating on employment contracts. And labour regulation imposed on the employment contract accepts and reinforces this. Why is this so? It is taken that, under the employment contract and associated labour regulation, businesses could not operate if employees turned up to work only when and if it suited them. For example, most employment law in most countries even gives employers the right to require employees to do overtime. The employment contract and law, in this respect, operate to serve managerial interests and the convenience of the employer by requiring employees to attend work.

This requirement to attend work imposed on the employee by the contract of employment and by employment regulation is taken as a given in society and a product of industrialization. Take the example of 'our daily bread'.

In the industrial age, bread production moved from the family home and local village bakery to mass production in large factories. To assist smooth factory production after the Industrial Revolution, the law of employment reinforced the obligation of employees to turn up at the bread factory each day at specified times. This was done, so the argument goes, for good social and economic reasons. With massive industrial baking machines, employers' production requirements necessitated that the bread ovens were started at particular times and that all key employees were at their stations at those times. If employees were missing, the entire bread production process for that day could be at risk. So the law and contract of employment was (and is) a reflection of the fact that, if employees were not at work, the economic losses to the employer would be so large as to threaten the financial viability of the bread business. If employees across an entire country could attend work when they chose, employers could not organize their businesses for production with any certainty. If this occurred systemically in an industrial society, the entire ability of a society to produce could be threatened. This fear of collapse of production underpins the law of employment contract and supporting regulation. And this fact is expressed quite regularly in court decisions on employment contracts and law. So employment regulation reinforces and supports the employers' control over employees, but only on the grounds that such control serves the greater and necessary good of society.

On other matters, however, even though the contract of employment delivers control to the employer, the regulation of employment has taken control *away* from the employer. This is done because of concern about potential exploitation by employers of employees if employers' power is unrestrained. The examples are obvious.

Almost every country imposes minimum pay rates on employers. Most frequently, complex quasi-judicial processes are established which dictate to employers the actual pay rates that are to be paid. So the rate of pay and the processes for determining rates of pay are dictated by the state. In effect, this removes the right and capacity of employers to determine the rates they are prepared to pay. It diminishes employers' control over their enterprises and is done under the banner of 'workers' rights'. In this area, the rationale is that, if employers had unfettered power to pay employees what they liked, then employers would, naturally enough, pay as little as possible and so exploit employees and create poverty. Across the globe, countries have decided that this is not an appropriate power for employers to have and so have set up a wide variety of state institutions that determine and impose pay rates on employers. This, it is suggested, is how social justice is achieved.

But the other consequence of this regulation (that is never openly admitted) is that it quite frequently denies effective rights to employees to determine and create their own pay rates. The setting of pay rates under labour regulations and processes does not generally deliver to individual employees full capacity to sell their services to their employer in a way that would maximize the financial return to each employee. Hence the processes of pay regulation deny employees their right to control their pay rate. There are two justifications for this denial of power to individual employees. It is thought that if individual employees had complete capacity to determine their individual incomes in direct negotiation with their employers, then employers' superior negotiating position would force individual employees to accept lower wages than could be obtained by employees negotiating collectively. Since employee negotiating power over pay rates is thought to be greatest when employees act collectively, individual employees must not be allowed to weaken the collective. It is also thought that, if individual employees negotiated a lower wage for themselves, this would flow through to all employees, thus creating a wage race to the bottom. Collective wage negotiations are therefore organized and entrenched in different ways (and to different extents) in different countries to stop or minimize individual employees exerting influence over their own pay rates. Thus, where collective wage negotiation is enforced by employment law, an essential and important element of it is the denial of power to individual employees. In effect, this is the denial of justice to employees as individuals. There may by good social reasons for this, as is argued by people who support the collectivization of employee power, but it is a subterfuge whenever collectivization is justified without clear acceptance of the consequent denial of justice to employees as individuals.

This social policy dilemma plays out on a regular and frequent basis — and not always simply on pay rates but on other employee rights issues as well. One example was a high-profile case in Australia in 2004.

Electrolux

In September 2004, the High Court of Australia (the ultimate court of appeal in Australia) handed down a decision that tells us a great deal about the ideas that underpin labour regulation both in Australia and internationally.

The judgment expresses ideas, images and moral positions that are common to labour regulation world-wide. The judges' comments reflect the clash of mindsets that define the labour and business regulation debate that has developed since the Second World War: a clash which is played out differently in each country, but which has common and clear international themes and principles.

The *Electrolux* High Court[1] case involved the large multinational firm Electrolux which, in Australia, manufactured whitegood products: washing machines, clothes dryers, and so on. Electrolux had a collective agreement with its employees organized through a union. The union wished to insert a clause into the agreement requiring non-union employees to pay a 'service fee' to the union; Electrolux was to be required to deduct the fee from non-unionists' wages. Electrolux objected to this clause, arguing that non-union employees should not be forced to pay money to the union if they didn't so desire. But the union wanted to make forced payment of money by employees to the union a condition of employment with Electrolux, and indicated that it would call a strike if the clause was not included in its enterprise agreement with Electrolux. Electrolux went to the courts, arguing that the union 'service fee' did not fall within the jurisdiction of the Australian industrial relations legislation and consequently was illegal under Australian employment law.

Under Australian industrial relations law, employees are permitted to strike in the attempt to force employers to agree to certain conditions of employment. In the absence of industrial relations law, employees taking strike action could be sued for damages by the employer. Most industrial relations law across the globe replicates this basic structure in one form or another.

In the Australian *Electrolux* case, if the union service fee clause could be demonstrated to have nothing to do with the relationship between Electrolux and its employees, the industrial relations legislation would not apply, and Electrolux would have been free to sue the union and its employees for commercial damages arising from any strike action.

The principle at stake was (and is) the key to all industrial relations regulation and law in most developed economies. It is the principle that underpins the core activities of the International Labour Organisation, which acts as the 'parliament of principle' for labour law.

The principle being considered in *Electrolux* was contained within the issue of whether industrial relations law could be imposed outside the employment relationship. Under labour law, employees working through a union can pressure employers into a contract by striking. By contrast, under commercial law, the application of pressure by one party to another to enter a contract is illegal and invalidates the contract.

The practical question in *Electrolux* was whether an employer could require an employee to make a payment to someone else (the union) a condition of employment. The question, in effect, highlights the great global clash of ideas concerning differing concepts of 'rights' in the work environment. Unions argue they have a 'right' to pressure someone into a contract. But commercial law holds that everyone has a 'right' not to be pressured into a contract.

In the *Electrolux* case, the Australian High Court rejected the union argument and accepted Electrolux's argument. The Court maintained that, under Australian law, conditions of employment were clear and specific, and related to how much an employee was paid, hours of work, holidays and other such matters. The issue of whether a non-union employee could be required to pay money to a union was not a matter relating to the relationship between Electrolux's employees and Electrolux as an employer. Consequently, if the union or employees undertook strike action over that issue, they were not protected against any lawsuit for damages from Electrolux.

The High Court decision infuriated Australian unions and many labour lawyers and labour academics, who branded the decision a backward step and claimed that the decision would destroy the operation of labour law in Australia. Nor was the Court unanimous: one of the seven judges dissented from the overall judgment. A comparison between his comments and those of the other six judges illustrates the clash between the mindsets on labour law. They amount to two clear but opposing conceptions of justice.

The dissenting judge

The dissenting judge first relied on one view of the history and evolution of labour law in Australia since the Second World War. He said that when the Australian Constitution came into force in 1901 industrial relations law was restricted to issues of employment.[2]

But, he argued, the Parliament had moved on in its thinking beyond the strict employment contract to include matters raised by the International Labour Organisation. Interference in management issues was now seen as legitimate under labour law.[3] Further, by the late 1970s[4] labour law had moved beyond 'employment' to embrace 'industrial matters', in effect bringing managerial decisions within the jurisdiction of labour law and so creating a new constitutional paradigm. He argued that the Australian Parliament had, in effect, changed the Australian Constitution and hence changed the scope of labour law.

The judge also claimed that the Australian Parliament had intended to extend the reach of Industrial Relations Acts beyond the traditional idea of the employer–employee relationship.[5] He said it was clear that the Parliament had used new technical words in the *Industrial Relations Act* that meant the Act had new meaning and reach.[6]

By implication, he was critical of his fellow High Court judges, concluding that 'The statute has been changed. The understanding of the Constitution has advanced. A new and different constitutional head of legislative power has been invoked.'

The dissenting judge's other argument related to the role of unions in society. He saw unions as important and vital social institutions that needed protection from commercial litigation in order to perform their necessary functions.[7] He took the position that, in this instance of union 'service fees', it was justifiable to force non-unionists to pay fees to unions. 'Those to whom the Fee would apply are those who have not joined a relevant union but have stood to gain from the collective bargaining by the union on behalf of the employees of Electrolux'.[8]

The judge did concede that there was another point of view on the matter. 'I accept, focusing solely on the text of the Act read narrowly, that this is an arguable construction.' But in the end he said he was right: 'differences of interpretation suggest, or demonstrate, differing starting points or values that influence the decision-maker, consciously or unconsciously'.[9]

He was, in effect, emphasizing that the decision in this case was really one about values. He believed that values have changed since the Second World War and that the other High Court judges should recognize this and be prepared to incorporate these new values into their decisions.[10]

What does this all mean? It seems to the layperson that the dissenting judge is arguing the following. He reasons that, under the Australian Constitution of 1901, the original ambit of employment regulation was to be limited to the direct contractual relationship between common-law employees and common-law employers: that is to say, that the specific contract of employment discussed earlier was of the type that was subject to control by the state through labour regulation processes.

He considers that this historical constitutional ambit of labour regulation meant that the legislative reach of union activity in arguing, agitating and applying pressure on employee issues had to be limited to specific issues such as pay rates. It meant that issues affecting purely political issues, overseas conflicts or managerial issues were not matters that could be included in labour/industrial relations regulations. Those matters were subject only to commercial-type legislation and regulation. But, he says, over recent decades or so (he suggests perhaps from around the 1970s), the ambit of Australian labour regulation has expanded and has needed to do so in response to the changing industrial 'realities'. The dissenting judge does not specify what those new 'realities' are, but it is probably safe to assume that they relate to the declining numerical strength of unions and the new campaign techniques unions use to try to keep themselves relevant. It is clear, that, as union membership numbers have declined dramatically and globally (in the USA, some States have union coverage of only four per cent of the workforce), unions have sought to shore up their influence by extending their activity beyond the employment relationship to matters affecting broader social, political and, most significantly, managerial and commercial matters.

Then he claims that the new 'industrial realities' created by the activities of the unions have changed the social landscape, and this change has been, and must be, reflected by a new understanding of the legal ambit of labour regulation, at least in Australia. The dissenting judge is clearly highly critical of his fellow judges in this *Electrolux* decision. In his view, they made a decision that takes the ambit of labour regulation back to its original construct, namely, the direct contractual relationship between common-law employee and common-law employer. This return, he argues, to the traditional view of labour regulation would be a 'great misfortune' as it would expose unions to civil litigation and the awarding of commercial damages if they organized strikes or other industrial action that related to issues outside the common-law employment relationship.

By implication, the dissenting judge proposed that unions are an important social institution and they are needed to prevent the exploitation of, and damage being done to, workers. The decline in union membership, however, has reduced their influence to the point that unions are under the threat of becoming irrelevant. Further, the attempt by unions to retain their influence by extending their activities into managerial, commercial and other matters is legitimate because it serves a social good (namely, the protection of workers). This social good has been reflected in Australian legislation, he believes, through the insertion of the word 'about' in the legislation. In addition, rulings of the High Court of Australia over the last two decades have reflected this redefinition of the Constitution, and this redefinition should be accepted by all High Court judges.

Unfortunately for the dissenting judge, his fellow six High Court judges did not agree. They did not discuss the dissenting judge's line of reasoning but instead argued for different principles. In fact, the six judges argued for principles of contract integrity which, unlike the dissenting judge's reasoning, highlight the clash of moral principles that underscores the international debates on labour regulation. The clash of mindsets has everything to do with differing values and ideas of justice, and is at the heart of some of the great international moral debates over globalization, the social role of business and the nature of free markets.

The majority judges

What did the majority judges say, and what can be learnt from their views and decision?

The majority judges focused on the specific issue at hand, namely, the requirement under the *Electrolux* agreement that employees pay 'service fees' to unions. They argued that the bargaining fee 'seeks to impose upon an employer an obligation to act as a collecting agent for the union to deduct from an employee's remuneration, an involuntary payment to the union for a "service" which the employee has not sought and which may have been of no benefit to him or her.... Such a term ... seeks to impose an involuntary financial relationship between a union and a person who is not a member of it'.[11]

> The claim, implicitly if not explicitly, is that Electrolux is to act as the union's agent in entering into a contract with new employees which requires the employees who are not members, to employ the unions as their bargaining agent ... The agency so created is for the benefit of the union, rather than for the benefit of the employee upon whom the contractual liability is to be involuntarily imposed.[12]

The judges were alluding to a basic human rights issue. Can people be forced to pay money for services they don't wish to use simply because they have a contract with someone else? For example, if a person is buying a house, should the terms of the house-purchase contract be allowed to force the person to take a loan from a specified bank? This is not just a human rights issue; it is an issue that is vitally important to the operation of free market economies. It is critically important that every person in a society has freedom to choose which goods or services to buy or not to buy. It is a breach of human rights to force someone to buy something he or she doesn't want. It also destroys the consumer's rights to choose, the very foundation of competition in free markets. The majority judges alluded to this key right, but it was not the technical basis upon which they had to make their decision. They instead focused on whether the bargaining fee issue fell within the scope of the employment relationship. This is the key point because, as discussed earlier, the employment contract is about the removal of basic human liberties while at work. Conceptually, if the bargaining agent's fees could be declared to be part of the employment relationship, the taking away of employees' right to choose what services they used and paid for could be lawful. And that, at least, is the line of reasoning presumably underpinning the union's case for making use of this instrument.

The majority judges clearly recognized that the bargaining agent fee takes away fundamental rights. But the right which most occupied their minds was the common-law right to sue for damages. If someone crashes a car into your house, you have a legal right to sue the car driver for the damage to your house. The judges accepted that parliaments sometimes take away people's rights, for all sorts of reasons. But the majority judges said that if rights are to be taken away by Parliament, then the legislation should be clear that this is the intent.[13]

The judges explained that Australian industrial relations law 'operates to restrict the employers' common law rights of contract, tort and property'.[14] Further, the judges held that the clause the unions wanted inserted into the agreement amounted to coercion.[15]

A good deal was riding on this decision as it affected not just the bargaining fee but core rights in the community as well. Australian industrial relations law takes away persons' rights to sue for damages and allows coercion to make someone sign an agreement. Under employment contract and labour law, basic human protections that are enshrined in the commercial contract are taken away. The judges were saying that it was not their role to presume that Parliament wanted these human rights taken from people; if Parliament wished to take away people's rights, then the law had to be crystal clear that this was the intent.

The conclusion of the majority judges was that there was little, if any, evidence that the Parliament had intended basic rights to be taken away. They said that 'for an employer to collect money from employees and remit such money to a third party on behalf of employees had an insufficient connection with the industrial relationship to fall within the statutory description'.[16]

On what most people would see as a highly technical legal issue, the judges in fact made a decision based on a clear protection of human rights as has been embodied in common law for a considerable period of modern human history.[17]

The conflicting attitudes and central ideas that drive labour law and regulation in several different directions seem to have come together in this Australian judicial decision. But the attitudes and ideas were not invented on the spot by these particular seven judges. They have in fact evolved over a long period going back in Western thought to pre-Roman times. These attitudes and ideas underpin what it means for a society to be civilized.

Humans face a social organizational conundrum. We are both intensely individualistic and at the same time intensely social. In our own mind's eye, we each see ourselves as the centre of the universe. Yet we crave the company of others, and other people become as important to us as we are to ourselves. We desire and need to be involved with others to organize the world, to create, to build and to make our lives as comfortable, enjoyable and fulfilling as we can. We organize ourselves into large complex groups to achieve mutual benefit. Yet this results in the emergence of power relations which can strip some people of their own power over themselves and deny them their essential individuality, allegedly for the sake of the needs of the whole group. Yet the needs of the whole group are frequently defined and controlled by a few individuals who have managed to seize control of the processes by which the group works. And frequently those who have seized control of the group can garner the benefits of the operation of the group for themselves. The conundrum of human organization is that the collective is frequently controlled by an elite in its own interests. The law is the most important process by which we attempt to resolve that conundrum, so that the benefits of social organization are shared by all, and the members of the collective are not stripped of their individuality. The law of employment and the law of commercial contract are two different and largely opposing models of resolving the organizational conundrum. The two models are highlighted in the Australian *Electrolux* decision but cannot be fully understood without some simple notions of how the ideas have developed over the centuries.

Much of the history of human social and organizational evolution has been a battle between the rights of the individual and those of the collective. The collective, whether a family, a village, a tribe, a nation or an empire has always been seen as vital to the success of human life. A strong family in prehistoric times would provide the organization for hunting and for protecting the family members from wild beasts. A strong tribe, working together, could cultivate the land, hunt and protect its members from opposing tribes. So it has been and is with nations and empires. But in all human history and within each of these collectives, whether large or small, the collectives always select leaders or leadership groups. And leaders have always been, or have been seen to be, the strongest and the most forceful of the individuals in the group. Natural selection within the social dynamics of the collective delivers power to the strong. The history of humanity is, however, littered with leaders, whether as individuals or as institutions, who have always sought to impose their will on the group, often brutally, savagely, without justice and with little regard for basic human and individual dignity and rights. This has most frequently been justified on the grounds that the need of the leader to impose his power on the collective and each individual in the collective is necessary if the collective is to be strong and successful. The problem of the collective is that it has always been controlled by individuals. The employment contract is a derivation of this basic human trait. At law, the employer has a right to control the employee. The collective is the firm. The employer is the leader. The employer has the right to direct and control the activities of the employee for the greater good of the collective, the firm. The employees must accept this subjugation.

Thus, one of the greatest and most difficult journeys of humanity has been to create social systems that enable the collective to exist, to cause operating systems to function within the collective, to enable leaders to operate within the collective while at the same time preventing the leaders, whether as individuals or institutions, from oppressing all or some of the individuals in the collective. On the political front, democracy has been the system created to enable the collective to choose leaders but to constrain and frustrate the ability of leaders to oppress individual members in the collective. The idea and application of the law as being something morally superior and more powerful than leaders themselves is essential to this process. In economics, the market-based economy plays much the same role. All individuals have the opportunity and can, through the dynamic processes of the market, become wealthy and seemingly powerful. But the free market constrains and frustrates any individual of wealth and power from oppressing other individuals in the market. The commercial contract, being something more powerful than any wealthy individual, is the legal bedrock of the free market. Consumer, competition and anti-monopoly laws have added to the strength of free market economies by frustrating concentrations of economic power. In the areas of democracy and economics, the processes that humans have developed enable all and any individual the opportunity and right to become a 'leader' but frustrate the ability of leaders to oppress individuals in the collective. It's a complex process, reflective of the complexity of humans that is not simply, neatly or readily explained in academic dissertation.

Strangely, however, this process of evolutionary thought has not been applied to the firm and to employment. The prevailing conceptual and operational paradigm of the firm is that it is and must be a command system controlled by a leader. The employment contract is the social and legal glue that holds this system together. The right of the employer to control the employee is an unchallenged theoretical position thought necessary to the very existence of the firm. But concern about the consequent legal and actual potential of the employer to oppress individual employees in the name of the firm has been the obsession of international labour law through all of the twentieth century. Yet the processes of labour law have not dared address the inherent structure of the employment contract itself. Instead, labour law has sought to create institutions and laws which are imposed upon both the employer and employee. Labour law has sought to address the inherent power imbalance of the employment contract by creating a new power imbalance, a new oppressor—the state itself. This is the current dilemma and failure of labour law.

Denying the individual

As is now clear, the process of control by the state over the employment contract amounts to theft by the state of employer and employee control of their employment contract. And this state-sanctioned theft of control affects many other aspects of employment and of the operation of firms and relationships inside firms.

In the European Union (EU), for examples, EU directives require businesses above certain sizes to have 'works committees'. By EU dictate, these committees have effective control over many of the day-to-day managerial functions of businesses operating in the EU. The committees are made up of managerial representatives and elected or appointed employee representatives.

One committee structured along these principles in one firm, for example, had the authority to issue orders on work rostering, on when and how overtime was to be allocated, on what company trucks would be used for deliveries, and even on which truck drivers would make use of company mobile phones. Such was the control of the committee that the most important function of the managers of the business was to lobby the employees to have their preferred employees elected to the committee. Managers became political lobbyists rather than managers. Such committees, imposed by labour regulation, take away from employers large measures of control, usurping employer control under the employment contract. But the committees also take away from individual employees large measures of their control over their own job. Control is removed from employers and employees and placed in the hands of state-sanctioned institutions — in this case, works committees.

The process is one of collectivization of the control of the firm rather than allowing the firm to be controlled by each individual doing his or her individual job. It occurs as a reaction to the employment contract. It removes employer control, but it also prevents employees having control. The collective process abrogates the rights of the individual and transfers control of their contracts to the collective. This takes many different forms.

In France, for example, employment laws during the 1990s imposed ceilings on how many hours an employee could work in a week. Sold under the banner of workers' rights, the laws in fact prevent employees working the hours they may want. These French laws are now, to some extent, unravelling because they deny employees their rights and prevent employees having control of their own lives.

Control over absence from work is likewise removed by employment regulation not only from employers but also from employees. Most countries have employment laws that dictate to employers how many holidays must be given to employees and often determine when and how those holidays must be taken and how many days absence for sickness are allowed. The reasoning behind the laws, it appears, is that employers would never give holidays to employees if the law did not demand it. Further, if the law did not require holidays to be taken, many employees would continue to work, thus affecting family life and social cohesion. And holidays and other leave laws are presented, again as, 'employee rights'.

But the trick, once again, is that the law not only takes away control from employers but also denies employees control of their own lives. Leave laws do not deliver workers' rights but overturn employer and employee rights. The laws that mandate holidays for employees play a trick because, in dictating holidays, they require employers to reduce weekly pay to employees, withhold money from them, and pay that withheld money to employees only when the employees take their holidays. Why? The argument is that employees are not capable of putting money away for their holidays and that the state must therefore force employers to be a 'bank' for employees. But in effect the law creates a cash windfall for employers which they use to help finance their businesses. The employee is forced by law to become a financier of the employer's business. And if an employee asked an employer not to withhold holiday pay but to add it to the weekly wage, the employer would not be allowed to do so. This is another example of employment regulation denying both employers and employees the right and capacity to control their employment contract. And it's all done under the banner of social justice. But it is a pretence.

One of the most significant areas where the state removes employer control is dismissal. Across the globe, employment law removes from the employer the ultimate right to dismiss an employee. An employer who dismisses an employee can be subject to an 'unfair dismissal' action by the dismissed employee. The employee can go to a court or tribunal and claim that the dismissal was not just. This does not occur under the employment contract but under employment regulation. Unfair dismissal regulation takes the right of dismissal away from the employer and places it ultimately in the hands of the state. Under this regulation, the state normally has the power to reinstate the dismissed employee, but this rarely happens. More frequently, the state tribunal sees that reinstatement is not feasible and instead imposes a fine on the employer which is paid to the employee. The outcomes are odd.

In effect, unfair dismissal laws have turned a job under employment into a strange form of property right. A job exists because a business has a need for something to be done. If the business need vanishes, the job vanishes. If the employer and employee have a falling-out for whatever reason, under the employment contract the employer was once thought to have the right to find another person to do that job. But unfair dismissal laws have taken away that right. The job, which under the employment contract was in the possession of the employer, has now become a property which ultimately is controlled by the state. The employee doesn't own the job. The employer has theoretical ownership of the job but the state has ultimate control over the job.

Unfair dismissal laws put the state in the position of second-guessing the behaviour and motivations of the people working in the firm. In most firms, the employer is a legal construct without any true human form. (The exception is small business, where the owner works in and daily manages the business.) As the business becomes larger, the employer becomes a system of cascading manager employees who are delegated the functions of the employer. The true dynamic in these firms becomes one of relationships and interplay between people of different employee rank within the firm. If a person is dismissed, the dismissal is a result of a decision of one employee or group of employees against another employee. When the state then considers an unfair dismissal application, it is mostly considering what occurred between two or more employees and is imposing a view of the rightness or otherwise of the behaviour and the dismissal decision. The process is supposed to provide justice based on some measure of whether or not the dismissal was 'unfair' or 'fair'. But any study of unfair dismissal cases and decisions shows that the criteria adopted in such decisions are not objective, predictable or certain. Consequently the process of dismissing an employee has become completely uncertain and the idea of 'fairness' has become a farce. From the perspective of the employer (or rather the delegated employees of the employer), unfair dismissal laws have actually created a process whereby the job has to be purchased back from the dismissed employee. And employees know this.

Most employee dismissal actions now involve a calculated guess as to what the cost of the dismissal will be. Most of the time, employers will offer money up-front to employees when dismissing them, in the hope that they will choose not to take an action. If an action is initiated by the employee, the employer knows that there is considerable legal expense associated with defending the action. Consequently, most cases are settled without going to court because it saves on legal expenses and management time. Ultimately, this behaviour makes a mockery of the notion that unfair dismissal laws actually have anything to do with fairness. Unfair dismissal laws have merely created a situation where an employer is forced to buy back the property known as a job so that the employer can hand it over to a replacement employee. The job has become a contorted form of property which is transferred between employer and employee—but ultimately under the control and at the whim of the state.

These laws, which allow the state to control employment, often even extend to when and how employees are to be promoted or demoted, create requirements for employers to report financial and other matters to unions, create rules dictating when employees can withdraw their labour (strike) or employers lock out labour, decide the process of transfer of employees from one employer to another, and so on. When studied in depth, each of these examples shows that they remove employer control and, equally, employee control. The process is always one in which the state, in one form or another, takes control of the employment contract to itself.

But what occurred late in the twentieth century was a recognition of the economic underperformance that these laws cause. The evidence is mounting that firms in countries with heavy employment regulation are less productive and less profitable than those in countries with minimal employment regulation. This is causing firms to relocate their business operations to countries with minimal labour regulation. It has become a competitive issue recognized by economists and politicians.

As it is generally applied, labour regulation imposes one particular organizational model on firms, which is not necessarily a model that works competitively. Through labour regulation (in particular, unfair dismissal laws), the state is imposing a business model preference on firms that glorifies the idea of managerial control through full-time employment. This model is narrow and assumes that all businesses operate in an industrial-type environment. But this is not the reality of post-Industrial Revolution economies and societies. The principles of production have changed since the eighteenth century. The outcome is that businesses in heavily regulated societies have difficulty being internationally competitive, which means that national economies underperform. And some nations are trying to rectify this problem, a problem that is squarely of their own creation.

Italy, for example, has introduced 'on call' employment designed to allow Italian businesses to get around unfair dismissal laws which prevent them from adjusting the size of their workforce to match consumer demand. Italian employers can now employ a new class of person called 'on call' employees. Any on call employee who refuses a call to work can be dismissed. But the law goes further and places additional power in the hands of the employer by making on call employees liable for damages if they refuse a call to work. Likewise, Japan has introduced fixed-term contract laws which enable employers to take people on for fixed terms, but which prohibit employees from resigning at will during the fixed-term period. For budgetary reasons, the Dutch are looking at laws restricting access to unemployment benefits for persons who are to blame for their dismissal.[18]

As a consequence, employment has become odd, complex and convoluted. In trying to create 'fairness' and 'justice' by giving the state control of the employment contract, the economic processes within the firm have become messy, unpredictable, inconsistent and expensive. The state's control of the employment contract has greatly multiplied the transaction costs of employment within the firm. Those costs are unseen and unrecorded, and most consist of the destruction of productive time within the firm. But the costs are real. And it has reached a stage where, based on the most noble of intentions, employment regulation in the second half of the twentieth century potentially destroyed the employment contract as a viable and effective form of organizing firms and economies. How societies came to this current position has a 300-year history that runs in tandem with the development of the Industrial Revolution.

The academic moral underpinnings of labour regulation

All law is the codification and enforcement of human ideas. Where human ideas are sound, law is good. Where human ideas are flawed, so too is the law. Labour regulation and law are founded on the idea that, within firms, systemic injustice always exists and that the law is needed to create justice. This is the moral basis of the state's imposition of labour regulation. Its moral language is the language of human rights and of a never-ending battle for justice. And how this view of systemic and inevitable injustice in firms came about has a long history. Countless millions of words and very many books have been dedicated to the subject. Most of the moral dissertations will explain the logic roughly along the following lines:

Up until the seventeenth century, the common people of England had rights to fish in streams, take fruit from trees, collect wood and hunt for game in forests, and take stone and sand from communal quarries and pits to make buildings. These 'common law rights' were the backbone of life. They enabled ordinary persons, the common people, to build their homes and obtain food and warmth. During the seventeenth century, these rights were progressively taken away as the King and the aristocracy enclosed and fenced the common areas and prevented the common people from exercising their common law rights. The ruling class made and controlled the law and enforced the destruction of 'the commons' by brute force backed by the law. The reaction to the enclosure by the commoners was often violent but ineffective. It was robbery of the weak by the powerful.[19]

The common people were left with only one option if they wished to avoid starvation, and that was to work on the now enclosed land as wage labourers. They worked the land to which they no longer had rights, were paid a wage but were prevented from owning the results of their effort. Profit went to the landowners who could accumulate great wealth while the common people subsisted. This new enforced lowly existence was considered at the time by the common people to be little better than wage slavery. And the term 'wage slavery' entered the political and ideological vocabulary in the nineteenth century when Karl Marx predicted that wage slavery must inevitably lead to the violent downfall of the new emerging capitalist class at the revolutionary hands of the common people. Inevitably, Marx claimed, the common people must and will reassert their common rights and that property would have to return to communal ownership. This idea of the theft of common rights by the capitalist class and the forcing of people into wage slavery through lack of alternative work takes a view of history spanning close to 200 years. It's the glue that holds together the prevailing global paradigm of labour regulation. It's a view that in the twenty-first century is giving signs of potential implosion.

Labour regulation in the non-communist world developed during the second part of the twentieth century as the Cold War was in progress. Fearful that Marx's revolutionary predictions could prove correct, non-communist societies in part accepted, at least theoretically, that power relationships inside firms were unequal. Labour regulation was created to address the power imbalance and most of the moral reasonings of the twentieth century continued to draw from the experience of the 'enclosure of the commons' of seventeenth-century England.[20]

Social theorists explain and reason that the evolution of 'wage slavery' in the seventeenth century was a necessary legal precursor to the Industrial Revolution. By forcing people off common lands, England created a vast reservoir of poor and destitute folk who had no choice but to flood to the growing factories of England that emerged from the eighteenth century on if they wished to earn a living. The wage slave moved from the meadows of England to work in the filth and danger of early Industrial Revolution England. And this process was forced by law which reached a high point in England under the Poor Law Act of 1834. And, so the reasoning goes, as the Industrial Revolution swept the globe, so too did wage slavery! In England, this legally enforced oppression of the people was not addressed until the late 1870s, when various Acts of Parliament began to regulate conditions in factories, legitimized unions and protected the people from the conditions of industrial life.

In presenting this historical backdrop as the justification for labour law as it is currently applied, there has been an almost overpowering tendency in labour academic circles to extend the 'wage slave' oppression arguments beyond the specifics of the employment contract. Echoing Karl Marx, the 'unequal bargaining power' argument has been applied across the entire range of economic activities. The argument maintains that free markets by their nature and essence must oppress the worker and create capitalist winners and worker losers. This is the historical thread of ideas that unites vast numbers of people in the vast global 'anti-globalization' movement, which depends for its existence on the idea of the inevitably of exploitation, first in the firm and, as a consequence, then in free market activity.

A morality with limitations

But the oppressed worker argument has deep flaws, not so much in itself as an idea but in its practical application. Unfortunately, the near-religious zeal with which the idea is held blinds many of its ardent followers to its practical flaws. Ideas are valid only to the extent that they are borne out in practical application. On this criterion, the moral arguments underpinning labour regulation contain major practical errors.

The fact is that the argument of wage slavery only has relevance within the context of the employment contract. And the late twentieth-century employment contract (the contract *of* service) is a watered-down derivation of the system of wage slavery. The employment contract contains within it the elements of control found within the original master-and-servant contract that constituted the 'wage slave' contract of work that followed the eighteenth-century enclosure laws. But the employment contract of the early twenty-first century has relevance only to the extent that it is applied inside the firm between an 'employer' and an 'employee'. It is not a contract type that extends outside the firm to transactions between firms and consumers or between firms themselves. Consequently, to argue that free markets are systemically exploitative is not valid, because the dominant contract operating in free markets is the contract of equality, the commercial contract, the contract *for* services. If the systemic exploitation argument is valid, it has validity only to the extent that the pure form of the employment contract operates in firms.

Further, the concept of wage slavery, dependent as it is on workers not having work options across any given society, is no longer valid. Every person who works in advanced economies has a vast array of choices in how they work, including the option not to work under the employment contract. In free market economies, the organization of firms has long ceased to be dependent upon the employment contract. Employment-organized firms are now only one model in operation. Self-employment, otherwise known as independent contracting, is now an equally important organizational form for firms in the twenty-first century.

In addition, the practical operation of free market economies is not dependent upon the employment contract or upon any form of wage slavery. In fact, the employment contract operates in complete opposition to free markets and is a drag on free-market activity. Free markets are completely dependent for their operation and success on the wide acceptance and application of the commercial contract. The commercial contract is the contract of freedom. The employment contract is the contract of constraint. Labour economists, academics and labour regulation propagandists are wildly wrong when they assess free market activity within the narrow and false assumptions of the dominance of the employment contract. Such thinking ignores the practical truths of how people behave, most frequently leading to the theorizing of problems that do not exist and the construction of bad laws that purport to address fictional problems. The outcome far too often is labour laws that create exploitation and oppression rather than remedying them. In the twenty-first century, labour regulation systems falter when their sole or dominant moral underpinning is the idea of eighteenth- and nineteenth-century wage slavery.

This is not to question the moral sincerity of those who hold such views. There can be no question that, based on their arguments, those who continue to adhere to the 'wage slave' view of the world argue from high moral principle and are passionate in their belief that society should protect the weak, vulnerable and the needy. But the eighteenth-century view of the world has diminishing relevance to the twenty-first century world. And in promoting solutions to problems based on a vision of diminishing relevance, labour law risks doing as much harm as good. But the real issue is not the theoretical musings of academics. The core concept of the firm, what it is and why it exists, is the real battleground of ideas over labour regulation.

Maintaining the firm as a class structure: is the employment contract dead?

The changes that are sweeping the globe in relation to work present fundamental challenges to the concept of the firm developed academically around the 1930s.[21] The firm has been thought of as a control system dependent upon the employment contract. But social changes—that is, the behaviour of people—are challenging the traditional employment structure upon which the firm was thought to rely. In turn, these changed behaviours challenge the nature and type of regulation the state seeks to create in relation to work.

The example of 'our daily bread' gives a practical demonstration of the changes and challenges.

The large, industrial bread manufacturers are under severe pressure from commercial competition as a result of the rise of the small, local, hot bread shops. Somewhere around the 1970s, new bread-making technology was developed involving small ovens and mixers and new doughs and yeasts. This was combined with a surge in interest for healthier eating and saw the revival of the local baker. The local baker is located in shopping centres and malls but does not home-deliver bread; instead, the consumer comes to the shop and buys freshly baked bread. Hot bread shops are generally privately owned, but operate under franchise arrangements whereby the operator benefits from bulk buying of raw materials, standardization of bread recipes, group advertising power and so on. But the secret to hot bread shop profitability is minimization of waste. The owner/operator of a hot bread shop bakes according to need. She can look at her front counter, see what has sold and bake on the spot to replace sold-out lines. By the end of the day, a good baker will have little if any bread left unsold. The hot bread shop operator is in a position to ensure that supply closely matches demand. The large bread factories, however, do not have this advantage. They have to bake early in the morning, pack the bread into trucks for delivery to shops and supermarkets, and make quality guesses as to what will sell where and when and at locations miles from the baking site. Inevitably, the big factory bread manufacturers will always have unsold stock. Unsold stock constitutes loss of critical profit margin. The factory producer of bread cannot have the intimate, detailed minute-by-minute information on consumer demand that the small, hot bread shop owner has.

And this situation is replicated in thousands of different ways in large numbers of different industries. It is not confined to baking franchises but is occurring in almost every industry and every sector. Emerging new industries based on information technology, for example, are structured almost entirely without resort to any traditional industrial form. Industrial-type production of goods and services is having to compete with many forms of non-industrial-type production.

The implication for employment law is significant. Once, when factory bread production dominated, the bakers who were critical to running the factories were all employees. They worked under employment contracts with all the features of control that prevented them profiting from their effort. They were paid wages and did not have the opportunity to share in the profit of the total enterprise resulting from their effort. They also did not suffer financial risk. This was the dominant form of work available for bakers. Now a new type of baker has emerged.

This time the baker in the hot bread shop is the owner. She does not work under an employment contract but rather has a direct relationship with consumers whereby her contractual obligations are determined by the commercial contract she enters every time she sells a loaf of bread to a consumer. There is nothing in her contract which tells her she is obliged to be at work. Unlike an employee, she does not have an implied duty of loyalty to anyone. These concepts do not exist for her. Instead, her work is dictated by her own desire to satisfy the simple demands for quality bread from her customers. She is driven and motivated entirely by the belief that she can bring all the elements of her business together, do it well and make a profit. She knows that she takes a financial risk. She does not have to like her customers on an individual personal level, but she will display all the personal attributes of friendliness, courtesy and respect because doing so makes her customers happy and encourages them to return for future business. She is guided in all this behaviour by the commercial contract that civilizes human relationships in a most marvellous and simple way. It occurs without massive interference by the state.

The only time the state interferes in the contract is when the hot bread shop owner has a dispute with a consumer or supplier that the two parties cannot resolve. Significantly, state interference does not occur prior to the parties entering the contract. For example, in free market economies, the state does not dictate the price of the bread.

What is happening in the bread business is happening across the globe in thousands of different ways in millions of businesses and different business sectors in every country. It is a great but quiet revolution, a revolution of changing relationships inside the firm. It is a people revolution whereby, mostly without conscious thought, the employment contract is being rejected. But what now is the firm?

In the bread business there are now two dominant models of the firm. One is the command-and-control-employment structured firm of the factory variety dependent on employment contracts for control. The other is the franchised small business model of the hot bread shops. To a casual observer, hot bread franchises look like large conglomerates, as if they were a factory-type conglomerate. But they are very different. They are, in truth, a new model of the firm in which the conglomerate is deconstructed into integrated small firms, but which, as a whole, still have recognizable features of a large firm. Rather than being controlled by employment contracts, the franchise operation functions internally through commercial contracts. Each hot bread franchise owner has commercial contracts with his or her customers and with the franchiser. In one instance, a hot bread franchiser went broke and the franchisees pooled their resources and purchased the franchiser's business. In this instance, the franchisees have commercial contracts with a franchiser in which they are all shareholders.

Importantly, control within the franchise structure is as strong as, and perhaps even stronger than, that which is achievable under the factory employment control structure. Which one is better is hard to say. But what is clear is that the command-and-control employment firm is no longer the dominant model of the firm. It is under challenge and facing competitive threat from new and different control structures operating not under employment contracts but under commercial contracts. This trend has been in evidence for many decades. The impact across societies is already significant. But labour regulation regimes around the world have barely begun to understand the change or react to it.

Nevertheless, this does not mean that the employment contract is dead. In fact, it is most likely to continue to live.

One of the key features of the employment contract and of the employment structured control firm is that they exist as a consequence of a strong human trait. There exists a fundamental desire of humans to control other humans. It is not a civilizing trait, but it is embedded deep within the human psyche. It is ego-driven and it is self-fulfilment driven. Firms are often, in the eye of the owner, an extension of the owner's ego. And the employment contract gives an individual as an employer control over other individuals as employees.

This is frequently augmented by the argument that most workers want to be controlled anyway or have no personal skills that would give them the capacity for control of their work situation. This basic human desire to control others and the corresponding belief that some humans want to be controlled are likely to ensure that the employment contract will continue to exist in societies.

But there are also other more practical reasons why the employment contract is likely to continue. When a person starts a business as a self-employed person and is financially successful, there is inevitably a desire to expand the business. As it grows, other people are needed to run and operate the business. There is a natural inclination on the part of the entrepreneur who started the business to believe that he has worked hard and is deserving of the financial reward that comes to the business. He is naturally inclined to want to ensure that he is the recipient of the profits of the business and that those profits are maximized. The employment contract serves this end. The employment contract ensures that employees do not share in the profit of the business and that the employer can keep all of it.

That the employment contract so simply serves the entrepreneur's profit-seeking motive is a common dilemma confronting large firms with shareholders. When corporations have shareholders that are removed from the daily running of the business, the business is run by managers who are employees. The dilemma of the corporation, called by economists the 'principal–agent' problem, is that the owners of the business do not have effective, daily control of the business. And a constant battle emerges between shareholders and employees over who has control of the profits of the business. Senior managers are the delegated employers. They have effective control over the employees below them. Senior managers have a vested interest in keeping pay rates for those below them as low as possible. Senior managers take control of the process which determines how and what they are paid. Senior managers consequently have the opportunity to pay themselves handsomely, thereby limiting the profit available to the shareholders. It is one of the great problems of the modern corporation, and many examples exist of senior managers being paid scandalously high amounts even when corporations are making losses.

But what is not recognized is that this process whereby senior managers seize the profits of business for themselves is in large part dependent on the firm being command-and-control structured around the employment contract. Where corporations are not structured around the employment contract, this principal–agent problem largely evaporates. How this occurs is discussed in Chapter Seven.

But the point of this chapter, however, has been the issue of the global paradigm of labour regulation and the time warp within which it is conceptually stuck. Whether or not the wage-slave thesis was ever right or wrong is not the big issue. What is at issue is the challenge confronting the relevance of the twentieth-century construction of labour regulation in the twenty-first century.

And the challenge is not from any global capitalist conspiracy. The challenge is coming from the people; people who do not see the relevance of being in a 'controlled' relationship when they work; people who do not wish to have the framework of their own working identity created for them by the class structures of employment-constructed firms. This is the challenge.

Endnotes

1. *Electrolux Home Products Pty Ltd* v. *Australian Workers Union* [2004] HCA 40.
2. 'The Act and even the words of the critical section, pick up language with a long history .... First, the background to the problem.... Can be traced to the constitutional necessity of preventing the [Industrial Relations Act] from exceeding its constitutional mandate. At the time of those decisions, [in the 1950s and 1960s] that mandate was relevantly confined... [to employment].' — Electrolux at 186.
3. 'Yet gradually this Court reformulated its view ... so that implications of industrial demands upon management prerogatives came to be seen, in some instances as legitimate subjects of industrial disputes ... It was inevitable that this process would occur because ... all decisions of the applicable tribunals constituted interference to some degree in what had earlier been regarded as management prerogatives. It was during this process of evolution in the perception by this Court of what "matters" did, and did not, sufficiently "pertain to the relationship between" employers and employees that a broader range of subjects came to be seen as within the ambit of industrial conflict and employment disputation.' — Electrolux at 209.
4. 'By the late 1970s ... this Court began to evince a broader, and should I say, more industrially realistic, approach to the permissible subject matters of "industrial dispute" within the Constitution and the statute.' He quoted from an earlier High Court decision that 'The words [industrial disputes] are not a technical or legal expression. They have to be given their popular meaning.' — Electrolux at 210.
5. 'Even more important is the signal given in s170LI(1) [of the Act]. This makes it clear that the Parliament had decided to cut the Act loose ... In a stroke, a new constitutional foundation for federal regulation is created ... The Parliament has thus embraced a new constitutional

paradigm. It behoves this Court to approach it without the blinkers apt to the old thinking ... We now have to apply new statutory language.' — Electrolux at 215.

6.   'It was enough that the agreement should be *about* matters *pertaining to* the relationship. It was not necessary, as such, that the agreement should actually "pertain" to the relationship itself. Quite clearly, this parliamentary expansion of the ambit of the connection between the claim and the employment relationship was deliberate. It was designed to enhance the permissible scope of the agreement and the connection between its subject matter and the employment relationship ... If there could have been any doubt about this under the former definition of "industrial dispute" in the 1904 Act, it is removed by the addition of the word "about", by the inclusion of a double formula for connection and by the substitution of a different foundation of the employment relationship in question. — Electrolux at 214.

7.   '[T]he search for a rational and practical meaning to the language of the Act is the more urgent by the dramatic consequences of denying protection to a union for industrial action ... a high degree of certainty is essential as to whether industrial action can be taken lawfully ... To expose an industrial organisation of employees to grave, even crippling, civil liability for industrial action, determined years later to have been "unprotected," is to introduce a serious chilling effect into the negotiations that such organisations can undertake....' 'In my view, it is a serious mistake of interpretation to read the scope of the protection offered by the Act in the way favoured by the majority of this Court.... It is one that has the effect of defeating a specific remedial protection against civil liability afforded by the Parliament to industrial organisations, such as Unions.' — Electrolux at 189, 192 and 195.

8.   Electrolux at 216.

9.   Electrolux at 205.

10.   'The only impediment, suggesting that the claim pertains only to the "relationship" between the employees and the unions, is one that derives from old thinking.' — Electrolux at 217.

11.   Electrolux at 240.

12.   Electrolux at 55.

13.   'There is a presumption that ... the legislature does not intend to deprive the citizen of access to the courts [to sue]...' although 'modern legislatures regularly enact laws that take away or modify common-law rights ... The courts should not impute to the legislature an intention to interfere with fundamental rights. Such an intention must be clearly manifested by unmistakable and unambiguous language.' — Electrolux at 19 and 20.

14.   'Thus, by conferring specific immunity from civil liability, ss 170ML(2) and 170MT effectively abrogate the common law rights both of participants to the negotiations and of third parties who may

suffer actionable damage.' — Electrolux at 107; *ibid.*, at 116.

15. 'The elements of the conduct prohibited ... are action, or threats of action, with intent to coerce another to agree, or not agree, to the making of an agreement.' — Electrolux at 26.

16. Electrolux at 10.

17. 'The question is not one involving s51(xxxv); it is simply a question of the meaning of the definition of "industrial dispute" in s4(1). And although there are some minor differences between the definition and the relevant definitions previously found in the [1904 Act], the requisite nature of the subject matter of a dispute remains precisely the same, namely that it pertain to the employment relationship involving employers, as such, and employees, as such.' — Electrolux at 157.

18. According to a newsletter produced by the global legal firm Baker & McKenzie, Vol IX No 2, January 2004. www.bakernet.com

19. The story given here draws largely on a version of it published in an article by Australian sociologist Scott Burchill, 'A short history of self-defence', *The Australian Financial Review*, 21 July 2000. Burchill is a lecturer in international relations at the School of Australian and International Studies at Deakin University.

20. The 'enclosure' of the commons should not be confused with the often discussed problem of the 'tragedy' of the commons which looks at poor use and over use of 'common' resources—for example, over-grazing and over-fishing of common lands. The 'tragedy' of the commons highlights the claim that when property is 'owned' by the collective, invariably no-one takes responsibility for looking after it properly. People want the benefits of the collective property but not the responsibilities. This is why private ownership is often considered a superior form of title, because people will care for their private property in a way that a collective will not.

21. See R.H. Coase, *The Firm The Market and The Law*, University of Chicago Press, 1988.

7: Markets in the Firm

The real voyage of discovery consists not in seeking new lands, but in seeing with new eyes

— Proust

Understanding the problem of the firm

The essential problems of the firm—considered during most of the twentieth century as a command-and-control, employment-contract-dependent structure—cannot be resolved. The reason is that the problems confronting the firm are products of the very structure of the employment-controlled firm.

The firm is supposed to be a system of transaction-cost management which enables entrepreneurs to develop, produce, market and sell products and services, and thereby make a profit. Control of the firm is theoretically delivered through the employment contract. But the employment-based firm suffers systemically from problems of poor accountability, low transparency, and corruption by executives and underperformance by de-motivated staff. The firm works—but it is far from ideal.

These problems of the firm are in large measure a direct consequence of employment because, under employment, the individuality and independence of employees must be suppressed if they are to be subject to control by the employer. Suppression of individuality de-motivates employees and creates poor accountability and low transparency. This is enforced by law under the employment contract.

With the suppression of individuality and independence, all power in the firm flows to the executives who sit at the top. They are thus routinely delivered the opportunity and ability to corrupt the processes of the firm to benefit themselves. In effect, they monopolize the benefits of the firm. This problem occurs where the controllers of the firm do not own the firm. It is an endemic problem in firms and is well recognized as the 'principal–agent' problem. What is not recognized is that it is a direct product of, and entrenched within, the firm by its employment-dependent control structure.

The extent to which executives makes use of this opportunity to benefit themselves is ultimately determined by their individual sense of probity and goodwill. The constraints on them from within the firm are few. Some executives rort the firm for their personal benefit. Most executives, however, are true to the greater needs of the firm. But the extent to which the firm does not become corrupted by executives is not a product of the employment system of the firm but exclusively the product of the honest and trustworthy behaviour of most executives who run firms. The system of employment control doesn't constrain corruption but constantly creates opportunities for corruption.

Within the employment construct, executives can corrupt the firm because they are at the top of the employment chain of command. They are the delegated employer even though they are employees themselves. Employees below them are not supposed or allowed to question the directions they are given because they are employed. Consequently, the very people who are most able to identify and expose rorting and corruption—namely, subordinate employees—are not allowed or required, under the terms of the employment contract, to do anything about it. And the problem of countering this executive opportunity to extort has become a principal but still unfinished task of corporate governance laws which, unfortunately, treat the problem in band-aid form rather than dealing with the root cause. It is one of the great conundrums of the firm as currently conceived.

The other great problem of the employment-based firm is that employees are far too often de-motivated. They see themselves as caught in a bureaucratic machine in which their sense of self-worth and their ambition are suppressed by the machine-like processes they must fulfil. They are trained, cajoled, induced and goaded into accepting their position, and sometimes even convinced that they enjoy it. This is the function of the human resource industry—to motivate the de-motivated employee. But why motivate? Because de-motivation spawns individual and collective underperformance. Again, it is the system of employment control that is the systemic cause of de-motivation. And all the efforts of the human resource industry don't remove the problem—they only mask it. Simply, the firm does not belong to employees. They are subject to the dictates of the system of the firm and, despite all the countervailing efforts of the human resource industry to create bonding to the firm, de-motivation must inevitability occur. Human nature is such that people are not innately motivated to commit to things that they neither own nor control.

Both of these problems—executive corruption within the firm and employee de-motivation—are consequences of poor accountability, low transparency and bureaucratic control, and both stem from the employment contract. The employment contract is a contract under which the employer tells an employee what to do. The employee is required to accept those instructions and carry them out with diligence. The control process involves a relationship of dominance by the employer over the employee. It requires the employee to be quiet and accept an instruction whether it's right or wrong. If an employee is concerned that the employer's instruction is wrong or even dangerous, the implied terms of the employment contract tell the employee to follow the employer's instructions regardless. Some employees don't follow the instruction, use their judgement and question it. This may be good. But by doing so they are challenging the authority of the employer, and this threatens the system of control within the firm. Most employees, however, simply accept instructions without question. The consequence is that the very people in the firm who are best placed to keep the systems in the firm accountable and transparent—the employees—have implicit counter-instructions in their employment contract not to question the system. Since this makes for systemic low levels of transparency within the firm and system-wide low levels of accountability, firms have to develop extensive processes running on top of, and parallel to, the employment contract to create transparency and accountability. Firms are forced to do this to overcome the problems of the employment contract. Government regulators, likewise, are forced to create countervailing regulations imposing external counter-corruption discipline on the firm because discipline fails to operate in the firm. Transparency, accountability, employee motivation and responsible executive behaviour occur despite the employment contract, not because of it.

The conclusion is that the firm, as a command-and-control, employment-dependent structure, works but has systematic weaknesses which cause the firm to underperform when measured against the human potential contained within the firm.

Employment as a cause of these problems, however, is not a topic that is approached or discussed by business theorists, management academics, managers of firms, economists or business regulators. Why? Because the prevailing concept of the firm is so wedded to the necessity of the employment contract that to question the desirability of the employment contract is conceived as threatening the very existence of the firm.

Free markets provide resolution

The problem of the firm as an employment control structure runs parallel to the problem of economies as command-and-control structures.

One of the greatest lessons learned during the twentieth century is that command-and-control economies perform poorly. Command-and-control economies cause the human capital of a nation to achieve well below its potential. Central control of economies by governments has been shown, time and again, to cause human misery in which corruption at the level of government is endemic. Controlled economies enable the controllers at the top of the system to rort it for their personal benefit. These facts are well recognized. But it took most of the twentieth century for that fact to be recognized and accepted. Once it was realized, however, the speed with which command economies were rejected globally, and free markets embraced, provides testimony to the utter failure of command and control at a national level.

What emerged during the twentieth century was a growing recognition of the superiority of free markets and of the appropriate role of government in free-market economies. Free-market economies are based on the recognition that humans have a natural desire to create, grow, discover and advance their personal position in life. People strive to improve their economic well-being and their physical comfort, and to find their own sense of self-worth and identity. Free markets cater to the physical, economic, psychological and, yes, even spiritual ambitions of humans. Free markets recognize that humans achieve these personal objectives through millions of different and changing personal actions and interactions. These interactions cannot be predicted, designed or determined by central planners. And the human desire to achieve, when allowed to occur within free markets, involves complex mixtures of both individual and collective action. It is rare for a human to achieve their ambitions in isolation. Few humans are islands! Humans achieve more by being communal. But free markets, unlike command-and-control economies, do not seek to dictate the communal form. Communal forms emerge from free markets and constantly change under free markets. This is the trick of free markets. They maximize both individual and communal action.

But government under free markets also recognizes that people have a natural desire to exert control. Humans will seek to maximize the benefits of their activities for themselves and to maximize the opportunity for realization of their personal ambitions. In seeking to maximize their personal opportunities, people are inclined to seek to stop others from having opportunity. They fear that other people's quest for achievement can restrict their own personal opportunities. It's a two-edged issue involving both desire for, and fear of, competition.

Under free markets, government has recognized the tension between these two human traits—to be ambitious and communal in achieving ambition, and also to control and maximize personal benefit by denying others the opportunity to realize those benefits. The role of government in free-market economies is to balance the tension between the two traits. It's a delicate and difficult balance.

Governments in free market societies have a complex task. They must set the framework in which people can achieve their goals without allowing people to exploit one another. Government must deliver laws that allow the human entrepreneurial spirit to seek monopoly but prevent them from achieving it. And in targeting this delicate balance, government must recognize that it has the potential to become the largest of all monopolists and the chief exploiter in a society. Consequently, government in free-market economies has progressively confined its role to social and economic objective-setting and law-creation and enforcement, removing itself from economic service delivery. This process is evolutionary, experimental and often poorly carried out. But the principles are being progressively accepted.

Oddly, however, these free-market lessons of the twentieth century have not been applied to the firm. Firms exist within free-market societies like islands of command-and-control socialism. And within government policy settings and the academic conceptual framework of the firm, the command-and-control socialism of firms is not questioned. Worse, the government's approach to the firm is to reinforce and support that command-and-control socialism. It is an oddity of free-market thinking that the socialist firm is thought so necessary and that the essential link of the employment contract to the socialist firm is not considered. This is why management concepts and government regulation are lagging behind human behaviour in firms.

A firm move to free markets
As an employment construct, however, the firm has been under challenge and threat for some time. But the threat and challenge come not primarily from the realm of ideas but from the combined behaviours of people. In effect, command-based, socialist firms are facing internal demise and external competition.

How is the socialist firm being challenged?

The 'independent employee' is the great internal threat to the employment firm. Independent employees may accept the command system of the employment firm in which they work, but they are not happy with it and comply with it only as a means to earn an income. And they emotionally react against it. They may become belligerent, aggressive, frustrated or benignly compliant. In extreme cases, they may become whistleblowers if they see wrong in the firm, and as a result they usually suffer exclusion from the firm and usually have their honesty and integrity impugned when the command-based firm seeks to protect itself. Witness Corinne Maier of France![1] Occasionally the firm invites independent employees to be independent, accommodates them, sometimes even encourages them, because to do so assists accountability and improves the firm's performance. Some of the great inspirational management performance gurus of the latter part of the twentieth century in effect appealed directly to the potential to the firm offered by the independent employee.

But, by whatever means, the independent employee is inevitably breaking down the command-and-control employment structure of the firm.

The external threat to the command-based firm comes from firms that have internal markets. The new type of firm adopts the free-market model, even if it is not done consciously. Like most things in human evolution, the non-command-based firm has developed through minute experimentation, with things that work being adopted, and things that seemed to fail rejected. The process has been comparatively slow but is evident—although it has not been recognized academically or theoretically.[2] But the emergence of this new firm is unmistakable. And it's an exciting development. The firm that incorporates internal markets is not dependent on command and control. Even if the language of the employment contract is applied, the principles and operation of the commercial contract direct the internal processes of the firm. Where this occurs—that is, where 'markets in the firm' exist—it spells the death of the socialist firm.

And it is not something that is brand new, unfamiliar or strange. In fact, it is surprisingly familiar.[3]

Alfred P. Sloan was the leader of General Motors of the USA in the days when GM was at its zenith. Sloan guided GM during the 1940s and beyond, so that GM became the greatest industrial giant of the greatest industrial economy in the world. Sloan had a vision of how GM should operate. This vision carried and guided GM long after Sloan's departure. Generally, it is believed that Sloan was the greatest of command-and-control dictators who constructed systems through GM that perfected command and control. Sloan decentralized GM's operations into discrete business units. However, the decentralized businesses operated under a command-and-control regime. Or so it has generally been considered! According to one commentator, although Sloan wanted GM to be 'decentralised' '... he also wanted to run it on "a principle of coordination"—the principle it turned out, of central command and control.'[4]

But the words of Sloan himself suggest that his model was different from the current command-and-control model. Sloan said, 'The most important thing I have learned about management is to make men think and act with individual zeal and initiative, yet cooperating with each other'.[5] Near the end of his career, Sloan explained in a speech how GM actually operated under his guidance. He said:

> We have never consolidated the various units of personnel ... They have been left free to develop their own initiative so that they feel that it is theirs ... In one type of organization policies and methods are determined at the top and orders are issued down. The other type of management comes from the bottom up and arouses individual initiative. We choose the coordinated type, the one which would apply even to small businesses ... We do not issue orders. I have never issued an order since I have been the operating head of this corporation ... Two hundred and forty-seven men in one group have each day's pay determined by the number of finished motors that pass the last man in the group ... We put no limit on earnings and the men put no limit on production ... Where do policies come from, if they are to be useful in the business? Out of the business itself ... They must come from the men who are in daily contact with the problems ... Our policies come from the bottom. Everything possible in the organisation comes from the bottom.[6]

According to Sloan himself, his successful management concepts were opportunity and motivation. Motivation was achieved by introducing incentive compensation schemes based on production and cost reduction. This does not sound like an employment-based command-and-control company, but rather one in which the production line workers at least were treated as if they were their own business people who determined production and directly benefited financially from the production they controlled. This looks very much like a basic form of markets operating inside a firm. And if this is what Sloan had applied inside GM, it may be that, after he departed, the coordinating systems he layered through the firm were turned by others into command and control. Whatever happened, GM, along with the other USA car manufacturing giants, became disconnected from the market place and suffered dramatic decline when challenged by the Japanese manufacturers during the 1960s–1980s. GM has struggled ever since. Based on his description, Sloan's model seemed to be close to the 'markets in the firm' concept, even if it was not recognized at the time or maintained after his departure.

What appeared to occur in the car manufacturing sector after the Second World War was that the USA command-based giants became progressively less competitive. But at the same time new business models emerged that took market principles directly into their internal operations. One of the most common of these was the direct selling industry—modelled along similar lines with many well-recognized brand names. One of the most recognizable is probably Amway.

Amway was formed in the USA in 1959. By 2003 it was valued at around $4.6 billion and was operating in 91 countries with annual global sales of some $US1.2 billion. Amway sells its own brand of household consumable products, including laundry products, vitamins and cosmetics.[7] But these products are not found in any retail stores. Amway is sold by tens of thousands of individuals who operate as independent contractors, usually from their own homes. It is a globally organized, home-based small business organization in which every Amway distributor receives income based on his or her sales. Amway distributors are, in every sense, self-employed independent contractors operating under commercial contract arrangements with Amway. The independent distributors have to deduct their own operating expenses before arriving at a profit. Their status as independent contractors has been tested in courts in many jurisdictions and found to be self-employment. Tax offices internationally now accept the self-employed, small business status of direct selling. Amway is a prime and obvious example of a firm which uses the principles of free markets in its internal structures. The entire, direct selling, global industry with thousands of businesses and many thousands of brands is organized in this way.

Franchising is another example of markets operating in firms.

Ray Kroc was the genius who created the McDonald's empire.[8] In 1954, at around the age of 53, Kroc was a successful salesman who sold commercial food preparation machinery to hamburger and fast-food outlets throughout the USA. Kroc could have retired, but he came across two brothers, the McDonalds, who ran their hamburger store with military precision like no other Kroc had seen. They sold a better hamburger cheaper and faster than any other. Kroc took the McDonald's operating systems and replicated them, store by store, across North America by developing and applying the modern form of franchising. Eventually this turned McDonald's into the global giant it is today.

The heartbeat of McDonald's is the conglomeration of small businesses operating within the coordinated McDonald's system. This system is franchising, which has been replicated worldwide in thousands of different retail markets unrelated to McDonald's. The core concept of retail franchising is that small business retailers who own and operate their own businesses are close to and understand the customer. They have a passion for, commitment to, and focus on their businesses that cannot be replicated in large command-and-control structures. Retail franchising allows small business persons to operate businesses, but it gives them a successful operating system with which they choose to comply. This is similar to the Amway system. In the case of food, the franchising operating systems will include recipes and products, standardized machinery, hygiene and safety systems, and layer these with bulk-buying power, marketing, training, advertising and so on. Franchising combines the advantages of large corporate operating systems with the advantages of small business commitment. And the real key to understanding this is that the control systems in the firm are dominated by commercial contracts, not employment contracts.

McDonald's franchisees enter a commercial contract with McDonald's. The terms of the contract set out rigorous obligations to comply with the McDonald's' operating systems. But before being granted a franchise, a potential franchisee undergoes extensive training in the systems. This training includes considerable unpaid time working in McDonald's stores and unpaid time at one of several McDonald's hamburger universities located across the globe.[9] Only after extensive training at their own expense do potential franchisees have the opportunity to purchase a McDonald's franchise. The contract between McDonald's and the franchisee is clearly a commercial contract in which the franchisee is fully aware of the contract terms and enters the contract of his or her own free will. The franchise contract is the contract that governs the relationship between the McDonald's company and the franchisee. Even though McDonald's is a hamburger and food retail company, its core business is that of a franchiser that designs, organizes and runs the systems that enable its specific food-retailing operation to function. Layered commercial contracts are used to direct the system.

McDonald's as a corporation (as distinct from the franchisees) owns the properties and buildings in which the stores operate, and they charge the franchisees rent. McDonald's corporation is one of the largest landholders in the USA and its share price is underpinned by its land holdings. McDonald's works with manufacturers to design and supply the specialized cooking machinery and leases the machinery to the franchisees. McDonald's works with external food and packaging suppliers who manufacture and supply meat, fries, buns, wrapping and so on. McDonald's doesn't ordinarily manufacture these things itself but has the tasks done to its specification by external providers. All this is governed and controlled by commercial contracts. The core business of McDonald's, as distinct from its franchisees, is not the selling of hamburgers. The franchisees sell hamburgers and McDonald's organizes all the commercial contracts that enable the franchisees to sell.

The McDonald's form of the franchise system is now common and used widely in a large number of varied retail businesses worldwide that have nothing to do with McDonald's. It is a principal model of 'markets in the firm'.

Compare franchising with the traditional command-and-control retail department store business. Retailers' large stores are divided into departments along product category lines. Employed department heads manage each department. The department heads are paid wages. They work under all the elements of control that go with being employed. Head buyers do the buying for the multiple departments spread around the many stores that the conglomerate may own. Sales people, also employed, work on the shop floor under employment control through their department managers. The entire ship is steered from the top, with entrepreneurial direction the preserve of an elite of executives. It's an employment-based command-and-control structure. The system works. It has been hugely successful. But it is under stress. During the latter part of the twentieth century, the command-and-control department stores, worldwide, ran into trouble. Profitability plummeted and many collapsed. These traditional retail conglomerates are like huge ships which, when they get into trouble, can be painfully slow to change direction. And they usually seek to change by bringing in new chiefs who take helm of these ships and try to steer them in different directions. But their entrepreneurial flair is too narrowly constrained by an elite of executives who sit at the top of the employment chain.

Compare this with the internally franchised department store structure which has taken its lead from McDonald's franchising. In Australia, for example, the successful retail conglomerate Harvey Norman has taken important and profitable market share from Australian command-and-control retail giant Coles Myer. Both Harvey Norman and Coles Myer retail white goods, bedding, furniture, electronic and computer equipment, and so on.[10]

The trick with Harvey Norman is that it has taken the franchise model and applied it to each department within its stores. Every product department is a privately-owned small business that utilizes bulk buying and marketing advantages available through the Harvey Norman banner and organization. In the computer section of a Harvey Norman store, its small business owner will be on the shop floor watching, coordinating and serving. This small business structure, coordinated through Harvey Norman's franchise rules, keeps Harvey Norman intimately alert to the fickle and changing demands of consumers. Coles Myer, for example, cannot bring its employee staff to the same level of self-motivation that Harvey Norman can systematically achieve with its shop floor, small business entrepreneurs. And it's this fine and delicate level of contact with the customer that makes a critical difference in the retail sector.

Consumers are unpredictable, fickle, and have little loyalty. What clinches the profitable sale in retail is that little extra care and attention that is shown to the customer on the shop floor. Employees can and do show that extra care but the problem for the retail firm is how to systematically spread it throughout the entire business. As a system, the self-employed, small business model will always out-motivate the employment control system. Systematically nurtured self-employment releases entrepreneurial flair and drive throughout a firm, not just at its top, as is the case with the employment-controlled firm. And in retailing, this makes the difference between those firms that really succeed and those that merely plod along.

In retailing, the consumer is the factor that creates the cut-throat competitive environment of the marketplace. The consumer *is* the free market, and retail businesses that aim to succeed have to connect seamlessly with the free market. Where the structure of the business is market-orientated, the business is more likely to repeatedly connect with its target markets than if it is based on command and control.

But the franchise system of retailing does not guarantee success. Command-and-control employment retail firms can and do succeed. Command-and-control firms can and do layer human resource and marketing systems on top of the employment contract and achieve high motivation and profit. A marketing genius at the head of a command-and-control retail firm can produce stunning results.

Franchise retail firms do collapse. If a franchise firm is not good at managing the commercial arrangements with its suppliers and franchises, it may fail. Its products, positioning in the market place, and so on may be poor. But further, managing a firm through the use of commercial contracts demands higher levels of managerial skill than do employment contracts. With employment contracts the manager's word is law. With commercial contracts, the manager's word is subject to the terms of the commercial contract, and the franchisees and others can, should, and do question the wisdom, authority, and wants of the contract managers.

This is where franchising opens the firm to high levels of transparency and accountability on a daily basis. No one is master. Egos based on hierarchy collapse. Everyone is equal. Everyone in the firm has a client relationship with everyone else. Everyone is a consumer to everyone else. Under this structure, it's hard to rort or corrupt the system because everyone is watching everyone else. If an executive seeks to rort the system for personal gain, it is often at the expense of someone else with whom he or she has direct dealings. Rorting in the franchise system becomes more difficult than under command and control.

Both systems—employment contract control and commercial contract control—enable firms to function. But the questions are: which system is likely to continue to work and which system gives greater chance of success? If the macro experience of managing national economies is any guide, and if the experience of franchising in retail is any guide, then 'markets in the firm' is likely to systematically out-compete the command-and-control socialist firm.

But franchising is just one model of markets in the firm and it is not completely structured around the commercial contract. Retail franchising generally still makes use of the employment contract on the shop floor where the franchisee is the employer. The relationship between each retail franchisee and the people who work in the small business operations is normally still dominated by the employment contract.

The next model of markets in the firm involves replacing the employment contract in its entirety with the commercial contract throughout the firm. The terminology for this varies across countries and industry sectors, but is most comfortably embraced by the term 'independent contracting'. Sometimes it is called freelancing, self-employment, or consulting; but whatever the terminology, there is one key and necessary feature: the legal relationship between the individual and the firm is a commercial contract.

This means that the master-and-servant relationship created via the employment contract does not exist. When this occurs, markets can take full hold within the firm. Once again, this development has become surprisingly familiar in the latter part of the twentieth century, although government regulators and many businesses have not altered their terminology and generally still use the term 'employment' to describe it.

In North America, it is common to have to tip waiters, bellhops, and other people working in the hospitality and related industries. It is standard practice that the wages paid to these professionals by their 'employers' are comparatively low. Tips constitute a significant and important part of their income. Tips are frequently included as a certain percentage of a restaurant bill, but additional tipping is normal and frequently expected. Tips reflect the value the customer puts on the service delivered personally by a waiter at a restaurant. The waiter may work in the restaurant as an 'employee', but a significant part of the 'payment for service' relationship inside the restaurant is directly between the waiter and the customer.

What does this say for master-servant employment, even if government might use the term 'employee' as a statistical description of the waiter, and the restaurant refers to the waiter as an 'employee'? In fact, when tipping arrangements are in place, the waiter almost has an implied commercial contract with the customer, the payment for which is at the discretion of the customer. It's close to being a commercial contract but is without the prior agreement of payment. But it's certainly not an employment contract. The waiter has a contract with the restaurant, probably an employment contract, and many of the features of the contract may reflect employment. But certainly the tipping regime breaks down the legalities of the employment contract by allowing elements of independent contracting to flourish.

In addition, in North America well-positioned jobs as waiter, bellhop, concierge, and so on have a resale value and can be bought and sold for substantial amounts of money involving goodwill. Such jobs therefore look very much like independent contracting or self-employment. These people are running their own small business which has an accumulated potential, if not actual, goodwill.

The housing construction sector in Australia is almost exclusively structured around independent contracting. Bricklayers, plasterers, plumbers, carpenters, labourers and other tradespeople associated with the housing construction sector are predominately independent contractors. Few people who work in the housing sector are employees. The companies that build houses use designers, surveyors, supervisors, sales staff and so on who are also predominately independent contractors. The building companies do not actually build houses but coordinate and organize the contracts and people necessary for construction and delivery of end product to the purchaser of the house.

Herein lies the challenge to the idea of the firm as a transaction-cost minimization process. The employment control concept of the firm holds that firms exist because, if every small aspect of an economy were organized through commercial contracts, the cost of organizing and managing the contracts would be so great as to suppress the level of economic activity; as a result, firms evolve in which the employer controls transaction costs by means of employment contracts. It is argued that employment contracts avoid the transaction costs associated with commercial contracts. This concept of the firm was explained by Coase in the 1930s and is still generally accepted, at least by academic economists.[11] Coase was not wrong on his transaction-cost management theory, but was wrong to assume that transaction cost containment by the firm is dependent on the employment contract.

Employment contracts, certainly in the second half of the twentieth century, have generated significant transaction costs of their own, to the point where employment has ceased to provide any transaction-cost advantage. The case of the Australian housing industry proves that firms exist by managing transaction costs, but can do so by way of either commercial contracts or employment contracts.

The idea that the firm is dependent on the employment contract for its existence is not valid. Control through employment is just one of several models for the structure of a firm.

The information technology sector is another which operates 'markets in the firm' based on commercial contracts. Most information technology specialists are, in one form or another, independent contractors. The term 'employee' is often used, but this is principally to satisfy outdated government regulation requirements.

The information technology sector is characterized by the management of multiple cascading job contracts, which may vary in length from a day to several years. Commercial contracts apply both within and between IT firms. A large company, for example, needs an IT job done. It issues tenders. A large IT company picks up the tender, and then several things happen. The company may have staff who work internally, normally under commercial type contracts or even as employees. The IT project is split into many components and the people working within the firm may bid for aspects of the job. Groups or teams of different sizes form around particular aspects of the project. Team leaders or coordinators emerge; positions are not necessarily organized around any formal hierarchy. A person may be a team leader of a project one day and work the next day on a project to which he or she is a minor contributor. Teams bid for and seek specific people for specific jobs. Remuneration is largely set according to the laws of demand and supply, and may vary from job to job. Work on the project may also be offered to outside suppliers, which may be individuals or small, medium or large companies. Who is competing with whom becomes blurred. In letting work to outsiders, the IT company regularly uses the services of labour hire companies specializing in the IT sector. Individuals who work for themselves are regularly registered with several IT labour hire companies. They may even do part of a job through one labour hire company and another part directly for the IT firm. Some IT labour hire companies provide wide-ranging services to the IT specialists on their books, such as taxation deduction procedures, organizing insurance and superannuation, preparing taxation returns, leasing vehicles, and so on.

To an outsider, the labour hire firm may look like an employer, but it doesn't control any of the work. All that the labour hire firm does is manage the contracts. In the IT sector, the differences in the internal structures of the large IT companies and the relationships between external operators are blurred. The entire industry is a massive mix of cascading contracts in which the external observer has difficulty seeing order and pattern. But to the inside players it's perfectly ordered and logical. Each person knows where he or she is in the mix, and actively markets his or her talents and abilities as an individual business. The IT industry is very much a free market for labour that works both across and between businesses, and internally within businesses. The structure and operations of the industry closely parallel those of a stock exchange or network of stock exchanges in which commercial contracts are at play for peoples' services.

In Chapter Two the words of the sheep shearers in Queensland demonstrated the attitudes of independence and business-mindedness that come with being an independent contractor. The Queensland shearers also happened to work under labour hire arrangements which closely resemble those of the IT sector. Traditional labour hire involves the on-hiring of employees of the labour hire company. But in Australia a particular form of labour hire emerged in the early 1990s as a result of several court decisions. In this 'Odco'[12] labour hire form of work engagement, the people supplied are independent contractors in both a legal and a practical sense.[13] Operating in a similar way to the IT sector, Odco labour hire companies place independent contractors into a variety of jobs, including in health care, teaching, manufacturing, and many others occupations. It's a major business in Australia.

The essence of Odco labour hire is that the Odco agency does nothing other than manage contract transactions. Odco agencies are firms in their own right. The workers they supply to clients are self-employed people (businesses) in their own right. The agencies supply self-employed workers to other businesses that need the services. Everyone is a client to everyone else. Several layers of firms are in operation and connected, but no employment exists. Transactions costs are managed to the satisfaction of all parties concerned through the Odco agencies. It is another form of markets operating in firms.

Koch Industries

Perhaps the most startling of all examples of 'markets in the firm' is Koch Industries, headquartered in Wichita, Kansas, USA.[14] Koch is unique because not only is it structured around 'markets in the firm' principles but it has adopted them consciously. Koch is possibly the only firm in the world that has thought deeply about what free markets are and deliberately sought to replicate the operations of free markets in its internal structures and published information on its approach. Koch Industries has developed a unique, patented management system called Market Based Management (MBM). It funds a unit at George Mason University to study, develop, promote and train people in Market Based Management. Its managers are inculcated in, and operate around, Market Based Management.

Koch is an impressive firm. It is a privately held company that does not release any of its financial statements or data to the public, but was cited in 2000 by *Forbes* magazine[15] as having annual sales of $US35 billion. The firm began in 1940, and between 1961 and 2002 the value of Koch Industries grew by 1,300 times. By comparison, the average value of the Standards and Poor's top 500 companies grew in the same period by 95 times.[16] By 1996, Koch Industries was the second-largest privately held company in America and currently rates as one of the largest American companies. Rather than one business, it's a conglomerate of businesses. It operates globally in commodity trading, petroleum shipment, asphalt production, natural gas, gas liquids, chemical, plastics, fibres production, chemical technology equipment manufacturing, minerals, fertilizers, ranching, securities and finances, and holds numerous other varied investments. It's big! It's different!

Being as big as it is, Koch Industries has attracted its fair share of media attention, but surprisingly little attention has been paid to its market-based management approach. This is in spite of Koch's Chairman, Charles Koch, stating in 1993: 'We are convinced that Koch Industries' success stems primarily from our management philosophy, which we call "market-based management" ... Command-based societies have found themselves unable to survive when faced with market-based alternatives, and command-based companies will suffer the same fate when confronted with market based competitors'.[17] Koch Industries believes that its utilization of markets in its firm gives it a critical competitive advantage.

> Koch Industries says: MBM 'Requires managers to understand the major features of a market economy, then adapt these features as needed to improve management practice'.[18]

The structure of Koch industries is best described as a series of internal markets where units sell their services internally to one another and externally. The management structure relies on internal markets to allocate internal resources. So-called support groups or profit centres are expected to survive in the internal Koch market by offering services competitively to other such centres. With internal markets, for example, a machinery maintenance depot seeks to service manufacturing sectors in the firm. The manufacturing sectors are not obliged to use the internal maintenance group, which has to win its business in competition with other service providers from both inside and outside Koch Industries. In a further application of market principles, the pay of individual workers in the maintenance group is linked to their commercial success. Similar internal competitive markets can be applied to other activities within the firm, such as accounts, debt control, marketing, training, recruitment, design and planning. For internal markets to work, no profit centre must be allowed any exclusive right to deal with any other profit centre: that is, internal monopolies cannot develop.

> Koch Industries says: 'The knowledge needed for sensible business decisions is inherently dispersed among many people'.[19]

In these internal markets, the principles of commercial contract transactions between the units drive the relationships between the units. Koch Industries doesn't divulge everything about MBM or its internal structures, so it's not known how Koch Industries actually constructs or manages the internal contracts, but the principles of MBM certainly could not be applied without substantial freedom to contract. Bureaucratic employment contract, command-and-control systems would not be consistent with relationships between the internal units under MBM.

Certainly, employment contracts may apply within each Koch unit, but given that individual remuneration is significantly tied to the profitability of each unit, the financial motivations for each unit would take on many of the features of small business. That is, the people working in each unit would be fully appraised of the profitability of their individual unit and know that profitability affects their personal income. This close connection between each unit's profitability and the personal incomes of its individual members creates a focus and motivation that cannot be replicated in a command bureaucracy. In effect, the internal price mechanisms resulting from this structure send signals constantly through Koch Industries which focus and drive the behaviour both of the units and of individuals.

Under these arrangements, bureaucratic management, rules and regulations are replaced by market performance, price and behavioural signals. 'Management' doesn't have to 'order' anyone to do anything, because everyone in the firm becomes a self-manager. Class structure is replaced by performance structure. Performance is not determined by bureaucratic rules but by success in the internal market. Competition exists both within and between the internal units. But so, too, do cooperation and community.

> Koch industries says: 'Markets are a complex blend of competition and cooperation. Likewise, a market-based firm should promote cooperation while channeling competition into activities that actually promote the common mission'.[20]

Even though people working in each unit have their incomes tied in part to the success of the unit and need to work as teams, they compete with each other for jobs, position and decision-making authority. This is to be expected because this is the normal way people behave. But because individual success is tied to the success of the unit, people also find that they need to cooperate. They have to create their own community to achieve group success. But this community and cooperation doesn't have to be created artificially through set company rules or processes or demands from superiors. People in free markets naturally find their own processes of cooperation and internal community. If they don't, the risk is that their unit will not succeed and not be profitable. Individual failure to cooperate is not masked by an employment bureaucracy, but is exposed by the failure or limited success of the unit in the internal Koch Industries market.

> Koch Industries says: 'The goal is to understand the crucial functions played by private property in a market economy, and then allocate rights and responsibilities in ways that harness independent judgement, provide continuous feedback and capitalize the future impact of current decisions'.[21]

Presumably, within Koch Industries, MBM implies that failing units are allowed to fail. If not, MBM would not truly be an internal market process. But, just as in external free markets, a community still needs services, even if a particular service provider fails. It appears that Koch Industries allows different units to compete for the same internal services; and if one unit fails, another already exists that fills the potential service vacuum. But in any community, people become reliant on a service and don't want failure. So it would be expected in Koch Industries that if a unit is servicing other units badly, signals are quickly sent to the underperforming unit to lift its game. These signals will be price, purchasing decisions and, most significantly, direct discussions between people.

While this occurs, the ebb and flow of success and failure, which is a normal part of free markets, operates within Koch Industries. But, importantly, market signals limit the extent to which the failings of any unit can grow to the point where they infect other units and thus risk creating creeping and endemic structural failure within Koch Industries.

By contrast, bureaucratic command-and-control firms systematically mask failure, and so failure in one section of the firm can grow and infect other sections of the firm to the point where, all too late, the resultant collapse can be huge and life-threatening to the firm. With internal markets, failure is not masked but exposed. Hence failure, which always begins in a small way, is more likely to be discovered while it is still small-scale.

Failure is a natural and a necessary precursor to success. Failure is an essential ingredient of free markets. Free markets treat failure benignly and as 'water under the bridge'. Tomorrow is another day, when success is always possible. Free markets detect failure early on, allow it to occur while it is small, then do something about it and thus prevent it from growing. In this way, success grows by treating failure as normal. Koch Industries has consciously sought to allow this process to occur naturally inside its firm.

Koch Industries has sought to take these elements of free market operations, understand them and apply them in much the same way as they occur in free markets. No one directs behaviour, but the system of free markets enables human behaviour to lean toward success.

According to Koch Industries, internal markets can have a profound effect on productivity. It claims that introducing the price mechanism to the internal workings of the organization encourages staff to think and act like smart purchasers. When each unit is allowed to operate independently as a small business, relationships between units take on the features of relationships between firms in supply chains. And supply chains are about people making purchasing decisions. But it would be a mistake to view purchasing decisions as price-oriented. In fact, price is only one factor. More critical to purchasing decisions in supply chains is cooperation.

One of the earliest developed secrets of the success of McDonald's, for example, was the realization that its suppliers had to make a profit. McDonald's needs products supplied at cut-throat prices.[22] But McDonald's operates on the view that in order to achieve low purchase prices for its supplies it needs to cooperate with its suppliers to achieve required quality and delivery capability. The art lies in identifying preferred suppliers with whom relationships can be developed to achieve these ends. Alternative sources of supply may be available and the buyer may shop around for alternatives to lower the price. But there is always a price in any market below which lower prices will always result in an inferior delivered product. McDonald's knows this and works with suppliers to get the lower price, but with the required quality. This is an unceasing and delicate balancing act involving technical knowledge of production issues, supply chain issues, money and human relationships. Importantly, if the supplier is not making money, its long-term viability is uncertain, thus placing the stability of the buyer at risk. The interdependence between suppliers and the purchaser is strong.

> Koch Industries says: 'Accountability must extend to the level of the individual. A person or team is free to utilize local knowledge, make judgements and bear the consequences. Assigning a kind of ownership for every activity, action and result'.[23]

The trick of being a smart purchaser in Koch Industries is to combine all these factors so as to make correct and sustainable buying decisions. In Koch Industries, MBM seeks to encourage staff to think and act like smart buyers. This involves all the processes of service delivery within each unit and between units. It's not a competitive price-driven process, but involves many factors, in particular to do with quality.

> Koch Industries says: 'This authority system applies both to internal resource allocation and external purchase decisions, and it has allowed Koch to abolish centrally approved budgets. In place of command and control budgeting, Koch tries to approximate the market's allocation through profit and losses').[24]

Take one simple example. The story goes that Koch Industries decided to implement MBM with a head office department that produced company reports. Before MBM, the office operated under a budget and diligently produced reports that were supplied to units across Koch Industries. When MBM was applied, the units suddenly became customers of the office. The units were free to choose to buy the reports. Predictably, after the change, the office soon discovered that many units chose not to buy the reports, and it lost revenue. This prompted the office to try to discover what sort of reports the units wanted: what format, how often, at what price, and so on. In effect, the office undertook market research of its potential customers. The office then redesigned its entire approach to reporting and consequently increased the sales of its products. This simple story demonstrates many of the elements of free markets operating inside the firm.

This process is standard within Koch Industries. Units market-research each other through formal and informal processes, always investigating whether they are satisfying their internal customers. The internal culture of Koch Industries is targeted to being one of intense client focus. That is, everyone in Koch

Industries needs to view everyone else in the firm as a client. And this focus is not directed from the centre or confined to specialists within the firm; rather, it's a daily necessity. This presumably means that, when Koch Industries deals with external clients, client focus is natural and immediate. This surely would result in higher-quality external client interface than occurs with command-and-control firms. In command-and-control firms, relationships with external customers have to be different from those within the firm.

> Koch Industries says: 'MBM does not mean a mindless copying of external market practices inside the firm ... It does not mean merely turning everyone in the firm loose to do whatever they think will make money'.[25]

Koch Industries makes it clear that market-based approaches to the internal structures and operations of the firm are difficult to implement and cannot always be applied. Safety is one such area. Koch Industries operates a wide range of highly technical production plants involving hazardous and dangerous substances. Environmental safety is a constant obsession with Koch, which claims that MBM does not necessarily work in this area. Presumably, Koch Industries has a number of health and safety manuals that dictate operating instructions. But this does not necessarily detract from the internal market principles. Free markets are an approach to systems of human behaviour and interaction that allows people to maximize their individual choices. But free markets and human choice cannot defy the physical laws of the universe. It is perfectly consistent for free markets to regulate according to the known or believed physical realities but to allow individual choice within those constraints. So Koch Industries has to be cautious about where and when MBM can be applied. Choice is sometimes limited, just as is the speed at which we are allowed to drive our cars.

Further, Koch Industries operates in law-based societies and its systems must comply with the law. As has been discussed in this book, many laws assume that firms are employment-based, command-and-control bureaucracies. By default, those laws sometimes almost impose employment-based command and control. No firm, including Koch Industries, can afford to act in defiance of the law. Indeed, to do so would not be consistent with a 'markets in the firm' approach in a market economy. And because Koch Industries operates in many different countries, it would encounter wide international variations in the extent to which employment regulation allowed or inhibited MBM. In the USA, for example, employment regulation is minimal by comparison with Germany, Italy, France and other European nations. It is speculation, but presumably Koch Industries would find MBM easier to apply in some countries than in others, which may have an influence in investment decisions.

> Koch Industries says: 'But it would be a mistake to view market-based management as always requiring more decentralized decision making. ... misplaced authority can be just as disastrous for an organization as having top management make all decisions'.[26]

Free markets economies are not unregulated; indeed, they are highly regulated. But one main purpose of regulation is to ensure that the free market can operate and is not corrupted. For example, free market economies have significant laws that seek to prevent monopolies forming. In the USA, 'Combines' legislation gives central corporate regulators power to investigate monopoly activity and force the break-up of companies that have become excessively large and dominant. USA regulators have done this on several occasions in the past, and subjected Microsoft to Combines investigation during the 1990s. Eventually Microsoft reached agreement with the regulators to modify certain behaviours to ensure that the USA IT industry remained competitive. Microsoft was not as a consequence broken up in the USA.[27]

Likewise, Koch Industries indicates that there are times when the centre must impose authority. But, as with free market regulation, it is assumed that such central intervention would be to ensure that the principles of MBM were being applied in practice. The Koch Industries' centre would have the same interest as government corporate regulators, that is, to ensure the integrity of (internal) free markets. And like corporate regulators, when to intervene and when to step back can be a fine judgement call. Further, Koch Industries would obviously need to intervene if an internal unit broke or risked breaking national laws. Once again, the judgement of when to allow units to freely operate and when to impose central authority would be difficult. But the difficulty for Koch Industries would be parallel to the difficulty faced by governments committed to free markets.

> Koch Industries says: 'The systems a company uses to generate new ideas and select those that will be tried should be designed to avoid as many command-based shortcomings as possible'.[28]

In any society, the difference between success and failure, wealth and poverty, progress and regression is often the extent to which the society allows its members to be creative.

Creativity is not a rare or limited human quality. In fact, creativity is mostly found in the millions of little ways that we all find every day to do things a little better. Creativity is the individualized human 'x' factor that free markets release. Creativity is suppressed under command and control and released under free markets.

By exposing everyone to competitive pressures, the 'markets in the firm' approach produces results by preventing the destructive and negative game-playing that can poison a company. But more importantly it allows human economic creativity to flourish. On this level, the approach of Koch Industries is even more interesting. For Koch Industries, internal free markets are not just about structures, transactions and money; they are also about how people choose to relate to one another and treat one another. And it's through this interpersonal conduct that creativity is allowed or prevented.

Creativity is a dominant human attribute. In command-and-control economies, creativity is crushed. This is why those economies are stagnant. Creativity is not something that can be 'created' or 'motivated'. It is not the preserve of elites. It is not confined to the arts or to any single activity, but it probably emerges in one of its most common forms in business activity. The act of supplying a good or service demands high levels of creativity involving thousands of integrated actions to achieve a result. In business, the creativity of every person working in the firm is essential to success.

Creativity is not a human attribute that can be predicted or detected before it emerges. It will appear, however, only if given the freedom to appear. It cannot be demanded. When it emerges, it often surprises the individuals or groups from whom it emerges. It is the unquantifiable potential of the human spirit. We do not know how to cause it to emerge, but we do know how to crush it. Command and control is the crushing process. Command and control suggests that creativity is the preserve of those who do the commanding and controlling.

By not seeking to command and control, Koch Industries has consciously sought to provide the environment in which creativity can emerge. And when it does, they let it flourish and grow. This it does in practical ways through the market design of its systems rather than through management control.

The fact that individual Koch Industries units can grow according to their success and that individuals within units can be remunerated according to the success of units is the primary foundation from which creativity can emerge. This replicates the small business unit in the external environment. But it seems that Koch Industries seeks to harness creativity in very real additional ways.

Koch Industries has an investment unit, advertised on its Website, with an open invitation to anyone with an idea to present it to the unit. Once again, Koch Industries doesn't divulge much about the operations of its investment unit, but some things can be surmised. Applications to the investment unit come from within Koch and also from outsiders. The indication is that numerous applications are made to the investment unit each year, which the unit analyses in detail. For those proposals that fit Koch Industries' business plans, an investment is made in such a way that the new business becomes part of Koch Industries itself. This should be comparatively easy for Koch Industries to do because its internal markets are like external markets. Good ideas or developments that have the potential to compete with Koch Industries are nurtured, developed, encouraged and become part of Koch Industries. Potential competitors become allies—but within an internal free-market framework.

In this way, Koch Industries is able to embrace new ideas, to be at the leading edge of developments, and to continue to grow. The key to this form of organic growth is that the people who have developed the new idea find it advantageous to work within Koch Industries rather than to compete against it. Koch Industries grows, but it is not a Big Brother. Its internal free markets allow individuals to be self-fulfilling entrepreneurs within a supporting framework. It won't always succeed. It won't be perfect. The process must be combined with astute business decision-making. But internal free markets supply a structure in which business creativity has higher chance of success than in command and control.

> Koch Industries says: 'The size and complexity of resource allocation decisions within the firm sometimes rival the size and complexity of decisions in the external marketplace ... An attempt to create internal markets without profit centers and carefully defined roles and responsibilities will create chaos'.[29]

None of this, however, is to suggest that 'markets in the firm' creates some new business or social nirvana. It doesn't. It's difficult and 'markets in the firm' is better only than the alternatives. Command and control functions on the pretence that perfection in organizational structures can discipline people into a smooth operation. But this denies the reality and vagaries of human nature. Free markets do no more than recognize the oddities and imperfections of human nature and allow humans to decide what they want to do—but this is done within a structure. This does not create or deliver a perfect society or a perfect firm. Rather, it allows the imperfections of humans to become glaringly obvious. But it also allows the better sides of human nature to emerge.

The structures that enable free markets to operate are more complex than command and control, because they must be created and applied without control. It's a high-order social task. And, like free markets, 'markets in the firm' is not chaos. It's structured. And it's demanding and difficult to achieve. Koch Industries insists that its MBM system is an imperfect journey. MBM is not applied to every aspect of its business. It does not assure Koch of success. But it is its preferred structure. And one of the elements of its structure is the way internal markets require specific forms of interpersonal human behaviour.

In this context, an important contribution that Koch Industries has made to the understanding of free markets is to explore the interpersonal relationships that are necessary for a free market to work. Its training manuals place a heavy emphasis on interpersonal skills. To succeed at Koch Industries, it appears, a person needs to behave in a particular way. Inappropriate behaviour would tear its internal markets apart.

It appears that, at Koch Industries, anyone who is brutish, arrogant, rude, pushy or a bully is unlikely to survive. Koch Industries' training manual explains the behaviours and understandings that it believes people need in its MBM approach. Koch Industries' manual (*Models Collection*) devotes much space to discussing the operations of markets in both a theoretical and a practical way. It discusses markets in a way that relates to everyday life, talking about the processes and events that occur in the servicing of one's motor car, for example. It asks the reader to consider the interaction between the garage and the client. If the business is well run, relations between customer and supplier are highly courteous. This does not mean that people need to assume a bland persona to work under MBM. People's personalities are very much part of the relationship. But Koch Industries says that there are identifiable ways of behaving in interpersonal relationships that enable free markets to operate. They involve, among other things, passion, humility, intellectual honesty, integrity, desire to learn, long-term perspective, respect for self and others, courage and initiative. The manual looks at customer understanding, value-creation processes, vision development, time allocation and so on. It discusses these in the context of functioning free markets. To Koch Industries, the market process is very much a process of human behaviour. It argues that for market principles to work in its firm, human interrelationships must replicate those that make markets work.

Whether or not Koch Industries' processes are right or wrong, whether it has understood market operations correctly or not, or whether its systems perform internally the way they appear to is not the point for the purposes of this discussion. The point is that Koch Industries seems to have studied market operations more than any other firm and has deliberately sought to apply market principles, structures, processes and relationships in its firm. In this, it appears to be unique and to provide at least one obvious model of the process for others to contemplate.

'Markets in the firm' is not some new business guru-led fad. It is, instead, a slowly evolving business structure being quietly driven by several factors. Humans have discovered that free markets are the best model for the forward advancement of the economic well being of societies. Oddly, this works by maximizing the choices that individual people are able to make within an over-aching social framework that primarily acts to protect individual free choice. It is a complex and difficult balancing act but, somehow, when it is achieved, effective structures emerge in societies which enable them to function with high measures of success and growth. This idea of free markets has seeped deep into the psychological recesses of the post-World War 2 generations. And, without even thinking, these same generations are taking their culture of success through individuality into the firm, thereby creating structures and business frameworks outside of the prevailing academic frameworks. The development of 'markets in the firm' is a process of osmosis driven by values which hold the supremacy of the individual above all else.

In this environment, employment, which requires the individual to be subjugated to the needs of the business, is struggling for relevance and acceptance. Within the core structures of firms we are witnessing a quiet struggle over values. One value holds the firm to be supreme. The other holds the individual to be supreme.

Endnotes

1. See 'Is slacking the only way to survive the office?', *The Scotsman*, 16 August 2004; 'What's that stench in your office? Inertia', TimesOnline 16 August 2004 at www.timesonline.co.uk
2. The only publication known to this author that is dedicated to discussing markets in the firm is Tyler Cowen and David Parker, *Markets In The Firm*, The Institute of Economic Affairs London, 1997.
3. Nothing in the following sections of this chapter should be taken as an endorsement of the products, services, general activities or corporate behaviour of the firms and companies discussed. The point of the exercise is to present and analyse the different ways in which 'markets in the firm' have developed in different sectors and places around the world. The firms in question are cited merely to illustrate these differences.

4. James Champy, *Reengineering Management*, Harper Collins Publishers, 1995, page 13.
5. Alfred P. Sloan, 'The Most Important Thing I Ever Learned about Management' in Peter Krass (ed.), *The Book of Business Wisdom*, John Wiley & Sons Inc, New York, 1997, pages 168–174.
6. *Ibid.*
7. Fiona Carruthers, 'Asia icing on Amway cake', *The Australian Financial Review*, 14 January 2005.
8. John F. Love, *McDonalds: Behind the Arches*, Bantam Books, USA, 1986.
9. 'Because of McDonald's international scope, translators and electronic equipment enable professors to teach and communicate in 22 languages at one time. McDonald's also manages ten international training centers, including Hamburger Universities in England, Japan, Germany and Australia.' http://www.mcdonalds.com/corp/career/hamburger_university.html
10. Coles Myer also retails food and other lines which Harvey Norman does not.
11. See R.H. Coase, *The Firm, The Market, and The Law*, University of Chicago Press, 1988.
12. The name 'Odco' was the name of the company involved the court decisions of the 1990s, but by 2005 had become widely used as a reference in Australia to the particular type of labour hire engagement resulting from the legal judgments.
13. *Odco Pty Ltd and Building Workers' Industrial Union of Australia.* No VG 151 of 1988 Federal Court of Australia.
14. Koch Industries' Website is located at: www.kochind.com
15. *Forbes Magazine*, October 2000; www.forbes.com.tool/html/00/oct/1002/mu8.htm
16. www.kochind.com/about/financial.asp
17. C Koch speech 1993, 'How to succeed in interesting times' from: www.kochind.com
18. *Market Based Management Models Collection.* A management training manual of Koch Industries Inc., Version 27, August 1998, page 45. Note: all descriptions of KI operating systems based on interpretations derived from *Models*.
19. *Ibid.*, page 5.
20. *Ibid.*, page 13.
21. *Ibid.*, page 29.
22. John F. Love, *McDonalds Behind the Arches*, Bantam Books, USA, 1986. Chapter 9.
23. *Market Based Management Models Collection*, page 30.
24. *Ibid.*, page 31.
25. *Ibid.*, page 12.
26. *Ibid.*, page 47.
27. Microsoft underwent some disaggregation in the EU in the sense that 'unbundling' of some software was required and some interoperability issues needed to be overcome if Microsoft was to avoid sanctions. This did not occur in the USA where agreements were reached to improve the competitive environment in different ways.

28. *Market Based Management Models Collection*, page 50.
29. *Ibid., pages 41 and 61.*

8: Values

The best form of efficiency is the spontaneous cooperation of free people.

— Woodrow Wilson

What has this book been about? On the surface it's been about the law of contract, employment, self-employment, the nature of the firm, doing business and how we choose to regulate and control these things. But these are just technical issues, which overlie a deeper issue. This book is really about our values, about how we choose to define ourselves as individuals, particularly in the work situation in a seemingly complex world.

One objective of this book has been to look at how in the past we have thought of ourselves in the work and broader social contexts and how these contexts affected the way we have defined ourselves as individuals. By looking at our past we can better understand our present.

For most of human history, it has been thought that social stability and order required that the individual be subservient to the greater good of the collective. Class consciousness and class structures required people to be happy with the station into which they were born. 'Others' who were powerful by accident of birth, wealth or physical capacity made decisions that controlled society. Social cohesion required all to accept their station and its duties.

Political freedom
But then ideas of democracy and social equality took hold. Every person, it was argued, is born equal and entitled to equal rights and equal treatment. Nations exist for 'the people' and not for the privileged—that is what democracy means. We have taken this to heart—and so we should.

We have learnt that, for a human society to be effective, successful and unified, it does not need to be 'controlled' by a few powerful people at the top (even though it may need political leaders). In fact, the reverse is the case. Democracy diffuses power. Everyone in some way, however seemingly minor, becomes a player in the decision-making processes. And out of this emerges structure, order and stability. It's far from perfect, forever changing, often tenuous but always striving for perfection—even though we know that perfection is probably unattainable.

In this environment of diffused power, institutions are always challenged. Decisions are always open to challenge. Social stability is a conundrum. Social stability means not being static but being in a state of constant movement. But, somehow, out of this constant movement, humans create order.

But societies that diffuse power, unlike command societies, don't have the appearance of simple, solid social structures into which we easily fit. Instead, democratic societies are big, complex and hard to fathom. It's hard to work out how a free society works and where as individuals we fit. But it does work and we do fit.

And it works and we fit because, in democracies, in free societies, where the powerful are constrained, the individual is supreme. All individuals are supreme. What matters in such societies is the personal happiness and fulfilment of each individual. The collective is made up, not of a hierarchy which dictates to those below, but of a collection of individuals, moving, shifting, chasing; finding their own values, their own meaning, their own purpose and place; securing their own contentment. But, oddly, it's not a social structure driven by selfishness.

Humans are an odd cluster of contradictions. For societies to operate, logic would seem to dictate that individuals should consciously put the collective's need above their own. Simple logic would suggest that this defines selflessness. But this is not the case. In fact, a counter-intuitive logic applies. A society that focuses on individuality in fact strengthens itself and achieves community. When humans are allowed the freedom to be intensely individual, they strive also to be social. We crave the company of our fellow humans. We find and define ourselves by the people around us—our families, our friends, our clubs, our churches, and the many and varied institutions in which we congregate for mutual self-interest. We find ourselves by being intensely individual but in the same instant intensely social. Culture is thus created, not by the efforts of the few geniuses we so often admire, but by the millions of small creations of each individual brought together because we choose to come together. We humans create order out of this.

Economics

It is the same with the way we run our economies. We have learnt the same lessons as we have with democracy. Economies do not become successful by being command-driven. No-one masterminds the whole. No-one is an earthly economic god. Instead, the individual is supreme. Individuals decide how and when they spend their money. Individuals determine the food they buy and the clothes they wear. As individuals, we strive to look after our own economic needs. But as individuals we also strive to look after the economic needs of those around us, and those that depend on us or who need our aid. And the more we are left to look after our own economic needs, the more we find we can do it. Somehow, order emerges from what might otherwise be considered the inevitability of chaos if command structures were not in place. The contradictions of human nature are in play.

Free-market societies have learnt the subtle game of enabling the free economic individual to flourish without letting any individual dominate. We have learnt that for any individual to be free, no other individual can dominate. Free-market societies have learnt that to achieve this it is necessary to underpin economic life with a very specific type of structural control. But it's control which has one principal and narrow objective—namely, to allow each individual their economic freedom but prevent any individual denying that same freedom to any another. This requires carefully crafted laws that never lose sight of this central objective. It requires institutions and people who understand this objective and who can apply crafted law in conformity with it. This is the economic management process of monopoly prevention. Our laws allow each individual to aspire to and achieve great wealth. But our laws must ensure that anyone who achieves wealth and economic might cannot use that might to prevent other individuals from also aspiring to and achieving individual wealth.

This is a difficult task. But when successful, societies move forward and can do so in spectacular ways. And from this comes order, an order which is a miracle of human ingenuity, an order in which no-one dominates but in which everyone is involved, more or less, on their own terms. This is why the commercial contract is so important and why the commercial contract has been referred to so often in this book.

The commercial contract—freedom

This book has spent a great deal of time explaining, discussing and praising the commercial contract, because the commercial contract is a bedrock of our personal economic freedoms. It must be understood that to damage the commercial contract is to damage our personal economic freedom. It must be protected also because it is the bedrock for successful, free, open market economies.

The commercial contract is an everyday experience for each of us. When we buy candy from a store, we have engaged in a commercial contract. No-one makes us buy the candy. No-one forces us to buy the particular candy we have chosen. The purchase is, in fact, the most basic expression of our individuality and of our freedom. There is no control over us. Yet we have engaged in a human action involving a contract which protects our individuality and freedom. The commercial contract ensures that we cannot be forced to buy the candy but that, if we do buy it, what is advertised on the wrapper must be what is inside the wrapper. Our choice is protected. Because we have bought that piece of candy nothing requires us to buy another piece of candy or anything else in the store. The seller of the candy has no rights over us other than our obligation to pay for the candy. And as far as the commercial contract is concerned, anyone who engages in the contract is equal, no matter what the colour of their skin, their religion, their comparative wealth, their political power, their sexual preference or any other matter. Whether the shop owner has equal wealth to us, or is a powerful retail baron or corporation, does not matter, because for the purposes of the commercial contract we have equal power. The commercial contract plays one principal role, that of ensuring equality and fairness between us.

In this sense the commercial contract is value-laden, but not value-laden in the way we normally think of values. Rather, the commercial contract is value-neutral and that is it's most important value. The value that the commercial contract has for us is the social value that we are all equal. It may be thought odd to conceive of a contract having a social value but it's helpful to think of it this way. It helps us to understand the role the commercial contract plays in society in protecting each individual.

The commercial contract protects us because it doesn't care who we are or what we do. It has no emotional attachment to us but is emotionally neutral. But it is this emotional neutrality that enables the commercial contract to treat us all as equals. The commercial contract is devoid of feeling, which is why it can treat each of us as equals.

And this is what makes a free-market economy hum—because it is controlled, run and organized through layers of fast-moving, interconnected commercial contracts. There is no overseer. There is no master controller. The candy we purchase from the store is purchased by the storekeeper using a commercial contract. The delivery is made by means of a commercial contract. The manufacturer purchased the ingredients through the commercial contract. The advertising was organized through a commercial contract. The paper to wrap the candy was obtained through a commercial contract. And throughout this ongoing, fast-moving process, the commercial contract never changes. It remains at all stages value-neutral with respect to the choices individuals make. It neither knows nor cares who the parties to each contract are. All it must care about is its own integrity to its value neutrality.

In this process, the commercial contract forms an essential and necessary part of the bedrock of free societies, free markets and free economies.

Free but not free?

But, oddly, even where societies are not free democracies, if the commercial contract is protected, those societies can still have hugely successful and strong free-market economies with widely distributed wealth. Freedom has seeming contradictions.

How can economic freedom exist without political freedom, it may be asked? But it can. Political freedom and economic freedom are not dependent upon each other; whether or not that is good or bad! Such is the power of the commercial contract that, as long as it is respected, economic freedom can be preserved even when political freedom is restricted.

But the care and management of the commercial contract is a difficult task—one which is easily damaged by any government which does not understand that that is one of its primary roles.

The power of the individual

Quite obviously this book considers the commercial contract to be of immense importance. The value-neutrality of the commercial contract makes it incredibly difficult for any single person or group in a society to economically dominate a society or the individuals in society. If protected and layered with other anti-monopoly devices, particularly the prevention of monopoly economic power being garnered by the state itself, absolute economic power in a society is thwarted by the commercial contract. Economic power in a free-market society exists, but monopoly power is thwarted by other countervailing and competitive economic powers.

The result is that where the commercial contract prevails, the most powerful economic unit in society is the consumer. In this sense, a free market economy is the expression of economic democracy, where individuals, as consumers, cast their economic vote many times in every day—and, unlike in political democracy, they always get what they vote for. The economic ballot paper is the commercial contract.

But the focus this book is the fact that, unfortunately, these lessons have *not* been learnt in our working lives. This is a principal message of this book. Humans have learnt that we create social order when political freedom prevails. We have learnt that we create economic order when economic freedom prevails. But we have not learnt that order is created in firms when working freedom prevails. We humans are slow learners, it would seem!

Employment—a troublesome contract!

When it comes to our working lives, that is, the process by which most of us earn a living, the dominant ethos of the twentieth century has been that the lessons of the free market and the value-neutral commercial contract do not and cannot apply. When we have thought about the firm—that is, the entity that creates our goods and services—we assume that all the rules that make for democracy, for free markets, for free economies and for the supremacy of the individual cannot apply. We have assumed (and largely continue to assume) that within the firm, the value-neutral features that make up the commercial contract are of no relevance.

We see the firm as having to be the old, hierarchical, class-based structure that has been so solidly rejected in our normal, non-working daily lives. And this is dependent on the employment contract.

It is the employment contract that declares that one person, the employer, is more powerful than the other person, the employee. The employment contract is a contract about the legal and institutional cementing of inequality. This is not some figment of the imagination. The entire purpose of Chapter One was to present the evidence of what the employment contract is as determined by law. And there is no question that, on the evidence, the employment contract is a legal device in which the employee hands over to the employer the right of the employer to control the employee. But this situation occurs only inside the firm. And, strangely, we have done this and accepted the outcome, hardly questioning the contradiction between life within the firm and life outside it.

And this idea of the firm is not limited to profit-making private companies. In fact, the firm is a general idea for any human organization that functions to provide goods or services. This includes public service organizations, government-owned instrumentalities, not-for-profit charities and so on.

We now generally believe that economies function best with minimal intervention from a central command. We know that economies function best when central bodies create and enforce frameworks that ensure the value-neutrality of the commercial contract and all that goes with it. Yet, within the firm, the dominant assumption is that the firm must be driven by a single vision and orders from a central command. The mechanism is the employment contract.

At the level of society at large, we understand that culture is created by the interplay of the values of free people. Laws and government provide the frameworks within which the values of free people can mix. We recognize that attempts by individuals or groups to impose values on the collective are exercises in intellectual, cultural and personal arrogance. In democracies, arrogance has become a personal liability for aspiring political leaders. Yet, within the firm, we continue to believe that people cannot be free and must instead bend, be bent or at least cajoled into accepting the culture that has been determined from the top. Cultural arrogance is a dominant hallmark of the firm made possible by the employment contract.

We assume these things about the firm because that's the way it seems always to have been. Without thinking, we reach deep into core, human tribal roots and pull out a most basic of human instincts, the desire of one individual to control others, and assume that this must be the structure through which the firm must operate. We give this notion its full legal form by insisting on the employment contract. The employment contract tells us that we must suppress our individuality in favour of the higher needs of whoever are the 'tribal chiefs' in the firm. The employment contract instructs us that we have to be loyal to the system of the firm rather than hold true to our own individual integrity. The employment contract instructs us that, when we work, our identity, our world view, our sense of self-worth is determined by our place within the firm, and that the firm, like a wise and benevolent chieftain, will protect and look after us. In this we are supposed to feel comfortable, relaxed, at ease and at peace.

This may be right. This may be proper. This may be acceptable. This may be the way things have been done for a long time. But is this the only way? Does this not contradict what we have learnt about political freedom? Does this not contradict what we have learnt about economic freedom? Does this not contradict what we have learnt about the pathways to personal fulfilment? The evidence set out in this book suggests that employment is contradictory to our other normal freedoms which we hold dear.

Societies have moved on and continue to move away from our tribal roots. We have moved on from the idea that central benevolent bodies will protect us if we relinquish our individuality in exchange for blind loyalty. In free societies, in all other aspects of our daily lives, it is the ability to experience and express our individuality that has become one of our most cherished values. And the release of individuality, counterbalanced and constrained as it is by the free release of everyone else's individuality, is what brings political, social and economic well-being along with order to our societies.

Employment works against this trend. Demonstrating this point has been a primary goal of this book.

But is employment illegitimate? Oddly enough, the answer is 'no'!

Within society at large, we allow individuals to do their thing. And that applies equally to firms. If individual firms wish to follow the path of employment, we do, and must, allow them to do so. If the suppression of individuality and the imposition of central control is the route firms wish to pursue, then they have that right to do so. Firms that choose the employment route must accept, however, that the state will apply its employment regulation against them as a consequence.

However, neither the state nor society has the right to impose the employment model on to all firms. Yet this is what occurs. Through our labour regulation institutions, our taxing authorities, our work safety laws, our academic concepts of the firm and our views of how the firm should be regulated, we have created a paradigm which presupposes employment as the only model for the firm. Almost by default we insist on imposing employment as the required model. For an individual firm not to seek employment as its internal structure is to confront mighty and powerful institutions of the state. To seek not to use employment constitutes a serious challenge to the existence of those institutions and is often the cause of oppression by them as a consequence.

In addition, the enforcement of employment is powerfully supported by prevailing cultures of management. Managers of firms are themselves mostly employees operating within the cultural and legal authority levels created by the myth of the employer. Managers mostly see themselves as benevolent masters, and when managers get together they reinforce the benevolent master culture among themselves. For any individual manager to buck this culture either within an individual firm or within a given society is to challenge a powerful cultural norm. Only some individuals confront the norm and only occasionally!

A values revolution at work
But change is happening and it is a powerful force. This is another key message of this book.

The change is driven by individuals who see freedom in their political, economic and social lives as being normal, expected and a right. The employment paradigm of firms and regulators grates against these expectations of freedom. And people are responding.

A revolution, a very quiet revolution, is under way. It is a revolution without a banner, anger or mass demonstrations. It is a revolution where millions of individuals working in employment-structured firms, through their personal behaviours, reject the crushing of their individuality. These are the people this book has referred to as 'independent employees', people who are trapped within the contract of employment but who have personal independence in their souls. Management has had to respond to this by trying to create systems and processes which allow scope for individuality but retain 'control'. Within employment structures this creates tension. Indeed, managers themselves are part of this revolution and this tension—also insisting on their individuality and often encouraging the individuality of others.

But the process of change that is occurring is not thought of in this context as being about individual freedom. In fact, the people who are carrying out the change think of what they are doing as just a matter of being sensible, practical and respectful of themselves and others. In fact, people sense that there is something wrong inside firms but feel unable to pinpoint it. In reality, the problem lies in the core structure of the firm created by the employment contract.

But the revolution is more than just one of attitudes. Increasingly, the employment contract itself is being rejected. And this rejection of the employment contract now constitutes a substantial part of the world of work. More and more, individuals are using the commercial contract as the method of engaging in work, thereby replacing the employment contract. The people who do this have had many names tagged to them: freelancer, self-employed contractor, independent worker, own-account worker and so on. The term used in this book is 'independent contractor'. Chapter Two case-studied the independent contractor sheep shearers in Queensland, and found that the attitudes of independence and personal freedom are not just theoretical but real and living human values. And it's becoming clear that, in many societies, making use of the commercial contract accounts for somewhere in excess of one-fifth of workforces. This worries the employment regulators and the employment institutions because they have difficulty understanding the change, seeing it in conspiratorial terms as a threat to them and their familiar institutions.

But the use of the commercial contract as the guiding value-neutral structure, both within firms and between individuals, is an inevitable consequence of the development of free societies and free people. The shift to the commercial contract challenges state institutions only if the institutions act aggressively against it and try to destroy it. In fact, the commercial contract in the workplace is perfectly adaptable to the regulatory requirements relating to work safety, taxation, anti-discrimination and so on. The only area where it is not adaptable is state attempts to destroy the commercial contract itself.

For the firm, the unanswered question is how to accommodate individuality inside the firm and yet still retain internal control. On this issue there is a mental block. If the firm is not commanded and controlled from the top, surely chaos will be unleashed? But chaos is not the inevitable outcome — as we have seen in our understandings of how democracies and free markets work in general terms. In fact, a high degree of order and structure can be created in firms by using the commercial contract. This was the point of Chapter 7, which demonstrated the emergence of what can be called 'markets in the firm'. If the 'controllers' of firms conceive of themselves as encouragers and protectors of a system of commercial contract transactions inside firms, the way to create order while enabling individuality becomes clear. Initially the process seems complex and certainly is counter to basic human instincts to control. But it's perfectly feasible and is being done.

Democracies and free markets represent a higher order of human organizational achievement than do command and control. The key structure is the unleashing of individuality balanced by devices which frustrate monopoly. And democracies and free markets have developed high-order laws, systems and institutions to achieve this structure. Every firm is capable of doing internally what free societies have achieved externally to the firm. But it's not an easy path because it is not a familiar path. It's not a well-known path partly because it is not recognized in the realm of academic study. But it is a better path that leads to better outcomes — both for the firm and for the people who work in, or more exactly the people who work *with*, the firm.

This has huge importance for the individual. Working in the firm as an employee is often a frustrating and debilitating experience relieved only by the freedom achieved outside of the firm. This should not be the everyday human experience of the firm.

Working in, being part of, or interfacing with the firm as an individual can and should be an uplifting personal experience. For many people it is. Many people do find rewarding experiences working inside the employment firm. Some people can enjoy the apparent security of command and control. Many people learn to use the firm to achieve their own ends. But many people also go one step further and become their own firm. Being your own firm and economically interacting with, supplying services to, and receiving services from, other firms is the ultimate expression of economic individuality and independence.

This drive for economic freedom is very powerful because economic freedom allows the individual to find the mental space to discover spiritual and personal values of significance. By design and structure, the employment firm seeks to impose an identity on individuals, but it is an identity decided by the firm, not the individual. This command way of dealing with individuals is increasingly being rejected.

People want to define themselves. Free political and free economic societies provide the structures within which individuals can define themselves. Firms are under pressure to do the same and it is employment which is the great stumbling block. Consequently, employment, although it is unlikely to die in the immediate future, is under challenge from the drive for individuality and freedom. This is the ultimate message of this book. Human individuality joined with freedom is an unstoppable human force.

It is for this reason that independence will inevitably herald the death of employment.

Postscript: Political Developments Since 2005

August 2008

> At the beginning of anything out of the ordinary, the mass of the people always dislike it.
>
> — Mao Zedung (aged 19)[1]

Reflections on the new century of politics, history and change!

For most of the twentieth century, particularly since the Second World War, the big global battles of politics rotated primarily around the idea that capitalist bosses exploited oppressed workers. The idea that working-class people had to unite and grasp political power to prevent exploitation defined and focused the activities of communist and socialists revolutionaries. This single idea played out in the former Soviet Union and in China on grand scales. It permeated anti-colonial liberation movements. It was at the epicentre of the Vietnam War. It was the 'fear factor' that motivated Western powers to oppose communism during the Cold War.

But come the twenty-first century, the idea that free-market capitalism systemically exploits workers has slid away as the defining core of politics. It continues to slide into irrelevancy as politics becomes progressively more multi-dimensional, and issues other than class warfare make their way on to the political agenda. It has become widely recognized that free-market capitalism demonstrably delivers material benefits to the greatest spread of the world's population than any other rival economic system.

Many implications of this shift can seem counter-intuitive at first. For supporters of democracy, it is perhaps a shock that the economic success of China has demonstrated that political freedom and free-market capitalism do not necessarily have to be joined for material benefits to be delivered. Authoritarian regimes can successfully adopt free-market economic principles and still stifle individual political and social freedoms. Examples such as these show just how fundamentally the economic and political assumptions of the previous century have fractured into unpredictability.

The idea of independence and individuality at work has played and continues to play an important but probably unrecognized role in this development. At the core of the 'workers are exploited' view of politics is the notion that if workers see themselves as individuals and act accordingly, they will be exploited. Consequently, so the argument goes, it is essential that workers act collectively. But as the protective arm of legislation has made exploitation more and more difficult, workers have found themselves more and more capable of acting individually. As a result, the need for the collective falls away. This is a primary reason for the collapse in membership numbers that is confronting unions across the globe. Increasingly, workers can think and act as individuals and not suffer exploitation. Society has become better at balancing the competing interests of economic players, no matter what their apparent strengths or weaknesses.

In effect, people do not need to see themselves as tied to a class, whether it is the working class or some other. And this idea of non-identification with class is not an organized counter-revolution driven by intellectual considerations. It is instead a product of people changing their individual lifestyles and working life ambitions on the basis of very practical personal considerations about their quality of life. The movement is more a form of osmosis than a tidal wave, in that it is totally unorganized and undirected — but it is a movement nonetheless.

Perhaps, oddly, this movement doesn't have an organized voice or seek to have a prominent place in politics, or even within the international institutions which are structured around command-and-control employment law. But, just as oddly, it's a movement that has created a crisis for these same institutions because it undermines the values and assumptions upon which many of them have been created and upon which they rely for their continued existence.

This book was first published in 2005 — but only on-line. It had taken eight years to research and write. At the time of publication of this first hard-copy edition in 2008, the scale of the changes that have occurred in politics and in approaches to labour arrangements in the intervening eleven years could not have been predicted.

Perhaps the most important change occurred at the International Labour Organisation (ILO) — the United Nations organization that specializes in establishing labour law standards across the globe. (See Chapter 4, above.) What the ILO says on labour issues sets, at minimum, the moral parameters for labour relations internationally and can, under some circumstances, establish legal obligations. The ILO has historically worked from the premise that workers are an exploited or exploitable class in need of protection. It is the international reference point for all academic theses that take this line.

The ILO

At around midday, Geneva time, on Thursday 16 June 2006, the International Labour Organisation voted to adopt a new 'international instrument' on the 'Scope of the Employment Relationship'. This vote signalled an important shift in labour law and the philosophical underpinnings of labour law internationally. It signalled the end of the idea that workers are systematically exploited when they are engaged in economic activity.

The ILO Recommendation passed on that day clearly accepted and endorsed the status of independent contractors by declaring that employment law should not interfere in the commercial relationship. In doing so, it marked a paradigm shift for the ILO.

To understand just how important it was, it is helpful to understand the structures and operations of the ILO. The ILO operates on a 'tripartite', allegedly consensual basis. Unions and employers each have 25 per cent of the votes and governments have 50 percent of the votes when decisions are made on ILO declarations.

The tripartite structure of the ILO is based on the assumption that if employers can be engaged with unions and governments, then agreements can be reached that will create protections for employees. Such a 'rights'-based approach engenders a pervasive way of thinking which isn't fundamentally interested in the practical realities of commercial activity. But it is ideally suited to a political 'deal making' environment in which commercial realities are secondary to the horse-trading of political settlement.

In this respect, the ILO is caught in an historical and ideological time-warp which presumes that working relationships are always class-conflict based and can only be resolved by striking a middle deal which neither totally favours nor totally damages either party. The ILO accurately reflects and influences the orthodoxies of labour regulators and institutions that have prevailed worldwide for decades. It is a process which both requires and creates constant tension to sustain itself. It entrenches conflict because, for progress to occur, conflict must inevitably rise from each previous deal in order to create a new deal.

In this structure, unions are representatives of workers — but only workers who are employees, since it is only employees who are presumed to be systemically exploited. Unions have a formalized, institutionalized and significant voice at the ILO. Unions do not formally or informally represent independent contractors. And, significantly, there is no institutional representation for independent contractors. The idea that workers can act independently — that is, without the protection of the collective — and not be exploited, is not an idea that has a representative voice at the ILO. In fact such a notion poses a challenge to the very intellectual pillars upon which the ILO stands.

The scope of employment debate

Since 1996, the ILO had been attempting to create an 'international instrument' that would effectively enable labour regulators around the globe to declare a commercial contract to be an employment contract, something which would consequently allow them to declare independent contractors to be employees. It was an attempt that flew in the face of reality and would have led to labour regulation that would have produced severe distortions in commercial activity.

But the ILO had little mind to consider commercial issues. The attempt was made because of concern about plummeting union membership across the globe and the consequent collapse in union influence globally. For the ILO this threatened its very existence and justification for being. If one of the 'legs' of the tripartite arrangement were to fall off, the edifice could collapse. Many in the ILO, the union movement, government and academia identified the rise of the independent contracting sector as part of the reason for the decline in union influence. Further, if independent contractors were liable for their own actions, this removed the need for employee-like protections, which also undermined the assumptions upon which the ILO was built.

The general response to this was to argue that the rise of independent contractors was an employer conspiracy, that the phenomenon was a sham and that it only gained credibility because the definitions that marked the 'distinctions' between employees and contractors were not clear. The supposed solution was to redefine independent contractors as employees. This would neatly fix the institutional needs of the ILO—even if it was totally illogical from a legal and commercial perspective.

The ILO debate was a protracted one. It began in 1996, resurfaced in 1998, had a committee of 'experts' report in 2000 and produced a major 'Conclusion' in 2003. The 2006 debate aimed to achieve a 'Recommendation' which would finalize the issue.

Until 2003, the debate was circular and lacked an outcome. The 2003 ILO 'Conclusion', however, contained a statement that independent contractors were legitimate. This was an historic occurrence and a first in the ILO debate. It signalled that the ILO had made a significant first shift in recognizing that independent contractors are not employees and that they operate through commercial rather than employment contracts. Further, it indicated that the illogicality—both commercial and legal—of declaring a commercial contract to be an employment contract had finally dawned on the ILO. If the ILO were to have passed such a resolution, it itself would have appeared stupid and irrelevant in the world's eyes—not something a prestigious international institution could afford.

The 2003 event triggered further developments. In 2005, the ILO released a major discussion paper on the issue which displayed a further significant shift in its thinking. It was an academic research paper which accepted, at its heart, the legitimacy of independent contractors.

2005: ILO Report

In the first half of 2005, the ILO office in Geneva produced a 90-page Report and questionnaire in preparation for the 2006 debate.[2] The Report raised the question of protecting commercial contracts.

> Throughout the discussions on the employment relationship, [2003] the concern was expressed that regulation in this area could interfere with the right of a person to contract for services by another person on a civil or commercial basis. (Paragraph 239)

What the report recognized was that the 'right' of employees to be protected cannot interfere with or damage the 'right' of people to engage in commercial contracts. This was important for the ILO because, as an institution motivated by 'rights' issues, the Report was now accepting that the 'right' to engage in commercial contracts was equally as important a 'right' as protections for employees. Because an independent contractor is an individual who undertakes work through commercial instead of employment contracts, to 'protect' independent contractors would require 'protection' for commercial contracts. The ILO had become aware that it was engaged in a balancing act.

Achieving this balance required precision in the ILO's use of language, given that ILO language influences and impacts on global policy and law. In the ILO 'scope of employment' debate and in debate on labour regulations in general, a key feature had been the imprecise use of language. This had resulted in much confusion.

Before 2003, the ILO had referred to 'employer', 'employee', 'employment' and other related language in a general way. For example, it had assumed—laxly—that an employee is a person who works. But the ILO and labour regulators are in the business of the law. They create regulations via legal instruments. At law, an employee and an employer only exist because they are parties to an employment contract. And an employment contract is a very specific legal object. This has been discussed at length earlier in this book.

In contrast, the ILO 2005 Report took a great step forward by identifying the international definitions of 'employment', 'worker' and 'non-employment', and by securing greater clarity of those definitions across a range of jurisdictions.

In particular, the Report detailed the results of the first serious survey and thorough review of employment definitions used across the globe. On the facts, the ILO found that, contrary to expectations, the definitional differences between employment, independent contracting, the employment contract and the commercial contract were clear and consistent around the world.

It stated:

> What is surprising is the amount of convergence between the legal systems of different countries in the way they deal with this [distinguishing employment] and other aspects of the employment relationship, even between countries with different legal traditions or those in different parts of the world.... Irrespective of the definition used, the concept of a worker in an employment relationship has to be seen in contrast to that of a self-employed or non-dependent worker... (Paragraphs 86-87)

This one statement signalled a turning point in the understanding of labour relations. It recognized that self-employed persons (independent contractors) are non-dependent workers and are in fact clearly different from employees or dependent workers. No longer did the academic assumptions of the ILO throw all workers into the one box—that of systemically exploitable people—instead it recognized and accepted that some workers are not systemically exploited as a consequence of the economic system. This changed the entire framework and understanding within which the ILO and labour regulators had conducted their thinking since the inception of the ILO in the 1920s.

The report looked at common-law countries and found that similar terms and definitions were used throughout. Countries it cited, for example, included Kenya, Nigeria, Lesotho, Indonesia, Ireland, New Zealand, Cambodia, China, Malaysia, Australia and Pakistan. These countries used terms such as 'to serve an employer', 'contract of service', 'contract of employment' and so on.

The report also looked at legal definitions used in a range of non-common-law countries. These included Argentina, El Salvador, Chile, Colombia, Cost Rica, Venezuela, France, Benin, Burkina Faso, Democratic Republic of Congo, Gabon, Niger, Rwanda, Portugal, Morocco, Bahrain, Qatar, Angola, Botswana, Slovenia, Mexico and Nicaragua.

The defining terms from these countries included 'dependency', 'subordination', 'permanent dependency', 'delegated direction', 'conditions of subordination', 'direction', 'supervision', 'control', 'orders' and 'for the employer's account'. These terms, used in non-common-law countries, all point to an idea of employment consistent with that of common-law countries.

The ILO report was clear and significant. For the first time, based on solid research, the ILO stated that the specific idea of employment was a contractual relationship in which one party (the employee) is 'dependent' on, or in some way subject to the 'control' of, the other party (the employer).

Such a relationship is normally tested or discovered through a court process, the details of which may vary between countries and jurisdictions. But the discovery process always focuses upon a central theme—namely, indications of dependency or control—and the ILO found a substantial degree of convergence and commonality of approach on that theme.

Consistent with the 2003 ILO Conclusion, the 2005 Report approached the definitions under three elements:

- *Worker*: This is a generic term that can mean an employee or a self-employed person.
- An *employee* is an individual working under a contract of control or dependency—in other words, an employment contract.
- An *independent contractor (self-employed person)* is an individual working under a commercial or civil contract. Such contracts are not denoted by control or dependency.

Significantly, the report dropped the term *'dependent contractor'*. It refers to a 'dependent' worker as an employee. This was an important development because the term 'dependent contractor' had been used in the past as the key term by which to attack the legitimacy of independent contractors. The fact is that it is not possible for an individual to be both an independent contractor and dependent at the same time. Legal dependency in this area is exclusively denoted by employment.

This finding of definitional consistency and the clear identification of employees and independent contractors as markedly different subsets of the more general class, 'worker', enabled the labour regulation debate—and specifically the ILO 2006 scope of employment debate—to move forward in a more constructive way than in the past.

The 2006 Recommendation result

The 2006 debate was exhaustive, hard-argued and contained an element of drama not usually found in ILO processes. The ILO prides itself on the fact that, for most of the time, unions, employers and governments come to a consensual agreement in their debates. It is unusual if one party in the debate refuses to budge on an item and a vote, with all its attendant unpredictability, is required.

In the case of the 2006 debate, most of the clauses in the Recommendation were agreed upon. It was not an easy process, as each word, line and paragraph was argued piece by piece. There were some clauses which were not agreed upon and the employer group determined that they would push the entire Recommendation to a vote.

The employers did not like the clauses which attempted to define what employment is and, in particular, they objected to those clauses which would have allowed legislatures to create assumptions of employment in specific instances. The employers argued that, on this issue, legislatures should presume nothing and leave it to the courts to make decisions based on the evidence of each case that came before them.

On the day of the vote, the main hall of the ILO assembly in the Palais des Nations in Geneva, Switzerland was unusually full. Even though most of those present were sure that the Recommendation would pass despite the bloc vote by the employer group against the Recommendation, the outcome remained uncertain. When the successful vote for the Recommendation was announced, the hall erupted in cheers. Union, government and ILO officials hugged each other and gleefully shook hands. It was indeed a resounding outcome for independent contractors—their status had at last been endorsed by the ILO.

Palais des Nations. Geneva

The moment of the vote

The Recommendation has significant and important positives for independent contractors. The Recommendation contains some 600 paragraphs which are mostly preamble and a record of the debate spread over 80 pages. Twenty-three clauses make up the substance of the ILO's decision (included as the Addendum below).

The key statement is *clause 8*. It reads:

> National policy for protection of workers in an employment relationship should not interfere with true civil and commercial relationships, while at the same time ensuring that individuals in an employment relationship have the protection they are due.

The remainder of the ILO Recommendation hangs upon, and has to be read within, the framework of clause 8.

Given that the defining mark of an independent contractor is that an individual earns his or her living through the commercial contract, this statement represents a balance between two key issues. First, the ILO recognizes the legitimacy of independent contractors defined as working in commercial relationships and, second, it recognizes the operation of labour law to provide certain 'protections' to employees.

The outcome, as a matter of principle, is that employees are regulated and find their 'protections' under employment law and independent contractors are regulated and find their 'protections' under commercial law. It is a simple principle but it has far-reaching implications, primarily because the high priest of labour law internationally, the ILO, accepts that labour law should not intrude into commercial law.

For the purposes of protecting independent contractors, all other clauses in the Recommendation are predicated on this statement. But, so what? The International Labour Organisation, like the United Nations, can make all the statements it likes but if the statements are not backed by action or if they have no consequences, they are simply reduced to symbolism. However, in the case of Australia, the June 2006 ILO Recommendation had immediate flow-on effects of a concrete nature.

The ILO Recommendation, Australia and the future of politics

Australia introduced a world-first *Independent Contractors Act* in late 2006. The Act achieved several things. First, it settled once and for all that the identification of an independent contractor rests upon the standard tests as applied under common law. This is consistent with, and reflective of, the ILO Recommendation.

The Australian Act also introduced a world first by introducing provisions which outlaw sham contracts — that is, contracts that purport to be commercial contracts for independent contractors but are in fact employment contracts. Anyone who intentionally constructs sham contracts now faces prosecution and fines in Australia. The Act also contains provisions protecting independent contractors from 'unfair contracts'. This is also consistent with the ILO Recommendation and in fact takes up some of the ILO's key concerns.

The Australian Act is all the more significant because it was introduced and passed in 2006 by a conservative government, allegedly of a right-wing persuasion, but by mid-2007, the Australian Labor Party, allegedly of a left-wing persuasion, was also committed to the principles of the Act. With the change of government, the ALP retained the *Independent Contractors Act* and does not have a policy to abolish it. This demonstrates a strong measure of cross-party political support for the Act, a fact which itself is significant.

This cross-party political support for the *Independent Contractors Act* signifies something much larger that appears to be happening within political orthodoxy in Australia. This change arguably reflects a global trend. It is a phenomenon which reflects an important political shift — namely, the collapse of the belief in communism/socialism, itself driven by a recognition that, in well-regulated economies, free-market capitalism works. It is not a shift that is steady or certain and there are many events and policy areas which, it can be argued, still run counter to the trend, but it is a shift in the central thread of politics nonetheless.

In Australia, the major and most influential writers from the Left have been saying for about four years that the Left has lost the ideological battle.

They say that market-based capitalism has proven that it works. They no longer hate it. This may seem a simple statement, but it is staggering in its consequences for Australian politics.

As a result, the old left-right battle, conducted along class lines, is now no longer primary to understanding the fundamentals of Australian politics and much of politics globally. Deeper analysis must be undertaken and deeper meaning teased out.

The shift has been blunt. The central plank of Leftist politics has always been that the capitalist system necessitated war between two classes: the workers and the bosses. But, in the past few years, the Left has accepted that this assumption is false, particularly as it applies to Australia. That marks a huge step for the Left. It recognizes and accepts that market-based capitalism clearly delivers sustained economic growth and maximizes equitable distribution of wealth. Exploitation is not inherent in market capitalism. The Left no longer hates market capitalism. They have embraced it.

This doesn't mean that some sort of political nirvana has been achieved where consensus reigns supreme. There remain widely divergent views about how equality and fairness can be achieved within free market economies. Market-based capitalism is not totally perfect; neither are human beings. Understanding how to regulate market-based economies appropriately is one giant part of a complex exercise. But what the shift by the Left means is that their starting point for political discussion is different from the past. They no longer hate the free market, nor seek to destroy it. They want it to serve social purposes.

This shift is relatively new and can be identified in fairly recent writings of leading left-wing academics. It has also had rollover effects for party politics in Australia, witnessed, in particular, by a significant repositioning of the Australian Labor Party. In many respects, it explains why the Australian Labor Party achieved a political dominance in Australia during the period around 2007, controlling every government in the country at the State and Federal level. With the conversion of the Left to free-market capitalism, the economic rationalists within the ALP and the Left found it possible to accommodate remaining differences and largely work together without suspicion.

This core change inside the ALP had been a long time in the making. It started with practical people recognizing that the electorate no longer defined itself along class lines. This developed into practical political strategies that have affected Labor philosophy. This does not mean that the task of government or politics is easy. There are huge tensions to be managed. But it does mean that Labor governments in Australia are not internally torn over economic fundamentals. To understand the ALP now means appreciating different tensions. This requires more than simply thinking in left-right frameworks. Political considerations have a new complexity. And it's where considerations surrounding independent contractors come into play.

When regulating free markets, the primary task is to understand how to regulate commercial activity. There is a simple equation for this. The less regulation, the more commercial activity is likely to be generated with consequent increases in prosperity. But history has shown that where there is no regulation, parties will seek to exploit one another and rorting and criminal activity will come to the fore. At minimum, fair, independent and uncorrupted courts are needed to settle commercial disputes between parties, and enforcement agencies are needed to ensure that court orders are applied. It is a matter of ensuring that, in the eyes of the law, all parties, no matter what their apparent strength or power, are equal before it.

It is from this policy perspective that independent contractors become important. When two large companies confront one another in a commercial dispute, it is accepted that it's a battle of two powerful forces. But if a large organization is in a commercial dispute with an individual, it is assumed that it's a battle between one party with great power (the company) and a single individual with little if any power. Not only in commercial disputes but in contract negotiation as well, it is assumed, and probably reasonably so, that the large party has power and the small party does not. But this should not be the policy or political assumption upon which independent contractor issues should be approached. Rather, the starting point ought to be that the independent contractor has power because of the commercial contract—power which an employee does not possess. This is why it is said that employees are dependent and independent contractors are not dependent. This is the meaning and consequence of the 2006 ILO Recommendation. It is part of the consequence of the Left's accepting the ability of the free market to deliver economic results. It is the starting point which the Australian Labor Party has now accepted. It is the key point of this book. Being independent means having power, that is, power to control your own career, future and work.

But rather than this being the end of a political or economic discussion, it is only a new and exciting starting point.

Independent contractors exist, not because of commitment to an ideology or a philosophy about work, but because for each individual its suits his or her particular circumstances in life. What lies at the core of independent contracting is a motivation to be in control of one's individual working life. And this means the rejection of hierarchy and class-conscious subservience to allegedly superior individuals who control or seek to control those below them.

This rejection of class-conscious control challenges the political orthodoxy of the Left because it challenges the idea that the labour collective is essential if individuals are to have countervailing power against the ravages of systemic and inevitable exploitation. The Left in Australia largely seems to have responded to this. The Australian Labor Party has also responded. Certainly the International Labour Organisation has responded.

By contrast, there has been little in the way of response to the challenge posed by independent contracting to the very concept and historical understanding of the firm. Historically, academic and economic accounts of the firm have held that the firm exists because it manages transaction costs by engaging dependent employees. On this account, the firm is dependent for its existence on employees because the state of employment prevents workers from owning the goodwill and value they create when they work. This value is captured and owned by the firm. If, however, independent contractors own the goodwill and value they create, how can the firm exist? This is a conceptual challenge with which managers of firms will have to grapple. However, there are plenty of practical examples where the use of independent contractors by firms creates considerably more value, both for the firm and the individuals involved, because of the release of human ingenuity not possible when individuals operate in a state of dependency. In fact, there are new models for the firm which compete with the traditional model of the employment-dependent firm.

There are significant challenges here. They arise from a 'new' and developing politics which has emerged only relatively recently. They will spread out in thousands of different public policy, managerial, political, economic, social and psychological directions. Over the next few decades it will be interesting to observe how these challenges extend and stretch our thinking, both as societies and individuals.

Endnotes

1   http://www.time.com/time/time100/leaders/profile/mao2.html
2   International Labour Conference, 95th Session 2006. Report V(1) *The employment relationship.* International Labour office Geneva ISBN 92-2-116611-2 ISSN 0074-6681. First Published 2005
3   Extract from International Labour Conference Provisional Record 21 Ninety Fifth Session Geneva 2006. Fifth item on the agenda: The employment relationship. Report of the Committee on the Employment Relationship Wednesday 14 June 2006

ADDENDUM

Extract from International Labour Conference Provisional Record 21
Ninety Fifth Session Geneva 2006[3]

1. Members should formulate and apply a national policy for reviewing at appropriate intervals and, if necessary, clarifying and adapting the scope of relevant laws and regulations, in order to guarantee effective protection for workers who perform work in the context of an employment relationship.

2. The nature and extent of protection given to workers in an employment relationship should be defined by national law or practice, or both, taking into account relevant international labour standards. Such law or practice, including those elements pertaining to scope, coverage and responsibility for implementation, should be clear and adequate to ensure effective protection for workers in an employment relationship.

3. National policy should be formulated and implemented in accordance with national law and practice in consultation with the most representative organizations of employers and workers.

4. National policy should at least include measures to:
(a) provide guidance for the parties concerned, in particular employers and workers, on effectively establishing the existence of an employment relationship and on the distinction between employed and self-employed workers;
(b) combat disguised employment relationships in the context of, for example, other relationships that may include the use of other forms of contractual arrangements that hide the true legal status, noting that a disguised employment relationship occurs when the employer treats an individual as other than an employee in a manner that hides his or her true legal status as an employee, and that situations can arise where contractual arrangements have the effect of depriving workers of the protection they are due;
(c) ensure standards applicable to all forms of contractual arrangements, including those involving multiple parties so that employed workers have the protection they are due;
(d) ensure that standards applicable to all forms of contractual arrangements establish who is responsible for the protection contained therein;
(e) provide effective access of those concerned, in particular employers and workers, to appropriate, speedy, inexpensive, fair and efficient procedures and mechanisms for settling disputes regarding the existence and terms of an employment relationship;
(f) ensure compliance with, and effective application of, laws and regulations concerning the employment relationship; and
(g) provide for appropriate and adequate training in relevant international labour

standards, comparative and case law for the judiciary, arbitrators, mediators, labour inspectors, and other persons responsible for dealing with the resolution of disputes and enforcement of national employment laws and standards.

5. Members should take particular account in national policy to ensure effective protection to workers especially affected by the uncertainty as to the existence of an employment relationship, including women workers, as well as the most vulnerable workers, young workers, older workers, workers in the informal economy, migrant workers and workers with disabilities.

6. Members should:
(a) take special account in national policy to address the gender dimension in that women workers predominate in certain occupations and sectors where there is a high proportion of disguised employment relationships, or where there is a lack of clarity of an employment relationship; and
(b) have clear policies on gender equality and better enforcement of the relevant laws and agreements at national level so that the gender dimension can be effectively addressed.

7. In the context of the transnational movement of workers:
(a) in framing national policy, a Member should, after consulting the most representative organizations of employers and workers, consider adopting appropriate measures within its jurisdiction, and where appropriate in collaboration with other Members, so as to provide effective protection to and prevent abuses of migrant workers in its territory who may be affected by uncertainty as to the existence of an employment relationship;
(b) where workers are recruited in one country for work in another, the Members concerned may consider concluding bilateral agreements to prevent abuses and fraudulent practices which have as their purpose the evasion of the existing arrangements for the protection of workers in the context of an employment relationship.

8. National policy for protection of workers in an employment relationship should not interfere with true civil and commercial relationships, while at the same time ensuring that individuals in an employment relationship have the protection they are due.

II. DETERMINATION OF THE EXISTENCE OF AN EMPLOYMENT RELATIONSHIP

9. For the purposes of the national policy of protection for workers in an employment relationship, the determination of the existence of such a relationship should be guided primarily by the facts relating to the performance of work and the remuneration of the worker, notwithstanding how the relationship is characterized in any contrary arrangement, contractual or otherwise, that may have been agreed between the parties.

10. Members should promote clear methods for guiding workers and employers as to the determination of the existence of an employment relationship.

11. For the purpose of facilitating the determination of the existence of an employment relationship, Members should, within the framework of the national policy referred to in this Recommendation, consider the possibility of the following:
(a) allowing a broad range of means for determining the existence of an employment relationship;
(b) providing for a legal presumption that an employment relationship exists where one or more relevant indicators is present; and
(c) determining, following prior consultations with the most representative organizations of employers and workers, that workers with certain characteristics, in general or in a particular sector, must be deemed to be either employed or self-employed.

12. For the purposes of the national policy referred to in this Recommendation, Members may consider clearly defining the conditions applied for determining the existence of an employment relationship, for example, subordination or dependence.

13. Members should consider the possibility of defining in their laws and regulations, or by other means, specific indicators of the existence of an employment relationship. Those indicators might include:
(a) the fact that the work: is carried out according to the instructions and under the control of another party; involves the integration of the worker in the organization of the enterprise; is performed solely or mainly for the benefit of another person; must be carried out personally by the worker; is carried out within specific working hours or at a workplace specified or agreed by the party requesting the work; is of a particular duration and has a certain continuity; requires the worker's availability; or involves the provision of tools, materials and machinery by the party requesting the work;
(b) periodic payment of remuneration to the worker; the fact that such remuneration constitutes the worker's sole or principal source of income; provision of payment in kind, such as food, lodging or transport; recognition of entitlements such as weekly rest and annual holidays; payment by the party requesting the work for travel undertaken by the worker in order to carry out the work; or absence of financial risk for the worker.

14. The settlement of disputes concerning the existence and terms of an employment relationship should be a matter for industrial or other tribunals or arbitration authorities to which workers and employers have effective access in accordance with national law and practice.

15. The competent authority should adopt measures with a view to ensuring respect for and implementation of laws and regulations concerning the employment relationship with regard to the various aspects considered in this Recommendation, for example,

through labour inspection services and their collaboration with the social security administration and the tax authorities.

16. In regard to the employment relationship, national labour administrations and their associated services should regularly monitor their enforcement programmes and processes. Special attention should be paid to occupations and sectors with a high proportion of women workers.

17. Members should develop, as part of the national policy referred to in this Recommendation, effective measures aimed at removing incentives to disguise an employment relationship.

18. As part of the national policy, Members should promote the role of collective bargaining and social dialogue as a means, among others, of finding solutions to questions related to the scope of the employment relationship at the national level.

III. MONITORING AND IMPLEMENTATION

19. Members should establish an appropriate mechanism, or make use of an existing one, for monitoring developments in the labour market and in the organization of work, and for formulating advice on the adoption and implementation of measures concerning the employment relationship within the framework of the national policy.

20. The most representative organizations of employers and workers should be represented, on an equal footing, in the mechanism for monitoring developments in the labour market and the organization of work. In addition, these organizations should be consulted under the mechanism as often as necessary and, wherever possible and useful, on the basis of expert reports or technical studies.

21. Members should, to the extent possible, collect information and statistical data and undertake research on changes in the patterns and structure of work at the national and sectoral levels, taking into account the distribution of men and women and other relevant factors.

22. Members should establish specific national mechanisms in order to ensure that employment relationships can be effectively identified within the framework of the transnational provision of services. Consideration should be given to developing systematic contact and exchange of information on the subject with other States.

IV. FINAL PARAGRAPH

23. This Recommendation does not revise the Private Employment Agencies Recommendation, 1997 (No. 188), nor can it revise the Private Employment Agencies Convention, 1997 (No. 181).

Resolution concerning the employment relationship

The General Conference of the International Labour Organization,

Having been convened at Geneva by the Governing Body of the International Labour Office, and having met in its 95th Session, and Having adopted the Recommendation concerning the employment relationship, Noting that Paragraphs 19, 20, 21 and 22 recommend that Members should establish and maintain monitoring and implementing mechanisms, and Noting that the work of the International Labour Office helps all ILO constituents better to understand and address difficulties encountered by workers in certain employment relationships,

Invites the Governing Body of the International Labour Office to instruct the Director-General to:

1. Assist constituents in monitoring and implementing mechanisms for the national policy as set out in the Recommendation concerning the employment relationship;

2. Maintain up-to-date information and undertake comparative studies on changes in the patterns and structure of work in the world in order to:
    (a) improve the quality of information on and understanding of employment relationships and related issues;
    (b) help its constituents better to understand and assess these phenomena and adopt appropriate measures for the protection of workers; and
    (c) promote good practices at the national and international levels concerning the determination and use of employment relationships;

3. Undertake surveys of legal systems of Members to ascertain what criteria are used nationally to determine the existence of an employment relationship and make the results available to Members to guide them, where this need exists, in developing their own national approach to the issue.

No. 21 – Wednesday, 14 June 2006

www.ingramcontent.com/pod-product-compliance
Lightning Source LLC
Chambersburg PA
CBHW070408270326
41926CB00014B/2755